BRESCIA COLLEGE
LONDON ONTARIO

Blockades and Resistance

Studies in Actions of Peace and the Temagami Blockades of 1988-89

Blockades and Resistance

Studies in Actions of Peace and the Temagami Blockades of 1988-89

BRUCE W. HODGINS, UTE LISCHKE,
DAVID T. MCNAB, EDITORS

Aboriginal Studies Series

Wilfrid Laurier University Press
[WLU]

We acknowledge the financial support of the Government of Canada through the Book Publishing Industry Development Program for our publishing activities.

National Library of Canada Cataloguing in Publication Data

Blockades and resistance : studies in actions of peace and the Temagami blockades of 1988-89 / Bruce W. Hodgins, Ute Lischke and David T. McNab, editors.

(Aboriginal studies series)
Includes bibliographical references
ISBN 0-88920-381-4

1. Indian land transfers—Ontario. 2. Indians of North America—Ontario—Claims. 3. Indians of North America—Land tenure—Ontario. 4. Indians of North America—Ontario—Government relations. 5. Government, Resistance to—Ontario.
I. Hodgins, Bruce W., 1931- II. Lischke, Ute 1948- III. McNab, David T., 1947- IV. Series: Aboriginal studies series (Waterloo, Ont.)

E78.O5B56 2002   323.1′1970713   C2002-903295-4

© 2003 Wilfrid Laurier University Press
Waterloo, Ontario, Canada N2L 3C5
www.wlupress.wlu.ca

Cover design by Pamela Woodland.
Book series emblem by Hugh McKenzie.
Cover photographs by Brian Henderson and Pamela Woodland.

Printed in Canada

Contents

Part 2: Historical Perspectives on Resistance

Part 3: Varieties of Contemporary Resistance

At the end of the annual Wanapitei colloquium on politics and history in August 1998, participants gathered to decide what the topic would be for the next year's colloquium. After a very stimulating three days of papers and discussions, we wanted the next year's theme to be equally stimulating. Enjoying the final soft rays of sun at the end of a brilliant summer, hearing the lapping waves of Lake Temagami, we were immersed in the spiritual beauty of this gathering place located on N'Daki Menan, the tribal motherland of the Teme-Augama Anishnabai. As the group brainstormed, many who had participated in the Temagami blockades of 1988 and 1989 noted that the tenth anniversary was coming up the following year. The decision was taken that the next colloquium should commemorate the blockades.

Although the Temagami blockades in northeastern Ontario would become the focus of the next colloquium, other aspects of resistance—the ways in which Aboriginal peoples have articulated their legitimate rights through various political and socio-economic tactics—also needed to be addressed. As Christian Feest has observed in his volume *The Cultures of Native North Americans*,

> the history of America is also the history of Native American land loss. In the United States, less than 2 percent of the land, mostly of below-average quality, now belongs to tribes. However, that land is an important link between its current inhabitants and their past sovereignty. It is hardly surprising that land rights continue to be at the centre of controversy between Native Americans and federal and state governments.[1]

Note on page 235.

The blockades were but one source of many acts of resistance by First Nations to non-Aboriginal governments. Resistance has always occurred throughout Turtle Island (Aboriginal People's name for the geographical space of North America). Given the large geographical space involved and the number of resistance movements since the first days of contact, one exploratory volume cannot hope to cover all examples of resistance.

This book reflects the interests of the participants in the Wanapitei colloquium in 1999, commemorating the two blockades by the Teme-Augama Anishnabai of the Red Squirrel Road extension in the Lake Temagami area of northeastern Ontario in 1988 and 1989. Therefore, the focus of resistance, in this volume, is primarily on Ontario. It also reflects the close connection of the colloquium to Trent University, specifically the relationship of the Frost Centre for Canadian Studies and Native Studies to Wanapitei , and the role of Wanapitei itself in the Blockades at Temagami in 1988-89.

This volume is intended to represent a starting point for further research on the concepts of blockades and resistance. We hope that others will take the initiative to add their voices to the study of resistance that is happening across the country, from the Mi'kmaq at Burnt Church in New Brunswick to the Haida in British Columbia. Blockades and resistance by Aboriginal peoples are not unique to North America. They are global issues.

The overall purpose of this book is to address the issues of Aboriginal resistance in Canada by creating a meeting ground of knowledge for Aboriginal and non-Aboriginal peoples alike so that we may learn more about one another and be able to speak with one another more fully. To that end, the editors offer this book on *Blockades and Resistance* to explore and begin this process as the first volume of WLU Press's new Aboriginal Studies Series.

We would like to thank all of those diverse voices who have contributed to this volume. It is also with much gratitude that we thank the University of Toronto for their financial support. This book was conceived while Ute Lischke was teaching at the University of Toronto. Without the monetary support from the Provost, Professor Adel Sedra, and the Dean of Arts and Science, Professor Carl Amrhein, this publication would not have been possible. We thank them wholeheartedly for supporting this endeavour. Last, but not least, we extend many thanks to all the supportive editors at Wilfrid Laurier University Press who have given us so much invaluable advice and encouragement along the way.

Bruce Hodgins, Trent University
Ute Lischke, Wilfrid Laurier University
David T. McNab, Trent University

Actions of Peace

UTE LISCHKE
DAVID T. MCNAB

Introduction

More than eleven years ago, Canada witnessed the armed occupation at Oka. Now, as we enter the twenty-first century, there is
renewed resistance by Aboriginal people to the Canadian nation-
state. After the events during the summer of 1990, with the
Mohawk blockade in the town of Oka in Quebec, came the occupation of Ipperwash Provincial Park by the Stoney Point First
Nation (1995) and the Mi'kmaq fishing wars on the open waters
at Burnt Church in Atlantic Canada (1999-2001).

Aboriginal people have not forgotten the summer of Oka nor
the precursors to it in the Temagami blockades of 1988-89 nor the
successors to it at Ipperwash and, most recently, at Burnt Church.
The issues are extremely complicated. Yet, the fact that these events
are so recent cannot be used as an excuse not to tackle at least some
of the more significant issues. On 30 April 1999, Gary Potts, the former chief of the Teme-Augama Anishnabai, remarked in Toronto
that the next step would be a full-scale war on the ground by
Aboriginal people to protect their lands and resources—their

Notes on pages 235-36.

1

territories—from further incursions by non-Aboriginal people, governments, and private corporations.[1] This war would be a response to the
fact that non-Aboriginal people in Canada are no longer following the
legal decisions handed down by the Supreme Court of Canada. This
rejection of the Supreme Court's authority happened in 1999 when the
Supreme Court, after the Delgamuukw decision in 1997 (a BC case in
which the Supreme Court of Canada, respecting the oral traditions of
Aboriginal people across Canada, ordered a new trial), then handed
down its judgment in the first of two rulings in the Donald Marshall Jr.
case in September and October of that year. This ruling gave Aboriginal
people in Atlantic Canada the treaty right to fish commercially. The result
was a war on the waters of Atlantic Canada over the fishery at Burnt
Church and at other places in the fall of 1999, and again in 2000. Elsewhere, but especially in Ontario, the repeated actions by the Conservative government of Mike Harris since the death of Dudley George at
Ipperwash in September 1995 pushed Aboriginal people close to this
edge.[2] The breaking point is not far off.

Even after Ipperwash and Burnt Church, not enough has changed
for Aboriginal people. While much attention has been devoted in the
popular media to blockades and resistance movements, it has primarily
focused on the "bad news" aspects of violence and warfare.[3] Within the
growing discipline of Aboriginal Studies in Canada, the last decade has
finally seen significant growth in academic research and writing.[4]
Encouraged by this growing momentum, learning more about the particular events of the Temagami blockades, and about Aboriginal people
and their relationships with non-Aboriginal people (both present and
past), gives us a chance to understand why such events take place.

There is hope for peace in spite of apparent conflicts. Our common
and yet separate pasts reflect the existence of meeting grounds—parallel paths and places of fire where different peoples can meet and discuss these subjects. In times of peace, there has been always a time and
a place for a council between Aboriginal peoples and the immigrants to
North America.[5] These meeting grounds still exist today—not just in
the Great Lakes or the "pays d'en haut"—but throughout the continent.[6] This idea of meeting grounds is worthy of scholarly exploration.
One of the purposes of this book is to further debate whether the modern, scholarly discussion should include advocacy. Some, who represent the opinion that scholarship should be neutral and based primarily
on non-Aboriginal principles, will say that this volume represents only

the advocacy of blockades and resistance. But we think it is imperative that Aboriginal voices and perspectives be heard on the subject. The pointedly non-Aboriginal perspective does not lack a voice and has had the power to set the agenda on the ground for a very long time. Furthermore, there is no study which explores the rise of an opposing group—smaller and starting to get louder—that opposes the extension of Aboriginal rights and whose use of scholarship rests on the same divide between advocacy and academic analysis. The issue of scholarly independence and advocacy is complicated.

Aboriginal rights have been part of Canada's constitution now for almost two decades, and the Supreme Court of Canada over the same period has validated this historical and legal fact in its many decisions based on the constitution. There is no denying that Aboriginal rights are part of the law of Canada. The major opposition to Aboriginal rights in the last ten years has been fuelled by an emotional and non-Aboriginal racist backlash in response to blockades in local situations. This phenomenon is just now being given attention by the scholarly community as a way of increasing public education on the issues and in combatting the sort of racism that occurred in southwestern Ontario. The debate on the magnitude of racism against Aboriginal people in Canada at the scholarly level will be a significant one. There is also a need to explore the enormous discrepancy between Aboriginal and non-Aboriginal representations of Aboriginal people, a discrepancy which is at the heart of the blockades and resistance issues. Much of the institutional and popular racism relating to these issues can be directly attributed to misrepresentations of Aboriginal people resulting from a lack of public education. Such lack of knowledge and understanding will often lead to violence rather than peace.

What is peace? One example from the Haudenausanee traditions is embodied in the covenant chain of silver that is embodied in Gus Wen Tah—the two-row wampum. The two-row wampum has been defined as a "bed of white wampum shell beads symbolizing the sacredness and purity of the treaty agreement between the two sides":

> Two parallel rows of purple wampum beads that extend down the length of the belt represent the separate paths traveled by the two sides on the same river. Each side travels in its own vessel: the Indians in a birch bark canoe, representing their laws, customs, and ways, and the whites in a ship, representing their laws, customs, and ways. In presenting the Gus-Wen-Tah to solemnize their

treaties with the Western colonial powers, the Iroquois would explain its basic underlying vision of law and peace between different peoples as follows: "We shall each travel the river together, side by side, but in our own boat. Neither of us will steer the other's vessel."[7]

Through the chain, peace can be achieved through better relationships. As stressed by the Royal Commission on Aboriginal Peoples (1996), a new balance will hopefully be established in the relationships between First Nations and the Canadian nation state. This possibly was reiterated on 2 October 1990, when the then premier Bob Rae stated that we must first of all recognize and accept the basic historical premise of the relationship between Aboriginal and non-Aboriginal people:

> First came the land, then came the people, and the people exercised power and yes, sovereignty in a system of law over that land. We now begin to realize—I say "we," I mean non-native people— that there was a very sophisticated, very highly developed culture, civilization, and system of law.[8]

On the constructive side of the ledger are recognition, respect, and fairness regarding Aboriginal sovereignty. On the other side, as Rae also indicated, there is a denial of Aboriginal people and its accompanying racism:

> We are a new country. We represent something new in the world. And yes, we share the land. But we sure as hell haven't shared it very fairly, have we? And that is what is at stake here. I am not going to pretend that the issues are easy. We know the tensions that exist within communities. We know, bluntly put—and let's call it what it is—we know the racism that is still there, still a fact of our society. It is an ugly fact of our society.[9]

The racism which he spoke about still exists and it manifested itself directly in the confrontation at Ipperwash in southwestern Ontario on 6 September 1995.

Gary Potts opened the 1999 Wanapitei colloquium on Lake Temagami in the evening of Thursday, 26 August as our keynote speaker. Consistent with the oral tradition, his remarks were delivered without printed text. What follows is based on our recollections of Potts's talk to us.

> The Teme-Augama Anishnabai blockades of 1988 and 1989 were "like a moose call in the fall." This resistance was meant as a warning to non-Aboriginal people and governments alike. For far too long, N'Daki Menan, the Teme-augama Anishnabai homeland—four thousand square miles surrounding Lake Temagami—had been taken over by non-Aboriginal people and taken from the people who owned it. All these actions had occurred in spite of the laws of Canada. And since there has never been a treaty or surrender by the Teme-Augama Anishnabai of their motherland, all of these actions were illegal, against the wishes of the Teme-Augama Anishnabai. They were in violation of the Treaties of Peace and Friendship as well as the English King's own policy document—the Royal Proclamation of 1763 which is still part of Canada's constitution today.
>
> When non-Aboriginal people and governments violated these laws in the early 1760s, the result was swift. The Aboriginal nations fought back with resistance against the abuses and frauds by the English imperial governments and the depredations of the white settlers. This resistance came to be known as "Pontiac's War of 1763" (which was really two resistance movements, one initiated by the Senecas and the other by the Western or Lakes Confederacy).[10] After this resistance in the spring and the summer of 1763, the Aboriginal nations were not conquered. Peace came in the summer of 1764 at Niagara almost one year later. Thereafter, non-Aboriginal people tried to pity us. This was a mistake. Indigenous knowledge comes from the land and the land is the boss. We still have that indigenous knowledge.
>
> Native people also wanted the newcomers to expose themselves by their actions. It is like the action of lighting a piece of birchbark. We need to smoke our enemies out. After much hardship on our part, being driven forcibly from our lands in the twentieth century like wild animals, the Teme-Augama Anishnabai said it was time to act when, early in 1988, the provincial government tried to put a road through the north end of our territory to cut down the last of the "standing people" (the old-growth red and white pine around northern Obabika and Wakimika) and open up the last of our sacred places to others. We then decided in the spring of 1988 to initiate a blockade at Sharp Rock Inlet where the road was to be extended at the north end of Lake Temagami. Our actions then and thereafter were entirely peaceful in a cause of peace. They were not actions of war on our part. The blockades and resistance were entirely peaceful actions intended to retain N'Daki Menan—our motherland—our place for ourselves. The

> Temagami blockades were a resistance and a turning point. From that time on to now we will act to protect our motherland. This was my job and it is now finished.

With these words of peace, Gary Potts set the tone and the meaning of blockades and resistance as actions of peace.

This volume, then, is a book primarily about peace and not war (which is not to deny that there have been conflicts in the past). We will explore the growing debate about Aboriginal peoples' use of peaceful blockades and resistance: why they happen and what can be done in a practical way to address the issues in them, especially aspects of peace, before they lead to further violence in all parts of Canada.

In Part 1, "Personal Reflections," we have included the words of the participants that provide some insight into the experiences of the Teme-Augama Anishnabai. There were three Temagami blockades in 1988-89. The first and third blockades were by the Teme-Augama Anishnabai. The memory of these blockades is recorded in the remarks of Gary Potts (above) as well as in a brief sketch of his writings and sayings in chapter 3. In addition, we have included reflections by James Twain, a former chief of the Temagami First Nation, entitled "The Life and Times of the Teme-Augama Anishnabai" and by June Twain, entitled "The Joy of Unfolding Commitment: A Woman's View of the Teme-Augama Anishnabai Blockades." We have left their words to speak entirely for themselves without any commentary.

The second blockade, which began in mid-September 1989, was by non-Aboriginal people connected to the environmental movement. The experience of the third blockade is detailed in Bruce Hodgins's chapter entitled, "The Temagami Blockades of 1989: Personal Reflections." Hodgins reflects on his own experiences in supporting the Teme-Augama Anishinabe blockades in 1988-89 and, in the fall of 1989, his own arrest. It is clear that Hodgins and many more non-Aboriginal people were greatly influenced by the Teme-Augama Anishnabai blockades that came and were separate from the second blockade in early fall of 1989.

David T. McNab, who now teaches Native Studies at Trent University, worked for the provincial government between 1979 and 1991. He experienced the blockades from the other side of the barricades and provides some background on the blockades, as well as insight into how the provincial government reacted to and then was stymied by

the Teme-Augama Anishnabai blockades. The Teme-Augama Anishnabai had effectively "captured" the provincial government by
metaphorically, in Potts's words, lighting a piece of birchbark in
blockading the Red Squirrel Road extension. In part, the blockades
issues became part of the political baggage of the Peterson Liberal government and led, in part, to the demise of that government in the summer of 1990 and the election of the first NDP government in the
province's history. McNab's chapter is called "Remembering an Intellectual Wilderness: A Captivity Narrative at Queen's Park in 1988-89."
It is clear from the other chapters in Part 1 that the Temagami blockades
of 1988-89 were perceived by non-Aboriginal people to be a war or conflict among Aboriginal people, environmentalists, governments, and
private corporations over a "wilderness" issue. In fact, as Gary Potts has
pointed out, it was about peace and not war. This analysis warrants further scrutiny.

Ellesa Clay High, the head of the Native American Studies Program
who also teaches English at West Virginia University, provides in her
chapter "You Can't Chop Peace Down: Planting the White Pine Tree at
West Virginia University, 1992-99" a valuable comparative perspective
(as do chapters 12, 14, and 15 of this book) on the Temagami blockades.
In fact, the similarities of the themes are quite striking. High narrates
the experience and also explores the significance of resistance of Aboriginal people on the academic grounds of West Virginia University in
the 1990s.

In Part 2, "Historical Perspectives on Resistance," Rhonda Telford,
historical research consultant and a Ph.D. graduate from the University
of Toronto, explores the multifarious sources of Anishinabe resistance
in connection with mining and Aboriginal mineral rights in the making
of the Robinson Treaties of 1850. Her chapter called, "Aboriginal Resistance in the Mid-Nineteenth Century: The Anishinabe, Their Allies and
the Closing of the Mining Operations at Mica Bay and Michipicoten
Island," is a strong revisionist chapter that clearly shows how hard the
Anishinabe fought using peaceable means, wherever possible, to resist
governments and private non-Aboriginal individuals and companies
from taking their mines and minerals. Brian Osborne, a professor of
geography at Queen's University, in his essay, "Barter, Bible, Bush:
Strategies of Survival and Resistance among the Kingston/Bay of
Quinte Mississauga, 1783-1836," attempts to develop a theory of resistance from the themes of trade and missionary incursions among the

Mississaugas in the late eighteenth and early nineteenth centuries. Likewise, in a companion piece, Michael Ripmeester, a historical geographer who teaches at Brock University, examines the resistance of the same Anishinabe people one generation later in his "Intentional Resistance or Just 'Bad Behaviour': Reading for Everyday Resistance at the Alderville First Nation, 1837-76." Susan Campbell, a graduate of Queens University, chronicles the early twentieth-century resistance of the people of Longlac in her "'White Gold' versus Aboriginal Rights: A Longlac Ojibwa Claim against Damages Caused by the 1937 Diversion of the Kenogami River into Lake Superior." This chapter focuses on the significance of water in Aboriginal history in northwestern Ontario. Part 2 provides a view of how deep Aboriginal resistance movements have been since the late eighteenth century, and how their continuity remains to this day.

Part 3, "Varieties of Contemporary Resistance," looks at the continuity of resistance into the twentieth century. Kent McNeil, a professor of law at Osgoode Hall Law School, York University, in his "Aboriginal Title on the Ground: Establishing and Protecting Occupation of Land," focuses on the modern legal framework in Canada on Aboriginal land rights cases and how the courts have been used by Aboriginal people to resist and defend their interests since the Calder case (a British Columbia case named after Frank Calder involving Aboriginal title) which was decided by the Supreme Court of Canada in 1973. This is significant. Before Calder, the Canadian courts did not recognize Aboriginal title. There had been no legal venue at one time to even assert these rights. Similarly, the Canadian justice system has treated (and still does, treat) Aboriginal people in the prison system with an uneven hand, denying their rights while incarcerating proportionally more of them than any other cultural group in Canada. The next chapter in Part 3 provides a theoretical analysis of the blockades by James Lawson, in "Space, Strategy, and Surprise: Thinking about Temagami Ten Years after the Blockades." Peggy O'Reilly-Shaughnessy, in her "Echoes of Resistance: Coercion and Injustices in a Canadian Prison," details and documents the racism against Aboriginal people in Canadian jails which is starkly reminiscent of the earlier horrors of the residential school system that ended in this country only in 1986.

Not all of the chapters follow the international border between Canada and the United States. Ute Lischke, who teaches German and cultural perspectives at Wilfrid Laurier University, analyzes the significance of gender and resistance in Aboriginal literature by focusing on the disparate notions of Aboriginal and non-Aboriginal women in her chapter on "Female Narratives of Resistance: The Significance of Gender and Food in the Writings of Louise Erdrich." This contribution includes writing by both Aboriginal and non-Aboriginal women such as Maria Tippett, as well as the author of six best-selling novels, Louise Erdrich, who is from the Turtle Mountain Chippewa Reservation which lies on the Minnesota-Manitoba border. Lastly, Bruce W. Hodgins and John S. Milloy, in "The Resistance of Little Charlie Wenjack and His Legacy at Trent University," tell the sad and unforgettable story of Little Charlie Wenjack—a residential school non-survivor—and the failed attempts to have his name commemorated as a College at Trent University where today only a lecture theatre is named in his memory.

Part 1

Personal Reflections

The Life and Times of the Teme-Augama Anishnabai

Chapter 1

JAMES TWAIN, FORMER CHIEF OF
THE TEMAGAMI FIRST NATION

Beginning with the most recent part of our history, we have to look at where we are in securing a settlement of our people. We have been a very patient people and we have also been a very trusting people, which is a trait handed down from generation to generation. With the court decision (the Bear Island land rights case, 1978-91) coming down against us, we did not give up and are still determined to secure a just and proper settlement for our people. With hard work and determination, we will see that justice is done for the future generations on our land. After over 120 years of trying to get the best for our people, we will succeed. With all the history that has been brought to the attention of the courts and the public, I do not see how we can lose our struggle.

If oral history has been a way of recording all that has happened to us throughout the ages, I do not understand why it was not acceptable in the courts.[1] The lack of understanding about our people, and the main fact that writing in pen and ink was not part of our way of life, should have been taken into consideration

Note on page 236.

when we first went into court. It was at this time that our community elders held the power—which was the case throughout the history of Native people of this country called Canada. It was our way of showing respect and honour for the wisdom and knowledge of the elders. Even today, with all the modern technology, we still look to our elders for guidance, for teachings, and for all kinds of information about many different things. It is this respect that should have been shown to them in the court system of this country.

Throughout the history of our people, we have discovered many unique things about ourselves. One thing is that, through research, we know that we have been here at least six thousand years and maybe even longer. We also have discovered some interesting artifacts that show how we lived in past generations. More recently, grave sites have been located in different parts of the area which show that we did occupy this land before the coming of the foreign people. It is all of these things that will show our younger people that we are a special and distinct people.

The oral teachings of our people are good. One elder told about the little people, the ones who are known as the helpers of our people. They existed in our community along the bluffs at the north end of our island. Sometimes, when this elder and one of the parents were paddling along these bluffs, they would see these little people disappear into the rocks. This is also a teaching in different Native communities. Another elder talked about the drumming and dancing that took place on the island in the area behind Tillie Missabie's and George Peshabo's houses. It has been said that this happened in the early summer when everyone gathered at the "Shaking Tent" which was used on Bear Island. There was also another elder who talked about the same kind of ceremony. These are just a few things that happened within our community. There are many other legends that make things very interesting in our little community.

Some of the things that happened in the tribal grounds of our people are also fascinating. There are many stories of the events in the Maple Mountain area. For example, our people used to hold sacred and other kinds of ceremonies at the one end of our mountain. The extent of those ceremonies will have to be further explored. Another thing that was known about that part of N'Daki Menan, our tribal lands, is that there is a place where pipe stone exists. This stone is used to make pipes for different kinds of ceremonies. These lands should also be protected for our people. When these many different kinds of lands are uncovered, they should be documented and filed as sacred and historical sites.

One of the other things that our people did before they made contact with the people from the foreign lands was to tan their own hides. For example, they made gloves, mitts, and moccasins along with many other things. They were good at making their own snowshoes, canoes, paddles, and other tools that were a part of their way of life.

There are a lot more important facts about our people that should be recorded for the use of our children, such as the battle sites, and the loss of some trapping and hunting grounds due to the flooding of our lands and waters by the governments and other agencies that wanted to use this land for other reasons. Another very important part of our history is our language. When a linguist came to do some research about our language, it was said that our dialect was unique and very old. I believe that this is one important part of our history that should be retained forever. It is so different from our neighbouring First Nations. If we were to lose our language, then most of our children growing up now would lose a key connection to their culture and would not be able to speak our dialect.

It was not that long ago when we did not have all the modern conveniences we have today. Before hydro and the telephone, everyone had a set of rules that they followed around the house to insure that there was water and wood enough to last until the next day. This, I think, was a very healthy way to live and we were self-sufficient.

The history of our people dates back a long, long time. Now we can record our history in pen and ink. We should be looking at making sure that this is done appropriately according to our ideas. Our next generation will then be able to find out where they came from and who they are as a people. They will have all of this information at their fingertips. Knowing who you are and where you belong makes you a better person. You will possess self-esteem and a feeling of belonging to our lands, to Mother Earth. That has been what has made us strong—as a people and as a nation. This is just a small part of our history that makes us a unique and distinct people as Teme-Augama Anishnabai.

Meegwetch

The Joy of Unfolding Commitment

A Woman's View of the
Teme-Augama Anishnabai Blockades

Chapter 2

JUNE TWAIN

The unfolding of commitment was a joy to see. This joy was shared by all the people from our community who were involved with the blockade. I noticed no one ever mentioned a drink. I do not think anyone even thought about it. I believe there is something to this fact. They had a reason to be there. This was something major that would affect our lives and our future generations. I saw something very positive during the days that I was at the blockade. Some of the very positive feelings were caring, commitment, determination, unity, and putting aside our difference in feelings. Spiritually we were very strong, joining hands together, praying, sharing sweet grass ceremonies and tobacco offering which showed that we were as a nation of people. It was like it must have been before alcohol came into our lives. It was such a great feeling! Support came from all walks of life. Church groups, ministers, priests, chiefs, and other Native groups. There was even a sister (a nun) who was arrested.

Being out at the blockade was a good feeling of being close to the land. It showed our children something very positive and powerful through non-violent demonstrations. This is very important. I believe that our struggles are far from over. To have this land base for future generations to come was the Creator's plan. He gave us this land to care for and to keep. We are trying to follow through on this responsibility that was given to our ancestors. It has been written that "we do not inherit this land from our ancestors, we borrow it from our children." In this teaching, the responsibility is to take care of what you borrow, so when you return it, it is in good condition.

We are greatly misunderstood by other societies where, in the most part, the materialistic values are more important. It is very difficult to try to maintain the traditional values with so much interference from the conveniences of the world in which we now live. Honour and recognition for the Native war veterans was good to witness. To hear names of our ancestors who fought for freedom in various wars was a significant event in our history.

The idea of sharing our land is ours. We want to share our land but the decisions have to come from us about the way the land is to be used. This is our responsibility that was given to us at the beginning of time. It is an awesome duty.

Not everyone in our community will share our feelings on these issues, perhaps they never will. We cannot go back completely to our old ways. So many of us are victims of the twentieth century. We now have numerous diseases such as cancer, alcoholism, tuberculosis, and allergic disorders. All of these diseases were foreign to our people until about a hundred years ago.

Meegwetch

Gary G. Potts

Chapter 3

BRUCE W. HODGINS

Dr. Gary Potts, former chief of the Teme-Augama Anishnabai (TAA) and also of the Temagami Band centred on Bear Island (now the Temagami First Nation), was a major leader in blockades and resistance. He led and managed what was both the greatest and longest specific resistance—two blockades in 1988-89—which were also the most significant and most carefully orchestrated blockades in twentieth-century Aboriginal history. And it was done peacefully. Elected chief of the Temagami Band as a young man in 1972, he obtained a legally binding land caution the next year on 112 geographic townships of the so-called crown lands of northeastern Ontario, the TAA's N'Daki Menan. The caution prevented any sale, alienation, or new development except logging, on such crown land (that is, 98 percent of the land). The caution survived until 1996. His actions slowed down the commencement of construction of the Red Squirrel Road extension through N'Daki Menan, while injunctions and a ceremonial blockade prevented its construction in 1988.

In the autumn of 1989, following a six-week-long blockade by environmentalists (the Temagami Wilderness Society or TWS) to stop and then slow construction and thus save the remaining old-growth pine forests, Gary Potts organized and led the TAA-sponsored blockade. Construction was stopped each morning on the Red Squirrel Road until protesters were removed and arrested. These arrests created a provincial, even a national, media event and a sensation. In a variety of capacities, hundreds of people, both Aboriginal and non-Aboriginal, were involved. Although the road was "opened" just before Christmas, only one pickup truck passed over it. After the spring washouts, the road extension was never repaired and thus never used. Gary Potts was behind the road's closure and he did all this while maintaining excellent relations with the Ontario Provincial Police who had their responsibility to make arrests and protect the construction crews.

Bad publicity from the three Temagami blockades played a major role in toppling the Ontario Liberal government of David Peterson in September 1990, even though Gary Potts and that government had worked out a memorandum of understanding on 23 April of that year. On 30 May 1991, Bud Wildman, the new Ontario Minister of Native Affairs, spoke with Chief Gary Potts at a gala banquet in the great hall of Champlain College (Trent). The next day, Gary Potts received an honorary doctor of laws degree from Trent University for his efforts on behalf of Native peoples. Although the Supreme Court of Canada's ambivalent decisions of August 1991 "found" that the TAA had, through "passive adhesion," exchanged Aboriginal title to their lands for treaty rights to some of that land, the resistance and the negotiations have continued to this day.

IN GARY POTTS'S OWN WORDS

The land is the boss, not one human; humans cannot live without land.... To disregard the ways of the people who have lived on a particular land area for thousands of years imperils the integrity of any process which denies this reality. (Taped speech, 1998)

I can bring a message, but I can't institute a plan because I'm not an academic. I am a bushman. (Taped speech, 1996)

There is no easy answer to many things, but we know one thing— if our land dies, we die. This land is our crown. This land, along with the seasons affecting us, is our touchstone to past life and the gateway to future life both human and non-human. (Taped speech, 1992)

Our view is that holistic life includes all matters that we deal with on a day-to-day basis on our land. It includes the weather, the water, the forests, all the life forms that are interconnected and that the human life form needs to be living within that framework in a manner that does not destroy the framework. That is primarily the central principle of sustained life—that each generation has a right to use the land in the way they want, but they can only use it in ways which ensure its continuity. (Taped speech, 1992)

The Temagami Blockades of 1989

Personal Reflections

Chapter 4

BRUCE W. HODGINS

There we were, on a cold Saturday morning in December 1989, sitting on the rough gravel of the Red Squirrel Road extension, trying to stop equipment and personnel from moving west to the shifting construction site, deeper into the Temagami-Lady Evelyn wilderness.[1] That morning there were about twenty of us actually on the road—Anishnabai, Cree, Oji-Cree, and a few of us non-Native Canadians by the gate at the northeast end of Lake Temagami. Several people stood showing their support along the road's edges. All had gone through a campfire-centred sweet-grass and tobacco ceremony. "Sergeant, do your duty" firmly declared the OPP Officer in charge. "In the name of the Queen, make way," cried the sergeant. There I was, a seventh-generation Upper Canadian defying the order of my sovereign. A surge of undefinable emotion passed through me. I knew that what I was doing was right, even if it was illegal. The Teme-Augama Anishnabai themselves were sitting on their own unsurrendered land. We had been invited to join with them. For me, it was a defining moment. We were then individually carried, politely and carefully, each by four constables, to waiting police vans with their exhaust fumes visible in the clear cold air. We were transported to Haileybury, where charges of criminal mischief were laid before we were released on our own recognizance.

The night before, I had driven from Trent University to the turnoff north of the village of Temagami and onto the old, late 1960s portion of the snow-covered Red Squirrel Road. Then I walked just over a kilo-metre into the Wanapitei Wilderness Centre (located on the eastern shore of Ferguson Bay at the northeastern end of Lake Temagami) of which I was and still am the president. As I passed the flag pole, a strange impulse made me shine my flashlight up to the top. There flut-tered not the red and white maple leaf flag but the multi-coloured ban-ner of the Teme-Augama Anishnabai, the Temagami First Nation. We had been taken over. That I had offered the site to Chief Garry Potts and the Anishnabai as an advanced base for their blockade, only three kilometres to the northwest, was then irrelevant. That the Anishnabai had most carefully excluded the Wanapitei property and all other free-hold lands in their N'Daki Menan from their caution and their land claim was very important, but it was hardly germane to this friendly occupation. The occupation was a rare reversal of the common histori-cal pattern in Canada and in the Queen's former empire generally.

In 1974, Jamie Benidickson and I had made a solemn promise to research and write a major historical monograph, which became *The Temagami Experience: Recreation, Resources, and Aboriginal Rights in the Northern Ontario Wilderness*.[2] The book did not appear until late 1989, by which time a lot more water had passed under the Wanapitei bridge over the lower Red Squirrel River. The book was designed to explore the history of human impact on the Temagami environment, including attempts at resource management and recreational use of the Northern Ontario wilderness. Aboriginal rights and Teme-Augama Anishnabai experiences became integral parts of our story. In the mid-1970s, we had perceived the preservation of northern wilderness and the advancement of Indian land rights to be two very important, linked, but quite distinct endeavours and historical discourses.

It was the young, recently elected Chief Gary Potts and the Teme-Augama Anishnabai who in 1973 had obtained a caution (effectively lasting until 1996) stopping all sale and all new development on the so-called crown land of 110 geographic townships. What a staggering achievement! The Temagamis' aim was to stop development—at least until their outstanding, century-old land claim could be settled. Happily, the provincial Maple Mountain project of the 1970s was abandoned. Led by the Red Tory minister of natural resources, Alan Pope, the Maple Mountain area became in 1981, a focal point of the new Lady Evelyn-Smoothwater Wilderness Park. Wilderness and the Aboriginal presence were now inextricably linked. The land claim in 1974 went to the courts, where it dragged on in various forms until 1991. After 1991 there were protracted political negotiations, deadlock in 1993, and then only recently new negotiations. A picture from the largely ceremonial blockade of 1988 was on the cover of the *Temagami Experience*. Injunctions prevented construction and full confrontation that year.

By the 1980s, my passion for the Temagami-Lady Evelyn wilderness and my identification with it knew no limits: clear deep lakes, fast-flowing and free-falling streams, tall pines, historic nastawgan (canoe routes), and fantastic campsites; silent herons, noisy and mournful loons, and hungry dragon flies; cedarstrip wood-canvas canoes, pre-Cambrian bluffs, wind storms, slow orange and black sunsets; short summer heat, winter stillness with moose, beaver, and otter about; breaking trail in February across snow-buried swamps and marshes, spring break-up with the crinkling sound of black ice converting to aerated crystals. Indeed, our historical writings were becoming, in part, a panegyric on that refigured and peopled wilderness.

In 1987 I was appointed by the province to serve on the broadly based and deeply divided so-called John Daniel (President of Laurentian University) Study Group to try to solve the problem occasioned by the provincial plan to extend the Red Squirrel Road to the northwest and link it up with the Liskeard Lumber Road running south from Long Point (near Elk Lake) through the Lady Evelyn-Smoothwater Wilderness Park. In early 1988, when I became ill, my son Shawn (Managing Director of Wanapitei) took my place. The group failed when Daniel, in the spring and on his own, submitted a report that was unacceptable to most members of the group because it urged Ontario to proceed with the link. By 1988, Temagami controversies were moving inextricably towards extreme conflict and blockade, occasioned by the planned construction of the Red Squirrel Road extension. After the tentative blockade in 1988, there was a major conference in October 1989 on Temagami at Laurentian University where I gave a claims paper that was favourable to the TAA.[3]

The dual blockades took place during the autumn of 1989. First came the environmental blockade on the right-of-way for the road, deep in the bush and reached only by canoe or float plane. The site was close to the Wendaban-Obabika-Wakimika old-growth forest. The first blockade was run effectively, using radical measures, by its non-Aboriginal leaders such as Brian Back, Kay Chernook, Hap Wilson, and the well-financed Temagami Wilderness Society (TWS).[4] That blockade began a couple of weeks after the appearance of our *Temagami Experience* which, alas, could not address the crises of that year. Construction of the road did slowly continue as protesters were removed and arrested each day until on 11 November, the Teme-Augama Anishnabai sat down on the old part of the road itself (just west of Wanapitei), led peacefully by Chief Gary Potts and the Teme-Augama Anishnabai. Almost three hundred people were arrested. The protest lasted until mid-December. The battle was technically lost when one pickup truck passed over the full road, but the war was won. Parts of the road were washed out in the spring of 1990, and the new road was never repaired and thus never used.

My colleagues, Jonathan Bordo, and other Trent faculty and students were arrested on the environmental blockade. (Jamie Benidickson and I had visited the blockade and had camped there just before it actually involved confrontation.) Trent Canadian Studies students, while at their Wanapitei retreat, paddled into the site and overnighted at Lake Wakimika to demonstrate solidarity. Many of us were later arrested on the Teme-Augama Anishnabai blockade. They included Jamie Benidickson, my wife Carol and myself, many past and present Wanapitei staff, Trent staff and students, many students from the University of Guelph, and, of course, over two hundred Temagami and other Native peoples from all across Ontario. To be arrested once meant trouble; to be arrested twice (after a promise to not try again to block the road) meant jail. Few chose a second arrest.

Through the crisis of 1988-89, I saw my primary role as trying both to keep intact a shaky TWS/TAA entente which was always far apart on their objectives and also to forge a real alliance and understanding between the Native people and the environmentalists who included the canoeists. I helped succeed with the former but I failed miserably with the environmentalists. Naively, I thought that I had succeeded when both Gary Potts and Brian Back had visited us for two days, on my initiative, at Trent and both spoke in John Wadland's Canadian

Studies class. They were both also in attendance in my graduate studies Frost Centre seminar on Temagami. A few days later, however, Brian
Back was again in the press, criticizing Gary Potts for putting the land
claims ahead of the old-growth pines. Gary Potts reported that he and
his people would "not be put or kept in zoos." These were issues of the
Teme-Augama Anishnabai and not the non-Aboriginal environmentalists; moreover it was the TAA's blockade. James Cullingham, a Trent and
Wanapitei alumnus and a wilderness canoeist, also spoke at these Trent
sessions. He was now becoming a major CBC producer and a private
filmmaker on Temagami and other Aboriginal topics. On the interface
between preserving a pristine wilderness and restoring and safeguard-
ing the Aboriginal presence, he was unhesitatingly on the side of Aboriginal presence. So was I.

The blockades were over before the Christmas of 1989, but the
struggle for land claims and future use of the road continued. In the
aftermath, I continued to play a small but significant role. In April
1990, a temporary memorandum of understanding between the Peterson government and the TAA had been worked out. The road would
not be reopened, land claim negotiations were to commence and to
run parallel with the TAA appeal to the Supreme Court, and a joint
council to co-manage land and resources in an interior portion of
N'Daki Menan was to be established. But this did not save the Peterson government in that summer of Oka (in Quebec). Bob Rae, who
had been arrested on the environmental line (probably believing it
was an Aboriginal line), and the NDP won power that September. Rae
was committed to Ontario-Aboriginal government-to-government
relations and to the inherent right of Aboriginal people to self government. He was also committed to finding a solution to the Temagami
conflicts. All cutting of old-growth red and white pine was halted
throughout the Temagami country. In late May of 1991, Premier Rae
and Gary Potts established the co-management body called the Wendaban Stewardship Authority. It was to deal with four geographic townships around Obabika-Wakimika, the area at the heart of the forestry
and road controversy. It had six issues, six Ontario representatives,
and six TAA representatives together with a jointly appointed chair.

By then, Carol and I had been presented, in a winter ceremony on
Bear Island celebrating the fiftieth wedding anniversary of Bill and
Isabel Twain, with the TAA flag which had flown over Wanapitei during
the blockade. It hangs today in the dining hall at Wanapitei Camp. I was

appointed by Bob Rae and Bud Wildman (MNR and Ontario Native Affairs Secretariat [ONAS]) as one of the six Ontario representatives on the WCA. I had known Rae reasonably well, both personally and politically. One of his principal executive secretaries, Melody Morrison—a former Trent student of mine, a shareholder of Wanapitei, and a friend of both Gary Potts and myself—was very influential. I presumably represented myself as well as the moderate environmental groups on the lake, including the canoeing interests. These included the Temagami Lakes Association and the Association of Youth Camps on the Temagami Lakes. I was on the board of the former and the executive of the latter. I was also there, I assume, because of my historical writings on Temagami and my involvement in the blockades. Cocky Ingerson was a second and radical environmentalist on the WCA; her partner Peter McMillan was one of the TAA appointees, and he had been connected with Wanapitei. Cocky and I were very close to the six TAA appointees and to the second chairperson, Jim Morrison. Compromise was essential. Consensus (at least ten out of twelve) was the rule for all decisions. Usually we were able to secure unanimity, after hours of debate and a drink or two in the local pub. We all became friends. What an experience, and we made it work! A highly detailed plan for the future of the four townships was prepared, submitted, and accepted. Action, however, was always frustrated and curtailed by the local MNR bureaucracy which was determined to prevent us from having any authority on the land or from even succeeding. The WCA was a bad precedent, they feared. When ongoing negotiations and ratification of the agreement-in-principle failed, the WCA effectively ceased to exist when all funds were cut off in 1994. Our completed plan became a definitive part of the overall comprehensive plan for the Temagami Country.[5]

In late May 1991, John Milloy and I ran a Trent Frost Centre colloquium on the Temagami controversy and on current Aboriginal-settler relations in Ontario generally. Jonathan Bordo and I presented a paper entitled "Wilderness, Aboriginal Presence, and the Land Claim." David T. McNab also presented a paper. The proceedings were later published.[6] For the latter part of the colloquium, Gary Potts and Bud Wildman were in attendance. The colloquium was linked to Trent's conferring on Chief Potts an honorary doctor of laws, for his role on behalf of the Temagami First Nation and Aboriginal peoples of Ontario.

This happy event came about through the efforts of John Wadland, and I had the honour of writing and making the presentation. The colloquium and the ceremony were a precursor to the subsequent and ongoing late-August aboriginal history colloquium at Wanapitei.

Unfortunately the Supreme Court decision on 15 August 1991 was not a victory for the Temagamis.[7] Nor was it exactly a defeat. The struggle continues. The court "found" that the TAA had lost their Aboriginal title to the lands through what it called the community's passive adhesion to the Robinson Treaty of 1850. Yet the court accepted nearly all of the TAA's version of their own history. It found that they had exchanged Aboriginal title for treaty rights, and that the crown had failed in its fiduciary responsibilities to secure proper land and resources for the TAA under the treaty. Such lands and resources, the court anticipated, would now soon be secured through the political process. Although it still hasn't been secured, in 1994-95 a settlement had been very close. My role in the Wendaban Stewardship Authority and in the honorary LLD for Gary Potts all came about through both Carol's and my participation in the blockades and resistance of 1989, as well as through my writings on Temagami and my position at Wanapitei.[8]

Remembering an Intellectual Wilderness

A Captivity Narrative at Queen's Park in 1988-89

Chapter 5

DAVID T. MCNAB

The fire in the heart of Temagami became a conflagration within the provincial government between 1988 and 1989. The government did not know how to address the issues in the Temagami blockades. Crisis management was the watchword as the days turned into weeks and months. Separation of the issues into the usual categories of Euro-Canadian knowledge systems was useless. The way the state used power and authority revealed its soft underbelly. The result was a captivity narrative within government in 1988-89 over the Teme-Augama Anishnabai blockades, the government becoming the captive. It has had repercussions in the forests of Temagami and at Queen's Park to this day.

Colin Calloway in his *New Worlds for All: Indians, Europeans, and the Remaking of Early America*, defines captives and captivity narratives as follows:

> Many of these cultural converts entered Indian country as captives, against their will, but they were subjected to

Notes on pages 237-40.

powerful acculturative pressures by their captors, and some came
to prefer their new life to their old. Still others chose to live with
Indians, whether in preference for the Natives' way of life or to
escape from their own society. Some of these "white Indians" even
fought alongside their Indian friends and relatives in their wars
against the whites.[1]

The issues posed by the dichotomy of "civilized" and "savage" in these
captivity narratives can be seen in the Temagami blockades of 1988-89.
This time it was the government which was held captive.

It was my lot to be working at Queen's Park for the Ontario Native
Affairs Directorate during these years. Specifically, as a professional his-
torian, my job was to record the events as they occurred at Queen's
Park. This chapter reflects my record and recollections of these events.

Gary Potts has remarked on how the Temagami Aboriginal blockades issue was like a lit piece of birchbark used to smoke out the non-
Aboriginal people who were about to cause damage in the 1980s to
N'Daki Menan, the tribal motherland, as they had done for many
years before. Denial of the very existence of Aboriginal people is a
form of racism. The relationship between the Teme-Augama Anishnabai (TAA), and the province has been characterized by a stubborn
rejection of the TAA and their ancestral motherland, N'Daki Menan.[2]
After 150 years, Ontario has refused to acknowledge the people's
Aboriginal title and rights to their territory. Negotiations had
brought the TAA the Bear Island Reserve, less than one square mile—
they had to purchase it using their own monies or face eviction by
Ontario as squatters on their own lands. Land cautions (1973) were
placed on about four thousand square miles of N'Daki Menan. Such
a legal caution prevents first registration of titles by the Crown and
thereby effectively puts a cloud on the title of the lands, preventing
or inhibiting economic development such as mining or any new land
sales. The caution was followed by more than a decade of litigation
from 1978 to 1991.

In 1991 the legal case finally ended in apparent defeat in the white
man's court of justice. Development was stopped by the "frozen cautions." The antebellum status quo was maintained until the cautions
were lifted by a court action initiated by the NDP government of Bob
Rae in 1993, and then concluded by the Mike Harris government early
in 1996.[3] In spite of this recent litigation, the TAA's Aboriginal title and
land rights to N'Daki Menan has never been resolved and the situation

is much worse now than in 1973 when the cautions were placed on the land. Litigation in the white man's courts do not always work.

Ontario won its case in the trial when Justice Steele handed down his judgment late in 1984. But what had it won and at what cost? Like at Oka, millions were spent on a long court action that ended in 1996 with only the status quo. In many ways the cost was high, in both the material cost of building the road (about $4 million) and in terms of damaged relationships.[4] For example, the federal government created bitter feelings and increased suspicion and distrust. From the early 1880s it had supported the claim of the TAA. It had funded the land rights litigation with millions of dollars in grants and loans, at least until the trial decision. But near the trial's end, Ottawa withdrew its position and then took an opposite view that was against the TAA. Perversely, the government argued that this switch was for constitutional reasons, just two years after Aboriginal and treaty rights were included in Canada's constitution.[5]

In 1986, Ontario presented the TAA with a settlement offer of at least $30 million in land, monies, and other considerations, including Aboriginal governance. Ian Scott, then the Ontario minister responsible for Native Affairs (and the Attorney General), briefly informed the federal minister of Indian Affairs of Ontario's settlement offer before it was presented in 1986. It is clear that the federal government would not participate or accept its equal share of the $30 million offer (on the basis of the missing annuity payments between 1856 and 1883, plus interest since 1883. In 1986 this was calculated by provincial officials to be more than $12 million). The federal government took the position that treaty entitlement was land and land was a provincial responsibility. After the TAA rejected this offer, it decided to seek satisfaction in the courts.

Over the next two years, the issue escalated. The Ontario Ministry of Natural Resources (OMNR) took the deliberate position that the caution did not apply to uses of land like forestry insisting that the caution applied only to the narrow first registration of Crown patents or leases, or the staking and recording of mining claims. In 1988 the TAA decided to test this interpretation after Jim Bradley, the Liberal Minister of the Environment, signed an order under the Ontario Environmental Assessment Act. This order allowed the OMNR to begin construction of the Red Squirrel Road extension in April 1988 without a major environmental assessment of the impact of the road in the area, and without regard to its impact on the tribal motherland, N'Daki Menan. This government action was one of the factors that brought the Liberals down within only three short years after their election with a majority government in 1987.[6]

Why did Jim Bradley, the Minister of the Environment, sign the order in the spring of 1988? He had many alternatives. His ministry staff were opposed to beginning construction without a full-scale environmental hearing. He could have called for such a hearing. He could have delayed signing the order or not signed it at all. The order which he signed permitted certain environmental conditions applied only to the right of way. The major environmental effects were not on the narrow right of way but throughout N'Daki Menan. The road would violate the tribal motherland. Bradley was a political neophyte, and a junior cabinet minister. He did not take the advice of his own officials not to sign the order. Instead he bowed to the arguments concocted by the OMNR officials and Vince Kerrio, the Minister of Natural Resources, that the issue was only an OMNR road and not an Aboriginal issue. This was a huge political blunder by the Liberal government.[7]

The decision was put through Cabinet when Scott was out of town. In football jargon, it was a political end run by OMNR staff. The OMNR submission to Cabinet stated that the building of the road extension would have no general impact on Aboriginal affairs in the province and none on the TAA, their land rights, or the outstanding litigation on the Temagami land claim. Scott's political and other advisors never saw the submission until after it had been approved by Cabinet.[8]

Scott knew and understood the issues. He had been through this before when he was commission counsel with Thomas Berger on the Mackenzie Valley Pipeline inquiry in 1974-76. He helped Berger write the best-selling report, *Northern Frontier, Northern Homeland*, which parallelled the Temagami situation, on a grander scale.[9] But Scott had made enemies in the bureaucracy by ordering the OMNR staff to make a settlement offer to the TAA on 30 September 1986. The OMNR got its revenge a year and a half later. Beset by institutional racism, it railroaded the decision through Vince Kerrio, its minister. Exhibiting little or no empathy with Aboriginal people, he met with Aboriginal people only once during his tenure. He appeared to be a willing pawn of the bureaucracy and the white hunting and fishing lobby groups.[10]

A few months earlier, late in November 1987, the OMNR had hived off responsibility for land claims to Scott and the weak and understaffed Ontario Native Affairs Directorate. When the decision was made on the road construction, the Directorate was neither consulted nor advised of the decision before it was made. It was the OMNR's call. It must bear the responsibility for the millions of dollars spent on constructing a road that was the subject of two six-month TAA blockades and a $4 million road that has never been used.[11]

The TAA took action to protect their motherland in the spring of 1988.[12] Ontario had already signalled its intention to build the Red Squirrel Road extension which was to hook up with a main lumber road running south from Elk Lake. Since the 1970s, there was discussion about building the road through the Lady Evelyn and Wakimika wilderness areas. The road's purpose was twofold: to throw open the last remaining stands of old red and white pine forest to the lumbering interests, and to break the back of the cautions and hence the land claim. The response was swift and immediate. Taking the initiative, the TAA camped out on their lands at the north end of Lake Temagami where no usable road yet existed.[13] This peaceful defensive action by the TAA succeeded in holding the province captive for more than two years.

After the blockade was established at the north end of Lake Temagami, the OMNR officials claimed that they had not been prepared for either the blockade by the TAA or the outcry from the environmental groups, especially the Temagami Wilderness Society, but their claim lacked credibility. Their strategy was strikingly similar to that used by the OMNR officials in the fishing negotiations between 1982 and 1987. To build the road, it was necessary to create an artificial issue, a scapegoat, and in this instance the land claim and the TAA served that very purpose. A white racial backlash against the TAA would be concocted, if it opposed building the road. In the end, this OMNR strategy failed largely because the Native Affairs Directorate refused to negotiate the land claim which was then in the courts, on the basis that the road issue was an environmental issue. It was not a land claim. The OMNR was hoisted with their own petard. The issue was made worse when the environmental groups joined with the TAA in support of the land claim issue, if not on the blockades, over the next two summers.

The 1988 TAA blockade was successful in terms of the TAA's objectives. The road was not built that year. The blockade was purposely kept simple as only a TAA land rights blockade. It was completely separate from the white environmental lobby. They camped on their land where the road was to be constructed and where they could not be arrested, except for trespassing on Crown land under the Ontario Public Lands Act. They were not blockading a road—only the right of way where the road was to be built. They were doing nothing illegal, so they could not be arrested. They were also in the middle of the forest where it was difficult and costly for them to be arrested. Most importantly, the province was fearful of a public outcry if it sent in the Ontario Provincial Police (OPP) to arrest Aboriginal people on an environmental issue while their claim was before the courts. Led by its Deputy Solicitor General, Stien Laal, the OPP continued to refuse to arrest the TAA: they were doing nothing illegal, and the cost of arresting them would be too high.[14] Laal had been a claims negotiator in northern Canada and was aware of the tactics used by the TAA. He was also getting good advice from the OPP who constantly urged moderation and caution. This advice was provided to the Temagami committee which was the forerunner to the Aboriginal emergencies committee formed during the Oka crisis in the summer of 1990.[15]

The TAA had publicly stated its intention of continuing to maintain their camp with TAA members—over eight hundred strong—men, women, and children, even if they were going to be arrested. Scott and Bradley co-operatively attempted to resolve the issues during the blockades in both 1988 and 1989. It was an exercise in political damage control by the provincial Liberals. Their strategy was political and relatively simple: to minimize the political damage to the Liberal government. The focus was to be on the environmental issue for which Bradley was ultimately responsible. The onus was to be kept on the OMNR for getting the government into the mess in the first place. Once the OMNR ran out of its panaceas, a balance could be created among the Temagami groups. A broad environmental hearing on the road, which should have been done in the first place, could then be undertaken.[16]

As the province's chief law officer, and the minister responsible for Native Affairs, Scott kept the OMNR off balance by continually stating that the issue was not the land claim which was in the courts and thus could not be negotiated anyway. At the same time, he tried to create a balance by seeking court injunctions to end the blockade until the TAA had their day in court. The quid pro quo was that the court would also create a legal balance by ordering Ontario not to resume construction of the Red Squirrel Road extension until the Ontario Court of Appeal ruled on their land rights. Ontario then would have a reason not to build the road. It was given this reason early in December 1988.[17] There was a lull for two months. Both sides were tired and needed a rest.[18]

By the end of February 1989, the provincial government was in the middle of the anticipated next round of Temagami blockades. Construction on the Red Squirrel Road extension into the homeland of the Teme-Augama Anishnabai had not begun. Work could not begin in 1989 until after the spring breakup which was usually sometime in April. After the busy months of blockades the past year, it was a time to reflect on the events and attempt to develop a strategy for the months of blockades that were certainly still to come.

On 27 February 1989, senior staff of the Native Affairs Directorate were in the Ontario legislature along with Scott. The Directorate was then before the estimates which was the first time that the Directorate had come under scrutiny by the politicians in this way. (The estimates are the amounts of money which each government ministry or agency will spend in the forthcoming year, literally an estimate of the cost of items in their proposed budgets and what the money will be used for in the coming year.) A legislative committee can review (usually on a rotating basis) the budget estimates of a ministry and have an opportunity to ask questions about the items therein. The questions and the answers are part of Hansard and are recorded like the speeches made in the legislature. The minister, deputy minister, and the senior staff are present to defend and provide information on each item in the estimate.

A bulky speech of thirty-two pages was prepared for the minister to deliver to the committee outlining all the good things that Ian Scott and the Directorate had accomplished and were going to accomplish with the monies that were requested. If nothing else, Scott was going to read into Hansard the entire thirty-two pages of "accomplishments" churned out for him by Directorate staff. Written by a senior staff member of the Directorate, it was, even for a bureaucrat, mind-numbing, turgid stuff. However, the committee, which included some prominent members of the Ontario legislature, the Tories Robert Runciman and Ernie Eves, and the NDP members, Gilles Pouliot and Howard Hampton, wanted to get on with the questions and agreed to put the speech into Hansard as an appendix to the discussion.

Both Runciman and Eves were the Tories on the estimates committee. They were almost completely ineffectual, lacking knowledge of the issues. For example, Runciman wanted to know what would happen to race relations if "native policing" were to be introduced for Aboriginal communities in the province: that is, would there be a parallel police force in each community. Eves, as the Conservative critic for native affairs, expressed concern about a number of general issues which he claimed were brought to him by his constituents. His main concern was the Temagami blockade of 1988 for which he said merely that the government had not done enough for the local non-Aboriginal people, had been damaging to the "Native community" (as a result of a racist backlash against them), and that it had put the Milne lumber company into receivership. The Tories showed that they did not care about Aboriginal issues—they went through the motions because they had to be there. But then the Tory record, of which they were a part, spoke for itself. The Tories had decided to undertake the litigation against the TAA in 1976 and to go to trial in 1982. Scott took great delight in reminding them of their many past failures. I noted in my journal that "Ernie Eves was truly pathetic."[19]

The NDP members had the best questions and were generally up-to-date on their knowledge of the issues. Their focus was on Aboriginal justice and economic development in northern Ontario. They asked why more was not being done. They argued that the province was still hiding behind the federal government and "playing a form of federal-provincial ping-pong" at the expense of the First Nations in Ontario. Scott, a smooth politician, and much more knowledgeable on these subjects than his opposition counterparts, kept answering the questions with hard facts at his disposal. When he did not know an answer, he made something up which was sometimes even more plausible than the facts. He cited the progress made in the policing agreements, the Native justice-of-the-peace program, agreements with the Nishnawbe-Aski Nation, education, and the movement toward self-government. He noted the record of the Liberal government on land claims and self-government. Scott paid special attention to what he had done on the Temagami claim. The government had made a settlement offer in 1986 of $30 million, of which $15 million could be taken up and used by the TAA in land. That amount, he estimated, would mean the establishment of a reserve for the TAA of about 150 square miles. Prophetically, he indicated that the province would soon make another offer of settlement even if the TAA appeal were rejected.

Scott rejected the suggestion by Gilles Pouliot that, as Attorney General and as minister responsible for Native Affairs, he was in a conflict of interest. That is, on the one hand, Scott was suing the TAA for their own lands and on the other negotiating a settlement with them. Scott argued that there was no conflict because, in this case, the landowner was the Ministry of Natural Resources. However, in terms of the Temagami land claim, both in negotiations and in litigation, Scott was calling the political shots. He could do so since he had the complete support of the premier in both of his portfolios to act as he required. Moreover, since he believed that a negotiated settlement out of court was the best way to proceed, he argued forcefully that any settlement offer that was made to the TAA should come through the Cabinet and the premier as a corporate decision. Pouliot called him a "juggler," suggesting that Scott was politically a manipulator playing off both of his portfolios. Scott retorted that "if I am a juggler as you suggest, I am the best juggler in the business."

The NDP members then shifted their questions to Aboriginal economic development and why the Directorate had not spent a fund of $2 million for "Native Economic Development" which had been on their books as a line item in the Directorate's budget since 1985. There was no excuse for not spending the monies which had been set aside. Through bureaucratic squabbling, the Directorate simply could not decide what to do with the monies. Scott skated on thin ice through that one, stating that the Directorate was working on a plan to use the funds for community development. But the Directorate had no such plans in process at the time. They began the very next day as directed by Scott.[20]

As the committee adjourned for the day, we found out that the Ontario Court of Appeal had unanimously rejected the TAA appeal. It was now time to meet and make another settlement offer to the TAA, and to prepare for the TAA to seek leave to appeal to the Supreme Court of Canada. Appeal at this level is not automatic, but given the magnitude of the litigation, it was more than likely that an appeal would be granted by the highest court in Canada.

The Temagami emergencies committee met the next morning at 8:30. Scott made it clear that, in spite of the fact that the province had won the appeal, now was the best time to make an offer to the TAA to resolve the matter out of court. He emphasized that the message that should be given to the TAA was that Ontario was intent on acting fairly and justly in the circumstances. He pointed out that the offer to be made should be just as good as the one made in 1986. He rejected the suggestion that the province should remove the 1973 land cautions. He argued that it was likely the TAA would be granted an appeal to the Supreme Court of Canada and no court would grant the province the right to remove the cautions while the case was on appeal. He requested that the settlement offer should go to Cabinet the next day and that he wanted to announce it in the legislature that same afternoon, Wednesday, 1 March 1989.

I prepared the 1989 settlement offer. The settlement offer was approved the next day and sent to the TAA. Scott announced it in the legislature on the first of March. The offer was to negotiate a reserve at the original site at Austin Bay of one hundred square miles of lands and waters which would include both surface and subsurface rights. This area was worth more than $15 million because of the potential of the subsurface rights at Austin Bay. Ontario also offered to continue to negotiate a model forest management area (of a size to be mutually determined). The model was to be based on Bart Feilders's discussions with the TAA—that is, the Wakimika Stewardship Council as well as other considerations that were stated in the 1986 offer. (Feilders, as Ontario's negotiator, was a planner and career bureaucrat who worked in the ministry of Northern Development and Mines.)

The provincial offer was much richer, at least double, the 1986 offer of $15 million from the province alone. And it was not contingent on federal participation. It was for a specific site which was to be negotiated and for a specific amount of land. Most importantly, it included both subsurface and surface rights to the land at Austin Bay. If accepted, it would have been the basis for a settlement. But the timing and circumstances were wrong. Once again, in rejecting the province's enriched offer, the TAA held the government captive.

The TAA was justifiably angry with the Court of Appeal ruling. The offer was immediately denounced by Chief Gary Potts as being insufficient. He said the site at Austin Bay had been logged over twice already and the province was making a lesser offer. The primary rationale, of course, was that the TAA believed that they had to have their case brought before the Supreme Court of Canada. They felt that they could not let the Steele and the Court of Appeal judgments stand unchallenged. They were right to do so. But, in the end, the cost was very high.[21]

The Temagami committee met again, a few days later on Thursday, 2 March. Ian Scott reported that he had called Chief Gary Potts with the provincial offer and that the TAA were angry with the ruling and the settlement offer. They would never negotiate on the treaty entitlement issue. He offered however, to talk again the next week. Thanks to the continuous negotiating efforts of Bart Feilders with Chief Gary Potts, at least the lines of communication to the TAA were open. Meanwhile the Attorney General's staff reported that the Temagami Wilderness Society's (TWS) legal case was moving forward and would be heard in court in April. The Attorney General's lawyers did not expect that the TWS would win their case or that any appeal would be denied by the courts. They were right.

The OMNR wanted to announce the continuation of its survey on the Red Squirrel Road extension as of 13 March. This would take about one month. Construction could then begin in mid-May after breakup. This left everything the way it had been the previous year. The injunction of the Ontario Court of Appeal had disappeared when that court had handed down its judgment on the land claim. What would happen when the TAA blockaded the area again? Or if the TWS lost their case, as expected, in the courts, would they also blockade this, or another road in the Temagami area? In spite of having "won" in the courts, the Peterson government was no further ahead on the Temagami issues. It was a captive of the TAA. No one had any suggestions. Things drifted yet again for the province.[22]

On 23 March we met again on the Goulard Road which was on the southwest side of Lake Temagami. It was not connected to the Red Squirrel Road extension. It was a private road, not a public highway or a right of way. This was the first and only time that the TAA blockaded a private road in the Temagami area. The TAA blockaded the Goulard Road where a bridge was to be constructed. The owner of the road would have to go to court to get an injunction. But the purpose of the road was similar—to harvest the timber in the Temagami area.

Bart Feilders reported that the TAA were greatly concerned that the OMNR was going to allow snowploughs to come onto the Red Squirrel Road extension at the west end—the opposite end to where the blockade had been the year before—and to disturb a "circle of sacred rocks" near the right of way. He noted that Potts, in a speech made to University of Toronto students on Wednesday, 22 March 1989, made a strong hint of potential violence, saying that the TAA were getting angry and frustrated with the lack of action by the government. Potts advised the OMNR to be careful with their snowplough in that area. But senior government officials thought the greatest danger would occur if the TAA and the white environmentalists joined together in the event that the TWS lost their case in the courts. The government feared that the TWS would resort to civil disobedience on one or more roads in the Temagami area.

Provincial officials had no idea of the relationship between the TAA and the TWS or other environmentalists. They did not know that the TAA had always refused to let the white environmentalists take part in their issue and thus, perhaps, be co-opted or lost in the "environmental" issues. The province was fortunate that there was no alliance in place. Their strategy, if there was one, was short term. It was to keep talking and wait to see what would happen. The Temagami emergencies committee met to discuss the Goulard Road issue. Bart Feilders reported with some good news. He had been advised that the Goulard lumber company had called off their work crews and would undertake no further work on the bridge. The Goulard brothers had decided that the bridge was a provincial responsibility and that they did not need to get an injunction. It was just easier to close things down. The TAA would then call off its blockade. There would be no confrontation on the Goulard Road. There would be no need for an injunction either by the Goulard lumber company or by the province. At the same time, on the Red Squirrel Road extension, the OMNR had advised their snowploughs to go carefully and avoid the sacred rocks along the right of way, to avoid a confrontation. Fortunately, the situation on both roads had cooled down.

The Temagami committee met again on 28 March. There were reports of a demonstration at the Goulard Road where the company employees were repairing a bridge. No one could find Mark Goulard, the company's owner, to find out what he was going to do. Someone thought he was in Palm Beach, Florida, "on the beach." The demonstration was to be a one-day affair with no blockade. Laal counselled calm and caution. The OPP were trying to keep things under control. Scott then looked at the critical dates. 13 March—the date set for the beginning of construction activity for the Red Squirrel Road extension—had come and gone. The OMNR had got its survey crews into the Red Squirrel Road extension and had been carrying out their work unimpeded. There was no blockade. The 10th of April was the next critical date, when the TWS case would be heard in the courts. Scott asked what would we do if we won the case. What would happen if we lost the case? What was our long-term planning for this year? Bart Feilders would continue to keep the telephone lines open to Chief Gary Potts and keep offering to negotiate. But there was no response to Scott's question by the bureaucrats.

Still held captive, decision-making was by crisis-management as the province continued to lurch from day to day without any long-term plan for Temagami. Ad hoc decisions ruled the day. The Minister of Natural Resources, Vince Kerrio, advised the government to wait until 11 April to see whether the province would win the TWS case, so it waited. The province won the TWS case. The environmentalists could now move into action and blockade whenever and wherever they chose without having to worry whether they would prejudice the hearing of their case. They appealed their case and lost the appeal.

On Thursday, 30 March I headed off to Trent University to present a paper on "Official History: Its Pitfalls and Criteria" at a colloquium hosted by the Frost Centre for Canadian Heritage and Development Studies (now the Frost Centre for Canadian Studies and Native Studies). I was invited to come by Professor Bruce W. Hodgins, who was still involved in the Temagami case, both as a landowner (owner of Camp Wanapitei) and as a friend of the TAA. After the colloquium, Hodgins asked me whether something could be done to break the current stalemate and to reach an agreement between the TAA and the province on the Temagami issues. He said that he was arranging a symposium at the Frost Centre in a few weeks, on 19 April, and invited me to come. He also asked me to invite Mark Krasnick, then the head of the Directorate, to attend so that we could talk further with a TAA representative and others who were attending to arrange for a facilitation of the Temagami issues. I agreed to try to do so.

Back in Toronto, I asked Krasnick about the idea. I told him that we had to do something to move things along. Feilders had done his best but he now had no mandate from the province and nothing to discuss with the TAA. He was mired in an interim arrangements agreement upon which the two sides could not agree. The TAA wanted the Wakimika Stewardship Council to cover the entire four thousand square miles while the province was holding fast to the position that the council's responsibility should apply only to the Wakimika triangle area or, at the most, to an area of two hundred square miles. No one knew whether the province and the TAA were prepared to negotiate the land claim and the interim arrangements for a stewardship council together or for what specific geographical areas. Feilders wanted to leave the area open and try to reach an interim arrangements agreement first, and then move on to the larger land claim negotiations. The TAA saw no difference in negotiating the two together.

Krasnick was very reluctant to attend such a meeting. His main objection was that Feilders was the province's main contact with the TAA. He said that he did not want to do anything to "screw up" the relationship between Bart and Gary. But I reasoned that Bart had said Gary was off for a rest and nothing was happening. Feilders was making little or no progress and there would be blockades again as soon as breakup occurred in the Temagami area, by either late April or early May. Finally, he relented and agreed to attend but only on the condition that I call Bart and ask his advice and what he thought about us going. Bart was, as always, extremely constructive and helpful. He pointed out that nothing was happening between he and Gary; nor was it likely to happen in the next month or so. He saw no reason for not to try something different. To meet the TAA on their own terms, would break the captivity and end the blockade.

Krasnick and I went along to Peter Robinson College, Trent University near the Otonabee River on 19 April.[23] I had prepared a draft memorandum of agreement, or framework agreement which I had used in other negotiations to great effect, that specifically fleshed out the items to be discussed or negotiated between the TAA and the province. This draft agreement mirrored the TAA's proposal for a treaty of co-existence. I kept it very simple to not draw red warning flags for the TAA. No geographic areas were specified for any of the items. That was to be left for the settlement negotiations. And no time limits were imposed, either on the negotiations or on the litigation. The previous offers had been quite complex. Now it was time to do something different. The draft framework agreement included a treaty, land, a stewardship council, interim arrangements, and other considerations. I did not show it to Krasnick for fear that he would not approve it or even that he would use it as an excuse to decide not to come along on the trip.

The Frost Centre at Trent University did a fine job of hosting the daylong symposium, led by Professors Hodgins and John S. Milloy. Milloy, a professor of history and Native Studies at Trent University, acted as the chair for the day's events. Others in attendance included Brian Slattery, a law professor from Osgoode Hall Law School, the late William J. Eccles, a professor of history from the University of Toronto, Brad Morse, a law professor from the University of Ottawa, Bob Surtees a historian from Nipissing University in North Bay, and Tony Hall then in Native studies from Laurentian University in Sudbury. Jamie Cullingham, a Toronto filmmaker and producer, was also there. Hodgins had also got a TAA representative to attend the meeting, one of the councillors, Mary Laronde. It was an auspicious gathering and the papers were useful in focusing on the historical and legal issues in the context of the recent Ontario Court of Appeal ruling on Temagami. Papers were presented by Slattery, Morse, Eccles, Surtees, and Hodgins.

Later in the day, tempers got shorter, likely because of our presence. Tony Hall made one of his eloquent speeches about colonialism and the province's history, and to vent his palpable anger, he walked out. We took a break. Hodgins and Milloy went out of the meeting room to try to calm Hall down and restored some semblance of order. When the meeting resumed, Hodgins focused on the Steele judgment and the Court of Appeal decision, pointing out that, in spite of the court's rulings, there was considerable doubt about the historical facts. For example, it was not at all clear that Chief Tagawinine represented or signed on behalf of the TAA in 1850 or even that the TAA participated in the treaty after it was signed, as the province continued to maintain in its arguments before the courts. Hodgins noted that, according to Canadian law, any such doubt should not be held against the TAA but rather should be in their favour. But the courts had stated that the TAA had also acted as if they had signed an adhesion to the treaty, even though no such adhesion was ever made.

I commented that I recognized there was considerable doubt on the historical facts, but both judgments had gone against the TAA. I still had respect for the TAA's claim as a living thing, as well as the legal forum in which they had chosen to address it. I said that I was not at all sure what the connection had been between the real headman of the TAA, Peter Nabonaigonai, and another chief, Tagawinine, who received a reserve at Lake Wanapitei. Mary Laronde of the TAA asked who Chief Tagawinine was, clearly implying that he had not been one of the chiefs of the TAA in the mid-nineteenth century. Hodgins responded that in his view, there was considerable doubt on the historical facts of the treaty and on who signed, if anyone, for the TAA. This being the case, he asked why could there not be political negotiations and an agreement to resolve the Temagami land claim.

Then Krasnick really put his foot into it. Rather than listening further, he put on his lawyer's hat. He asked what were the assumptions in the Temagami legal case and then stated that the historical facts, as decided by the courts, were the legal underpinnings of the case and they had been narrowed by the courts so that the legal case was now a historical fact. He advised that it was on this basis that the province would settle the land claim. Brad Morse intervened and argued that his statement might be taken as "good or bad" but in other jurisdictions one distinguishes between the historical facts and the law.

It was at this point that Jamie Cullingham, the film producer, lost his temper altogether. He literally screamed at Krasnick: "You say you have respect for the land claim, you don't even understand it. You're a piece of shit!" He walked out of the room in a rage. Krasnick paled at this outburst and was visibly shaken. The chair called for a break at 3:30 P.M. Krasnick walked out. Outside of the room, I met with Hodgins and Milloy. They apologized to me for Cullingham's behaviour and said that Mary Laronde wished to speak to me. I spoke with Mary briefly and told her that I realized things were stalemated between Gary and Bart and that I had no intention of short-circuiting their discussions. I handed her the draft framework agreement and suggested that this approach might be a way to break the log-jam of negotiations. She said that she understood and agreed to take the draft document back to the TAA for their consideration. I told Bart Feilders the next week what had happened to warn him that he might be approached by Gary Potts on this subject.

Meanwhile, Krasnick was very angry. Perhaps, assuming that I had set him up to be called a "piece of shit" by the people at Trent University, he never forgave me. But Jamie Cullingham, a graduate of Trent University in 1980, was a strong activist for the TAA and had made a film for them called "Frozen Caution." His outburst was a surprise to everyone. In the end, Krasnick failed to listen to what people were saying, polarizing in the process positions that were already strained by a year on the blockade.

In retrospect, the occasion was worthwhile. Another approach had been offered to the TAA—a framework agreement—without any conditions attached. The TAA took the document and added their treaty of coexistence to it, as well as the discussions with Bart Feilders on the interim arrangements, and gave it to Bart and the provincial Cabinet. Just over a year later, on Earth Day, 23 April, a document was signed, which included a treaty of coexistence, a stewardship council, and agreement to enter negotiations. The way to an agreement on Temagami went through Trent University in Peterborough after more than one hundred years of negotiation.

The Temagami emergencies committee met again on 24 May. We heard updates on the roads, Milne and other lumber companies, the Temagami Wilderness Society and the upcoming construction season which was described as reopening a situation in Temagami like the civil wars in Beirut. Even with Milne lumber company in receivership, the OMNR was still planning, seemingly without any purpose, to complete the Red Squirrel Road extension, even after all that had happened the year before. They had opened a competition and asked four or five companies to respond to tenders for a licence to cut down the forest off the Red Squirrel Road extension. Construction on that road was scheduled to begin again in the middle of June. With the TAA neutralized by the injunction and the Court of Appeal decision, the primary fear at the meeting was that the TWS, having lost their court case (and with little likelihood of an appeal being granted by the courts) would become "desperate" to stop the construction and would begin taking direct action such as tree-spiking to protect the red and white pine.

The only suggestion to help counter this activity came from the Deputy Minister of Natural Resources, George Tough. He advised that the OMNR was going to hold an international conference in the fall of 1989 on the old-growth forests—too little and too late as always—and presumably it would be held while the OMNR was helping lumber companies cut down the forest it was discussing at the conference. It seemed a strange way of doing business.

Brock Smith, the Deputy Minister of Northern Development and Mines, chaired the meeting. Quite remarkably, he stated that, to avoid a repetition of last year's events, Scott wanted the officials to come up with a "strategy" for the construction season. The senior officials ignored this request. They had no idea what to do; they were being held captive and were being smoked out by the TAA. Governments and their officials may be "good" at ad hoc crisis management and "reacting" to events, but they are truly hopeless when thinking strategically to prepare for what is going to happen. Instead of developing a strategy to address crises, the bureaucracy did what it always did: after the fact it created a committee to respond to Aboriginal emergencies. The Temagami committee became this committee during the events at

Oka in the summer of 1990. The committee still exists in the provincial government to this day.

Feilders reported that Potts was taking a much-deserved leave and that the second chief, Rita O'Sullivan, was now in charge. The TAA were moving ahead with their appeal of the Ontario Court of Appeal ruling in February to the Supreme Court of Canada. The TAA would, now that the injunction was over, be free to determine the place and the timing of its next blockade. Feilders also reported that he was making some progress, which was quite remarkable in the circumstances, in getting the OMNR staff and the TAA talking to one another for the first time. (This was part of the framework agreement that I had given to Mary Laronde.) The subject was a research study by the TAA and some consultants mutually agreed upon by both, on the old-growth forest. It was proposed that the OMNR would pay the TAA $50,000 for this research study. It turned out that Mary Laronde became the TAA contact with the OMNR on this project. It presaged the work of the TAA on the Wendaban Stewardship Council from 1990 to 1995. To give him his due, Feilders was always tenacious and, as a professional planner, he was always a strategic thinker.

I prepared the strategy for the minister, setting out the three most likely scenarios if the road extension was going ahead that summer. My primary assumption was that the TAA would not want to blockade the road before its leave to appeal was granted by the Supreme Court of Canada. If the TAA did blockade, a court would likely grant another injunction to stop it, which might harm their Supreme Court of Canada case. If leave to appeal was granted, then the court would most likely do again what it had done the year before. An injunction would be granted but the court would also order a halt to any road construction pending the outcome of the TAA appeal to the Supreme Court, which could take a year or even longer. The strategy was outlined as follows: (1) if the TAA leave to appeal to the Supreme Court of Canada was not granted; (2) if the TAA leave to appeal was granted; and (3) if the TWS appeal was not granted, which was likely. The proactive strategy in all of these scenarios was to continue the province's dialogue with the TAA and to establish "bridgeheads." The TAA and not the TWS was the key to seeing that things would happen constructively in the Temagami area. The advice and the strategy was to concentrate on assisting the TAA positively in the areas of resource development, especially forestry, such as in Feilders's research study. A workshop hosted by the TAA was also recommended to keep them talking rather than fighting with the OMNR staff and to seek ways to maximize economic development. It worked over the next year, leading directly to the treaty of coexistence which the TAA, in its generosity, held out to the OMNR and the Wendaban Stewardship Council.

The Temagami emergencies committee met again on Wednesday, 21 June. With construction about to resume, Scott required updates and assurances that the province was in a position to respond to events when the blockade(s) also resumed. The government suspected, but did not know with any degree of certainty, that the TAA would either not join with the TWS or not let the TWS support their blockade. Their primary issues were quite different. The TAA would not want their land rights lost in the broader environmental concerns of the TWS on whether to cut down the Temagami old-growth forest. Besides, the TAA were not against cutting the old-growth forest but were rather more concerned about how it was done. By this time, even Kerrio had seen the value of the strategy of keeping open a dialogue with the TAA and working with them. He suggested that the OMNR expand its proposed "model management system" to include the environmentalists. It is a pity he had not thought that way a year before when it was possible to have a full-scale environmental hearing on the Red Squirrel Road extension. An incredible amount of time and money would have been saved.

All through that summer, the province was still held captive by the TAA in its blockade. Scott kept asking in our briefings whether we had a settlement proposal prepared to offer on the Temagami land claim if the TAA were denied leave to appeal to the Supreme Court of Canada. The bureaucracy did not have either a proposal or a strategy ready for this remote possibility. Neither did Krasnick ask me to prepare one. Perhaps he figured it was a certainty that the Supreme Court of Canada would hear the case. By 3 August, we knew that the Supreme Court of Canada would decide on the TAA appeal within two months. It was good to work on other things, especially the Manitoulin Island settlement negotiations which were progressing well. For a change, it was a quiet summer.[24]

By early September 1989, we knew that another blockade would take place soon. But Krasnick had implemented, yet again, another management reorganization within the Directorate. We had one on 1 February 1988 and again in the spring of that year. This was the third in a year and a half. It wreaked havoc on staff training and morale. In this round, the Temagami file went to someone else in the Directorate. When I handed over the file in my meeting with Krasnick, he questioned the deputy minister's and the minister's instructions to prepare another settlement offer to the TAA in the event that the Supreme Court refused to hear the case. His reasoning was that, in preparing another "rock-bottom offer" to the TAA, the government was merely reaffirming the negative messages it had constantly sent to the TAA. This was a serious misreading of the situation. I told him that he was wrong—that what was required was to build on the dialogue that had been established and to work with the TAA to develop a substantive framework agreement which would, among other things, include land as a substantive component. But he never had much information about what was happening on the ground. As a result, no offer was prepared and nothing was done. But the TAA got leave to appeal to the Supreme Court of Canada on 3 October. With Feilders as the provincial negotiator, the dialogue with the TAA that had been opened over the past year and a half had set in place a framework for negotiations and a Treaty of Co-Existence.

The OMNR began construction of the road. In response, the TAA blockaded the road again in early November. The highest court in the land agreed to hear the claim on 3 October 1989. The TAA sought an interlocutory injunction in the Ontario High Court of Justice on 27 October 1989 to stop the road construction. Their injunction was denied, without costs being awarded by the courts.[25] Ontario responded by seeking another legal injunction to stop the blockade which was granted by the courts. The TAA obeyed the law, not wishing their claim on appeal to the Supreme Court to be jeopardized. The TAA began the blockade on 11 November 1989. They were taken away gently by the OPP and many were arrested. They were not fined by the Ontario courts since it was recognized that they had an interest in the land.[26] However, this recognition did not help the white environmentalists who had already taken up the blockade of the Red Squirrel Road extension. The environmentalists had attempted to save the Temagami forests. When they tried in 1989 to stop the construction of the Red Squirrel Road, they were arrested. Many went to trial and some were either fined or imprisoned. They did not have the same sort of legal defence, i.e., a land claim, that the TAA had, now that the Aboriginal people were gone.

In the political fallout, Scott came under heavy criticism for using the law for purely political ends. Critics argued that he should have negotiated and not gone to the courts for an injunction. However, from Scott's perspective, several things were accomplished. The claim was not sacrificed for another issue. (Substantive negotiations were not seen by the Liberal government to be possible anyway.) The TAA refused to negotiate and wanted to have their day in court. The road became an environmental issue. Even Bob Rae, who had never before backed any Aboriginal issue, much less a land claim, allowed himself to be arrested in September 1989. But he had little interest in Aboriginal issues then or now, except as abstract constitutional matters.[27]

Unfortunately for Scott, the issue led, in part, to the defeat of the Liberals in the provincial election of September 1990. He was only narrowly returned to the political backbenches, and has since left politics altogether. Given his background, and initial high promise and depth of experience as minister responsible for Native Affairs, Scott was a large disappointment to First Nations in Ontario. He supported Quebec and the Meech Lake Accord over Aboriginal people. He let his inexperienced head of Native Affairs and his special assistant (both of them lawyers) "rule the roost" on Aboriginal matters. Their focus was on Aboriginal self-government modelled narrowly and conservatively on a municipal scheme. After four years in power, the provincial "Native self-government" policy, another political embarrassment when it was announced in the Ontario legislature early in December 1989, died still-born.[28]

The Directorate staff met with Scott on Tuesday, 3 April 1990 for a briefing session. One of the issues was Temagami. With the Red Squirrel Road extension completed, Roger Fryer had taken over the remains of Milne Lumber. If Fryer was not able to gain access to a supply of wood, he would be in financial trouble. Events were set in motion once again in a high reactive way. The OMNR had again authorized cutting, using the completed road. The next Monday, 7 April, the TAA would again blockade the road, stop traffic, and go to jail this time. And this time, since the road was completed, they would be doing something illegal. The issue now became whether the government would allow the OMNR to timber and permit the use of the Red Squirrel Road extension.

Earlier that day (7 April), Feilders had an extended lunch with Potts who had warned the OMNR to stop cutting. Potts wanted to meet with Scott on these matters. Feilders had told Krasnick that the TAA would show no movement on the issue, and Krasnick informed Scott. Scott said straight out that the OMNR should stop cutting for one month until

Scott got a proposal to Potts to break the log-jam and get an agreement that would give us a strategy that would also "see us through the next two years."

Temagami was the Directorate's senior bureaucrat's file but he was nowhere to be found. He had prepared no offer of settlement since 1 October, had no strategy prepared, and no proposal. Scott had lost confidence in him after he (Scott) had been "savaged" in the Ontario legislature early in December 1989, with the self-government proposal that the senior bureaucrat had prepared. Feilders was asked to prepare a proposal for Scott to give to Chief Potts. In the negotiations, Feilders would continue to act as the provincial negotiator. Scott noted he could do this because his role, as the Attorney General, in the Temagami blockades was as a "hawk," instead of a dove. Scott observed that he would surprise them with a proposal which would be in the TAA's favour in his role as an "advocate" for Aboriginal people. There was a private meeting between Chief Potts and Scott. But almost assuredly, this proposal became the memorandum of understanding and the draft treaty of coexistence that was signed by Chief Potts and by the new minster of Natural Resources, Lyn McLeod, on Earth Day, twenty days later. Ironically, Ian Scott did not sign the MOU, though Lyn McLeod did. However, Scott had to get his Cabinet colleague to agree that the OMNR would not permit logging or the use of the Red Squirrel Road extension. He succeeded. The OMNR was "tamed" for a time. Scott never got the political credit for getting the province out of the Temagami debacle or for the signing of the MOU.

On Earth Day in the spring of 1990, the TAA and Ontario signed a memorandum of understanding on a treaty of coexistence and the creation of a stewardship authority which effectively meant that the Red Squirrel Road would never be used to destroy the last old red and white pine timber stands in the Lake Temagami area.[29] A few months later, just as a provincial election was called in July 1990, another resistance and blockade occurred, this time over the pines at Kanesatake (Oka).

Since April 1990 there have been ongoing negotiations, with the signing of an Ontario-TAA memorandum of understanding on a treaty of coexistence, as well as the establishment of the Wendaban Stewardship Authority.[30] Ontario, despite the change in government from the Liberals to the New Democratic Party (NDP) in October 1990, took a legalistic, hard-line approach to the negotiations. The August 1991 Supreme Court decision undermined the TAA claim. The negotiations, under the auspices of the NDP government, were a failure. The NDP government made a settlement offer which was rejected, in November 1993.[31] Given the Supreme Court ruling in August 1991, and the subsequent non-Aboriginal and Ontario government institutional backlash, and the lingering controversy over the Algonquins of Golden Lake land claim centring on Algonquin Provincial Park, there was no room for optimism. There still remains a deep division between Ontario and the TAA on the matter of Aboriginal title which Ontario has never accepted in this, or any other Aboriginal title issue. Ontario continues to see the matter as one of only treaty land entitlement, as it argued in the courts, and not as a question of Aboriginal title. But for the TAA, the two cannot be separated.

This is a classic case of an Aboriginal people's resistance movement which has been a partly successful, hard fought, and frequently bitter experience. For more than two years the TAA held the province captive through its blockades in 1988-89. Ironically, the actions taken by the TAA since 1973 have been successful. Development was effectively frozen for almost thirty years. At least part of the Lake Temagami area has been preserved. N'Daki Menan has been partly saved from exploitation from private timber and mining interests, at least to date.

You Can't Chop Peace Down

Planting the White Pine Tree
at West Virginia University, 1992-99

ELLESA CLAY HIGH

Chapter 6

Trees brought me to the shore of Lake Temagami—the Great White Pine of Peace whose roots extend past human failings; an ancient Ontario forest refusing to become commodity; eastern woodlands still connecting Aboriginal peoples of places now called "Canada" and "United States"; the standing people— sycamore and hemlock, elm and oak—of my Kentucky youth. Their invitation was as clear as the one I received on paper through the mail. I would be lucky to learn the lessons I knew would be waiting at the 1999 Wanapitei colloquium, "Blockades and Resistance," commemorating the tenth anniversary of the Temagami blockades of 1988 and 1989. But then, I believe such writers as N. Scott Momaday, who says that the "imaginative experience and the historical express equally the traditions of wo/man's reality."[1] David T. McNab, an organizer of this event, had visited West Virginia University on several earlier occasions, including the 1998 annual colloquium on literature and film, where we first met. When I explained we had a small but growing program in Native

Notes on pages 240-41.

American Studies at WVU, formally begun with the planting of a peace tree on campus in 1992, he seemed both surprised and pleased. He visited the peace tree, and before leaving campus commented, "I've been coming to this place for three years [giving papers at the literature conference], and now I know why I had to come. I will help you build your program any way that I can." Thus began a friendship and some initial networking between our program and the Native Studies Department at Trent University, with which David is associated.

The Tree of Peace was in this way instrumental in my connecting with the Wanapitei colloquium. When I was invited to participate, I began by asking: What is the relationship between peace and resistance? Do Native peoples view such concepts differently than mainstream culture does? Do trees themselves have qualities that concentrate these related forces? And finally, might the blockades of 1988-89, by which the Teme-augama Anishnabai attempted to stop logging of their ancestral homeland, be viewed not as demonstrations of resistance but as acts of peace, or both simultaneously?

PEACE AS EMBODIED IN THE GREAT WHITE PINE

One of the best-known images of peace originating from indigenous peoples in North America is the peace tree, a tradition of the Haudenausanee or Six Nations Iroquois confederacy. This symbol, which dates back at least five hundred years and quite likely is much older, is part of the story of the Peacemaker, a figure who was able to unite warring tribes by redefining what it means to be human and by showing why peace can prevail (principles the "founding fathers" borrowed to create the American constitution and to unite the thirteen colonies; and which later provided a basis on a global scale for the United Nations. As with many Native contributions, however, it has taken a long time for this debt to Indian philosophy to be acknowledged). The full story of the Peacemaker and the founding of the league, the *Pax Iroquoia* as it sometimes has been called, takes many days to be told orally, and thus is beyond discussion here. What does concern us is how the Haudenausanee define peace, particularly as it has been embodied in the Great White Pine. As Paul Wallace states *in The White Roots of Peace,*

> Peace was not, as they [the Haudenausanee] conceived it, a negative thing, the mere absence of war or an interval between

wars...peace *was* the law. They used the same word for both. Peace (the law) was righteousness in action, the practice of justice between individuals and nations....Their own Confederacy, which they named the Great Peace, was sacred.[2]

So peace is not some static, resting period between conflict, but something much more vibrant. Again, Wallace notes that the root word for peace in Iroquois is:

The same as that used for "noble" and "the Lord" in their translations of the Bible....Even such renderings of the term in English are too abstract to catch their way of looking at it. Peace was the Good expressed in action, that is, the good life. It was also, in their thought, the ideal Commonwealth—not *Utopia* (No Place), but *Kayanerenhkowa* (the Great Peace) established so firmly at Onondaga.[3]

Again, notice the emphasis on "action," on taking the intangible and giving it form—in this case, in movement. As with much of Native thought, concreteness is important—dreams and visions (especially when they articulate paths to be taken and values to live by) must be further expressed through dance, song, ceremony, artifact, or practice.

IN COMPARISON, HOW IS PEACE DEFINED BY THE DOMINANT CULTURE?

If we turn to *The Oxford English Dictionary*, we find that the word *peace* came into Middle English from the Old and Middle French term *pais*, which, in turn, traces back to the Latin *pax*. The first written evidence of this term in English dates to 1297 as "a time of peace." The OED then lists six definitions, worth quoting in part: "1. Freedom from, or cessation of, war or hostilities"; "2. Freedom from civil commotion"; "3. Freedom from disturbance"; "4. Freedom from quarrels or dissension between individuals"; "5. Freedom from mental or spiritual disturbance or conflict"; and "6. Absence of noise, movement or activity; stillness, quiet, or inertness."[4] Thus, peace remains defined in a kind of "negative" fashion—understood more fully by what it is not rather than by what it is. I am reminded of a pool of water with nothing moving: it will stagnate sooner or later if a current isn't introduced! To give that "current" to the term in English, we must add a verb, as in "to hold one's peace," "to keep the peace," "to make peace," or "to make one's peace." Even with this boost, the concept of peace seems somewhat mired in itself.

To approach closer to the Haudenausanee concept of peace, the above definitions could use an infusion of resistance. Unlike peace, which has no verb form, as in *to peace*, the first appearance of resistance in English is to resist. This term, the OED again informs us, probably originated in Latin (*resistere*), then found its way into several romance languages, including French (*resister*), with Chaucer pioneering the word in written English (1374). The OED first lists it as a transitive verb: "1. to stop or hinder (a moving body)"; "2. to succeed in standing against"; "3. to prevent a weapon, etc.) from penetrating...to withstand the action or effect of a natural agency or physical force...an attack, invasion, blow...natural force, weakness or disease"; "4. Of persons: to withstand, strive against, oppose"; and "5. To stand against, to make opposition to."[5] There is a lot more action here to be sure! The OED also includes an interesting noun form, as in a *resist*: "In calico printing: a preparation applied to those parts of the fabric which are not to be coloured, in order to keep the dye from affecting them....Also, any composition applied to a surface to protect it in part from the effects of an agent employed on it for some purpose."[6] Such a definition might have special significance for Native people if applied to past interactions with the dominant culture, and perhaps this noun will gain wider circulation in the future.

The term *resistance,* the later noun form, echoes the verb: "The act, on the part of persons, of resisting, opposing, or withstanding." And the curious use of *resistance,* as in a piece of resistance, coming directly from the French *pièce de résistance*: "Our appetite demands a piece of resistance" (1797), smacks with positive, delicious connotations.

NOW WHAT DOES ALL THIS HAVE TO DO WITH THE GREAT TREE OF PEACE?

Perhaps it should come as no surprise that Native people often refer to trees in general as "standing people," with print evidence found in work like *Black Elk Speaks* by Nicholas Black Elk and John G. Neihardt, among others. This image not only acknowledges a direct and equal relationship between human and plant, but also reveals some of the innate qualities of trees. Indeed, trees are entities that continually stand, falling only to die (a quality reflected in such phrases as "a stand of trees," or a "deer stand," for hunting out of trees, etc.). Rooted in the earth, they also reach for the heavens, and thus become connectors and bridges. One of their most important functions is to stand, withstand, and resist. Yet they are filled with peace.

And while they stand, pieces of them travel—seeds whirling away to colonize other places, roots extending where no eye can follow. Western scientists proclaim them the oldest living beings on the planet, and the largest—a grove of aspen in reality all one plant connected through roots for acre upon acre—a corporate single.[7] Trees capture light with their bodies, which later can be released into fire, warming us like the star it came from. Wood, coal, diamond—a galaxy made human size, given enough pressure and time. Trees recharge the air and pump water between the earth and sky. They may recharge and pump a lot more while they stand.

All this, Native peoples have understood for a long time. As scholar and writer Paula Gunn Allen says, a "fundamental fact" for Native Americans is that "humans exist in community with all living things (all of whom are known to be intelligent, aware, and self-aware), and honoring propriety in those relationships forms one of our basic aesthetic positions."[8] And N. Scott Momaday notes in a foreword to *Keepers of the Earth* by Michael J. Caduto and Joseph Bruchac, "one of the most important of all considerations in human experience [is] the relationship between man and nature. In the Native American world this relationship is so crucial as to be definitive of the way in which man (this differs from Native belief which holds that all things, even stones, are living) formulates his own best idea of himself."[9]

Hundreds or perhaps thousands of years ago, the Peacemaker revealed the white pine as a symbol of humanity's "own best idea" of itself as we try to live in harmony with one another. According to Paul Wallace: "The Iroquois [Haudenausanee] fed their minds and guided their actions by means of symbols. When Deganawidah [the Peacemaker] stood before the first council of the United Nations at Onondaga and planted the Tree of the Great Peace, he planted in the hearts of his people a symbol that was to give power and permanence to their union."[10] As with many Native symbols, it was (and still is) easily discerned on the surface, but, like the intricate root system of trees, it is complicated and interactive on multiple levels "down under," the full meaning of which rightly remains hidden except for those few who have "a need to know." What *was* generally shared transformed the "European mind of 1600" from a medieval way of thinking into the "Modern World."[11] As John C. Mohawk continues to observe in his prologue to *The White Roots of Peace*:

> They [Europeans] learned to think in egalitarian terms, they heard themselves repeating the heresies which they heard from the Indians which questioned the doctrine of the divine right of kings. They began to adopt the Indian custom of democratic social ideals....A way of thinking was the most powerful change which Europe experienced in the Americas. It was to change the face of Europe and the world forever.[12]

Each part of the Great White Pine held ideas. Its branches provided "shelter, the protection and security that people found in union under the shadow of the Law," and its roots, which extend in the four sacred directions and thus encompass the world, "signified the extension of the Law, the Peace, to embrace all mankind. Other nations...would see these roots as they grew outward, and, if they were people of good will, would desire to follow them to their source and take shelter with others under the Tree."[13] The tree itself was evergreen and thus unchanging and everlasting in spirit.

Also important were the presences found at either end of the tree. Underneath its roots, the Peacemaker disclosed a stream that disappeared into the earth. For there to be peace, all weapons of war must be thrown into this current and then covered back over, thus originating the idea of "burying the hatchet." In the pine's top branches, the Peacemaker placed the eagle, that most sacred of birds, who would sound an alarm at approaching trouble, for peace cannot last "unless a watchful people stands always on guard to defend it...a reminder that the price of peace, as of liberty, is eternal vigilance."[14] This bolsters the notion that peace is not a "freedom from" or "absence of" condition, but a dynamic process, with disarmament and preparedness connected by the conduit of a "Standing Person." If we want more clearly to understand how to promote and preserve peace, we might try "to peace" together a model that functions in human society the way trees function in the larger domain, as suggested by the Haudenausanee so long ago.

BORROWED SYMBOLS

Some of the symbols established by the Peacemaker and others who followed him filtered later into the American colonies as they were established and remain today—the eagle, the arrow bundle, and the concept of the "long house" in such slogans as "united we stand, divided we fall." Unfortunately, some traditions, such as the use of wampum to verify truthfulness in treaties and the holding of condolence ceremonies to heal those who would take part in important meetings, were not embraced by the encroaching Europeans. And the symbols of peace? In most cases, the spiritual connotations seem to have vanished in translation. The eagle, which for Native peoples flies closest to the Creator and thus acts as holy messenger and intermediary, is depicted in aggressive, military stances, often found riveted to the top of flag poles (a mainstream version of the Peace Tree?) and appears most strongly connected with the armed forces and other agencies of the federal government.

A similar example passes through millions of unknowing hands a day—the American one-dollar bill, that building block of currency. Is it a coincidence that the front of it pictures George Washington, "founding father" and first president, while the backside features a pyramid with floating eye (another borrowed symbol from an ancient culture) and on the right the eagle? As is typical, the bird is shown "spread eagle," the arrow bundle fisted in one talon and a branch clutched in the other, with "E PLURIBUS UNUM" on a banner flowing from its beak, the American flag covering its body, and a star cluster floating overhead. The eagle as national emblem may be patriotic, but it is not spiritual.

For a widely acknowledged peace symbol, we must turn to such sources as the Old Testament—the dove with olive branch in its beak. Interestingly, here again is a bird and tree, though the tree is reduced to a twig and physical connection to the earth is lacking. No other generally recognized symbol for peace comes to mind, except perhaps for the finger-waving "V" which emerged in the 1960s and early 1970s (made suspect forever by then President Richard "I am not a crook" Nixon gesturing before cameras in this manner), and the graphic symbol (a hoop with a three-pronged stick turned upside down) of the same period, which today seems as quaint as a pair of bell-bottomed jeans— more fashion statement than icon. Perhaps, not surprisingly, at the end of the twentieth century, the dominant culture recollects its history more in terms of wars fought than peace maintained. This supports the idea voiced by John C. Mohawk, when he observes that of all the skills Native peoples shared with Europeans so they might endure on this continent, one was not "completely transmitted....It was the survival skill of negotiating a truly peaceful settlement and the vision of a totally peaceful future. It was the survival skill which we in the late twentieth century probably need the most."[15]

THE PEACE TREE AT WEST VIRGINIA UNIVERSITY

In 1992, coinciding with the quincentenary anniversary of Christopher Columbus's arrival in North America, WVU began a celebration of Native American heritage, with many events scheduled throughout the academic year. These included lectures, performances, and workshops by such notable figures as historian James Axtell, artist Don Tonaso, filmmaker and health educator Beverly Singer, storyteller Joseph Bruchac, writer Elizabeth Cook-Lynn, and the American Indian Dance Theatre, among others.

The event of widest impact, however, was the first to occur—the planting of a White Pine of Peace by Chief Leon Shenandoah, Tadodaho or presiding moderator over the fifty coequal peace chiefs comprising the grand council of the Six Nations Iroquois confederacy in upper New York. As Tadodaho, he represented a line of more than two hundred Tadodahos which stretches back to the time of the Peacemaker.[16] At a banquet the night before the planting, he spoke quietly and with tremendous authority about the importance of right thinking, reminding the audience that the Creator had taught his people the importance of "peace on earth, the welfare of all people and powerful good minds." He said, "I would like to go back one thousand years to the way of life [then]. Our land, water, and air are the three things we have to live for....Without Mother Earth we wouldn't survive. We need pure water and fresh air to fill our lungs." Then he warned of a strong wind that would rise little by little as the water and ground becomes more polluted. "The wind is going to be worse than it was in Florida [a recent hurricane]. It will be enough to destroy the world....One day the United States will come to us asking for help."[17] Then he finished by voicing his concern for the future of his grandchildren—his way of looking forward seven generations. Some of the three hundred in attendance looked forlornly down at their dessert plates, having expected a different kind of after-dinner speech. Others understood they had heard something far greater.

The next morning, a warm 12 September, a seven-foot white pine was planted across from the student union building, the Mountain Lair. Robert Talltree, a Chippewa flutist who also was an honoured guest that weekend on campus, assisted Chief Shenandoah. After performing a pipe ceremony to purify and bless the area, Talltree said, "Hopefully this tree will be remembered every year, and people will learn to start a new life. We have a long journey to help Mother Earth. With your help and understanding we'll make it through again."[18]

Then Chief Shenandoah planted the pine, invoking the earth, wind, and water as part of his blessing. He also said that the "roots of the peace tree go in four directions. Each nation can follow back to the tree and to the creator." Again he warned about an impending storm, pollution, and other disasters that could end this present world.[19] Because at least two of us who were involved in planning the event had seen in dreams that water was somehow tied to this particular ceremony, I presented gifts of spring water to both Robert Talltree and Chief Shenandoah, and water was poured on the trunk and ground as part of the planting.

Three more annual Peace Tree ceremonies followed, presided over by Peterson Zah, first elected president of the Navajo Nation (1993), Chief Oren Lyons, Faithkeeper of the Turtle Clan of the Onondaga Nation (1994), and Dr. Henrietta Mann, Cheyenne (1995). These ceremonies also involved Native people from our region (most notably those of Shawnee and Cherokee descent), as well as WVU faculty and administrators, students, and members of the larger Morgantown area. After four years of prayer and hearing words from "powerful good minds," our community's understanding of peace had grown, yet at the end of the fourth ceremony, something felt finished. I thought perhaps the four ceremonies had completed a spiritual cycle, yet I also felt an unease I couldn't explain.

It took almost a year for that unease to be understood. In the early morning hours of 10 August 1996, the Peace Tree was chopped down. The vandals were never identified, and no arrests were made. The shock and sadness caused by this act were compounded for many of us by the death seventeen days earlier of Chief Shenandoah, the Tadodaho who had planted the tree in 1992. Some people worried that if another tree were planted, it too would be felled, and that no action should be taken—that, in essence, the Peace Tree on our campus should be allowed to disappear. However, we told the press as a message to the vandals, whoever they were: "You may chop down the tree, but you can't cut peace down. What the Peace Tree symbolizes can't be destroyed." A function, after all, of the Peace Tree is to stand.

On Saturday, 19 October 1996, Chief Jake Swamp of the Mohawk Nation and founder of the Tree of Peace Society honoured WVU by coming to plant another Peace Tree. October in West Virginia can be gloriously sunny and balmy, but it can also snow. Because it was a slate-grey morning of rain and icy wind, Chief Swamp was greeted by university officials and regional Native people by the fireplace in the Mountain Lair. There, as part of his opening remarks, Chief Swamp recounted part of the story of how the Peace Tree originated—it was good to hear it again, this time by the fire. Then, warmed and heartened, we once more went outside to plant a Peace Tree, only a few feet from where the first had been cut down. Chief Swamp began the ceremony with a prayer in Mohawk "to gather the minds of those present and to give thanks" to all of creation. During the planting, he again mentioned how the Peacemaker over a thousand years ago had dedicated his life to uniting tribes in conflict—that the Peace Tree is a living symbol of that peace. He said, "We come from many corners to unite for the common purpose of promoting peace....The tree doesn't change color with the seasons, to show that the peace will never waver." He then remarked that although "much of the original knowledge had been lost, and the tree had slowly fallen," there was hope. "The children of peace are born today, [and as they begin] to spread the timeless message of peace, the tree is going to rise again."[20] As part of the planting, the crowd sprinkled "soil and tobacco around the base of the tree." Young school children helped to tie prayer ribbons marking the four directions and representing all peoples of the world. And Chief Swamp turned to them and said, "When the wind blows, the ribbons will touch each other," and many of the children smiled, because they understood his message of brotherhood. Then he gave a great gift to the university students also, by telling them that the tree was now "part of their family," and that those far from their homes could "overcome their loneliness and gain peace" under its branches—a kind of home-away-from-home. And some have found that comfort. Afterward, he stopped by the site of the first Peace Tree, where only a stump jutted from the ground, and he said that it showed "how hard we have to work for peace."[21] I don't think we really heard him, because after this replanting a quiet period set in. Although individuals prayed and visited at the site, a couple of years passed with no public ceremonies. But the Peace Tree remained, and it greeted David McNab when he stood before it in 1998.

TO WANAPITEI AND BEYOND

The previous sentence seems to signal that we will now move to some revelation that, if we're lucky, will illuminate this story and close it— reminiscent, perhaps, of an Annie Dillard, who, upon perceiving "the tree with the lights in it" shares a vision through which "the mountains open and a new light roars in through the crack, and the mountains slam."[22] But that's not the way it works—at least for me. Such "vision," if ever attained by someone like me, accretes in rings and at a pace a tree might find comfortable, the complete pattern of which can be seen only if the tree is cut down. Should I live to "old growth" myself, per- haps I'll be able to express in better terms the "dialectic, creative ten- sion between peace and war" embodied in the white pine, as David McNab suggested to me.[23] I don't know.

What I do know is that those trees are calling, and that they took me to Wanapitei. As I gave my presentation there, the wind came up, scat- tering papers across the room, and the slide projector burned out. Afterward, when I looked at Lake Temagami in the late afternoon sun, I saw that it teemed and flashed with spirit in the slant light, almost seething with tiny bodies—a countless gleaming. Dark forest lined its shores, a living frame, and then the lake just seemed like water again, but not quite. I have since learned, during the writing of this piece, that David McNab is Cree on his mother's side, who was a Kennedy or Canada. The family is originally from Pine Tree Island, Cumberland House, in present-day northeastern Saskatchewan. Kennedy in Cree is *konawpeki*, meaning "he who stands tall," and a logo of a pine within a circle, representing Pine Tree Island, tops David's faxes and other cor- respondence. And I am Cherokee back on my mother's side, and the name I have been given has to do with the dove and with water. White pines surround my house, here in West Virginia. So now I see that, even an ordinary person like I am is moved about the way trees move—rooted in many directions, travelling like a seed. I just hope my heart is good, and that I too can find shelter in such branches. For the

Great White Pine and its ongoing workings for peace, I give praise to the Creator, and I thank the Haudenausanee who continue to safeguard and nourish it, trying to live by the ideals it embodies. And to David McNab, who somehow is part of it all, I remain grateful. Also I've learned, from listening to the scholars gathered at Camp Wanapitei and to the Teme-Augama Anishnabai who kindly met with us there, about the many obstacles overcome by this nation—they are the same that Native peoples in West Virginia still face—issues of identity and homeland. To this day, no federally recognized or even state-recognized tribe exists in West Virginia. The prevailing historical accounts perpetuate the "fact" that these Appalachian mountains were merely hunting grounds (another term which remains undefined, particularly from a Native perspective), thus held in common and belonging to no one. Since none lived here, the land was easily granted away. And paper trails leading to other conclusions were "lost," destroyed when court houses burned during the Civil War or later coal mine "wars," or were ethnically cleansed from the beginning, the "Indian" not being an option on census records—only "white," "coloured," or "mulatto."

To the Teme-Augama Anishnabai, this story must have a familiar ring. Their hard-won successes make me feel proud and give me hope that with perseverance and similar effort, the First Nations of West Virginia may one day be recognized again. I salute the Teme-Augama Anishnabai for their courage and vigilance, and for their continued struggles as "the people of deep water."[24]

Unfortunately, the battle to save the red pines and other trees remaining on their sacred lands has not been won—the legal cautions put forward by the First Nation were denied in court, and it may be only a matter of time before more resistance is required. Most certainly, these trees remain flash points where the Teme-Augama Anishnabai will continue to "make their stand," their defence just one more step along what Gary Potts, chief during the blockades, called his tribe's "odyssey toward justice."[25] Trees may stand full of peace, but they recharge and pump a lot more.

In the larger scheme of things, demonstrations of resistance are also acts of peace, for there can be no harmony if one side is gone—if all ancient trees are cut down and sacred places bulldozed over. As Chief Leon Shenandoah said in his address to the General Assembly of the United Nations in 1985:

We must live in harmony with the Natural world and recognize that excessive exploitation can only lead to our own destruction....We were instructed to carry a love for one another and to show a great respect for all the beings of this earth....When people cease to respect and express gratitude for these many things, then all life will be destroyed, and human life on this planet will come to an end.[26]

When the Peacemaker's work was done, he covered his body with bark and went back into the earth. Before he disappeared, he said, "If men would ever become indifferent to the League...perhaps I may stand here again among your descendants. If the Great Peace should fail, call my name in the bushes, and I will return."[27]

So I look for him sometimes among the Standing People. He might have been in my dreams last night. A billow of smoke, thick and fast and yet somehow contained and thinking, both mysterious and terrifying in its power, flowed over the tree tops and then slid down the trunks in front of me and other people all having a good time. The good time stopped. When the smoke cleared, I could see nothing, but I knew an entity was there, waiting, because the spiritual had been forgotten. We tried to make amends, quickly lighting sage and sweet grass, reaching for tobacco, but the dream ended.

WORKS CITED

Allen, Paula Gunn, ed. *Spider Woman's Granddaughters*. New York: Ballantine, 1989.

Ankrom, Barbara Burke. "Native Tribute." *West Virginia University Alumni Magazine* 16, no. 1 (1993): 20-21.

Black Elk, Nicholas, and John G. Neidhart. *Black Elk Speaks*. 1932. Reprint, Lincoln: University of Nebraska Press, 1988.

Dillard, Annie. *Pilgrim at Tinker Creek*. 1974. Reprint, New York: Harper Perennial, 1988.

Hodgins, Bruce W., and Jamie Benidickson. *The Temagami Experience: Recreation, Resources, and Aboriginal Rights in the Northern Ontario Wilderness*. Toronto: University of Toronto Press, 1989.

Mohawk, John C. Prologue to *The White Roots of Peace*, by Paul A.W. Wallace. Saranac Lake, NY: Chauncy, 1986.

Momaday, N. Scott. Foreword to *Keepers of the Earth: Native American Stories and Environmental Activities for Children*, by Michael J. Caduto and Joseph Bruchac. Golden, CO: Fulcrum, 1988.

———. *The Way to Rainy Mountain*. Albuquerque: University of New Mexico Press, 1969.

Noisette, Tim. "Community Gathers for Tree Planting." *The Daily Athenaeum*, 21 October 1996, 1, 10.

The Oxford English Dictionary. Oxford: Clarendon Press, 1971.

Raine, Meredith, and Jennifer Dittman. "Native American Fest Kicks Off." *The Daily Athenaeum*, 14 September 1992, 1, 2.

Wall, Steve, and Harvey Arden. *Wisdomkeepers: Meetings with Native American Spiritual Elders*. Hillsboro, OR: Beyond Words, 1990.

Wallace, Paul A.W. *The White Roots of Peace*. 1946. Reprint, Saranac Lake, NY: Chauncy, 1986.

Part 2

Historical Perspectives on Resistance

Aboriginal Resistance in the Mid-Nineteenth Century

The Anishinabe, Their Allies, and the Closing of the Mining Operations at Mica Bay and Michipicoten Island

RHONDA TELFORD

In 1849, after years of dispute between the Anishinabe and mineral developers, a group of prominent chiefs and their allies took over a mining location at Mica Bay on Lake Superior. This action was a demonstration of Ojibwa ownership of and beneficial interest in the subsurface; it precipitated the Robinson Treaties of 1850. This chapter will examine the long-standing relationship between the Anishinabe and their minerals, the circumstances leading to the mine shutdown, and the prominence of minerals issues in the treaties. From the Aboriginal perspective, the Robinson Treaties recognized and respected their subsurface rights. But irregular colonial actions soon caused Anishinabe anger to rise to the level it had been in 1849, when they closed another mine on Michipicoten Island in 1854.

Archaeological evidence indicates that Aboriginal peoples in Ontario have used copper for seven thousand years and silver for about five thousand. Some archaeologists emphasize a continuity

---

Notes on pages 241-47.

of mining experience in the Great Lakes area, believing that Anishinabe and Iroquois of Lakes Superior and Huron are the descendants of the ancient miners. The Anishinabe believe that metals, rocks, stones, crystals, and sand possess power; some, but not all mineral locations were sacred places. Before minerals were disturbed, the ancient miners and their successors offered presents to their spirit-keepers.[1]

On numerous occasions, and for differing reasons, Aboriginal people chose to reveal mineral locations to non-Aboriginal people, thus facilitating most of the major "discoveries" in Ontario. Between 1534 and 1840, Cartier, Champlain, Brule, numerous Jesuits, Alexander Henry, William Johnson, Schoolcraft, and George Johnston among others were given information about copper, gold, and silver. In the seventeenth and eighteenth centuries, Aboriginal people shared their mineral knowledge with Europeans, largely, it would appear, as a means to cement trade and military alliances. During the nineteenth century, Aboriginal people used their mineral knowledge to elicit non-Aboriginal support for their land rights. As early as the 1840s, but more particularly since the 1860s, some revealed mineral locations for cash compensation.[2]

In August 1840, Chief Shinguacouse of Garden River petitioned the government, complaining about non-Aboriginal use of food and timber resources and emphasizing his nation's ownership of the land. Such disputes intensified after an American copper boom spurred several Canadian mining companies into action. Among these was the Lake Superior Company, established in 1845 by Allan and Angus Macdonell, with whom Shinguacouse shared his knowledge of mineral locations.[3]

In 1845, Shinguacouse stated that the first miners "came stealing along our shores...to look for metals which they heard were to be found in our land and asked us to shew them the copper but this we refused."[4] Colonial authorities did not stop these incursions. The mining licences were a source of revenue and used for patronage purposes: six of the first licences went to Tory executive councillors. Sixty-four locations on the shores of Lakes Huron and Superior yielded $400,000, payable over five years. By 1846, $60,000 had already been collected, but "not one shilling...has been paid to the Indians." Already tied to the Ojibwa because of their revelation of mineral deposits, Macdonell, a lawyer, stayed to help them obtain compensation from the Crown.[5]

When the Crown Land Department authorized Alexander Vidal to survey mining locations at the Sault in 1846, it exacerbated the situation

by ignoring Aboriginal title, thereby creating the basis for more grievances. Vidal was advised by Chiefs Shinguacouse, Nabenagoching, and
others that they owned the land and minerals, that he had no right to be
on their land, and that "had they not been too few in number they would
have prevented a party which has just gone off to explore." Vidal ceased
surveying for a few days, but returned to lay out additional mining locations, including two which covered Shinguacouse's village at Garden
River. Although Vidal informed D.B. Papineau, the Commissioner of
Crown Lands of Anishinabe land rights, nothing was done.[6]

In June 1846, Shinguacouse petitioned the "Great Father" in Montreal, demanding a cessation of mining operations that were threatening traditional lifeways and infringing on Ojibwa land rights. He said,
"great things have been found in these places. I see Men with hammers
coming to break open my treasury to make themselves rich and I want
to stay and watch and get my share." Insisting on compensation for the
use of his minerals, he demanded "a share of what is found in my
lands." This was a significant petition, the first of at least fourteen,
emphasizing Aboriginal knowledge and ownership of minerals. It was
ignored. In July 1847, chiefs representing the Ojibwa from Michipicoten to Thessalon petitioned the Governor General, unsuccessfully
offering to sell their land.[7]

In response to rumours that the Crown would ignore their claims,
the Ojibwa stated they would visit the Governor General. In open disagreement with the licensing policy pursued by the Crown Land
Department, Civil Secretary Major Campbell advised the executive
council that Ojibwa land rights should be obtained prior to the issuance
of mining patents.[8]

Neither the chief's request for a treaty, nor Campbell's position persuaded the Crown to act. Instead, that same July, the Indian Department failed to convince Shinguacouse to relocate on Manitoulin Island.
Rather than leave, the chief confronted George Desbarats, demanding
an end to his mining activities. Believing these unsettled claims would
result in violence, Desbarats implored Governor General Lord Elgin
to make a Treaty.[9] Although warned by a man-on-the-spot, colonial
authorities took no action. In November, Papineau, reported negatively
on the Aboriginal claims arising from the mining agitation. His views
clashed with those in Vidal's earlier report and in the Indian Department, which called for a treaty before the issuance of mining patents.[10]
Lord Elgin, however, did not act.

Obtaining no response to his petition, Chief Shinguacouse led a deputation to Montreal in June 1848. On returning, Ojibwa anger increased when they discovered that the Crown Lands Department had sold their village of Garden River as a mining location. Following this disclosure, the chiefs "spoke openly of resorting to force." In July, Campbell informed Anderson that the Ojibwa had told him their "hunting is entirely destroyed," that mining licences cover their villages, and that they are forbidden to cut timber and hay. Campbell instructed Anderson to investigate their claims and propose compensation.[11]

Anderson met separately with Chiefs Shinguacouse and Peau-de-Chat, reporting that the Ojibwa were undoubtedly the "proprietors" of the timber and minerals from Mississauga River on Lake Huron to the American boundary at Pigeon River on Lake Superior. Anderson recommended reserves and a treaty. Following his departure, Shinguacouse instructed Macdonell (now the chief's legal advisor) to inform the miners through public notice to cut no more timber.[12]

The American press printed an account of Shinguacouse's speech to Anderson which varied widely from the version he submitted to government. Among other points, the chief asserted that

> the miners are intruding upon our lands, without securing us a compensation. The Great Spirit, we think, placed these rich mines on our lands for the benefit of his red children so that their rising generation might get support from them when the animals of the woods should have grown too scarce for our subsistence. We will carry out, therefore, the good object of our Father, the Great Spirit. *We will sell you lands if you will give us what is right and at the same time we want pay for every pound of mineral that has been taken off our lands, as well as for that which may hereafter be carried away.*[13] [emphasis added]

The fact that Shinguacouse had demanded to be paid for all past and future mineral development was absent from Anderson's Report.

In the spring of 1849, Macdonell visited the Governor General in Montreal, but returned without a settlement. By this time, the Anishinabe had lost all patience and were openly "proposing to drive the miners out of the country." Macdonell promised to escort another deputation to the Governor "to prevent a resort to force."[14]

After his return to Garden River, he convened a council in June 1849. According to the Methodist missionary James Cameron, who reported the proceedings to the Indian Department, Macdonell obtained a variety of mining leases from the chiefs. Cameron noted that his rival, the Anglican Reverend Anderson, secured a lease of Garden village from the chiefs. Cameron implied that the chiefs were tricked, but it is more likely that their lease was intended to supersede those of the Crown Lands Department as it would have included part, if not all, of the area previously sold as mining locations. Cameron warned the Indian Department that a deputation of chiefs and Macdonell would go to Montreal to claim the mineral monies held by the Crown Lands Department and advised James Price, the Commissioner of Crown Lands, that a treaty should be concluded as soon as possible.[15]

In July 1849, Shinguacouse, Nabenagoching, Menissinowennin, Macdonell, and Anderson went to Montreal to speak with Elgin. Angered by the illegal sales to mining companies, they declared they would "this winter drive off the obnoxious miners" if their claim remained unaddressed.[16] This was the last time the Ojibwa spoke personally with the Governor General before taking over the mining operations at Mica Bay. The government moved slowly. Instead of sending treaty commissioners, they sent Alexander Vidal and T.G. Anderson to conduct another investigation.

While the Garden River deputation was in Montreal, the Fort William Anishinabe made a strong demonstration of their anger and rights. In July, Peau-de-Chat "arrived at Mica Bay with a large band of his people, and told the parties in charge [that is, John Bonner] and also the miners there, *that unless a settlement was made with them for their lands,* they (the miners,) must leave the country"[17] [emphasis in original]. Following his return, Macdonell received word from Peau-de-Chat to meet him forty miles up the lake. Instead, Macdonell sent word that a treaty would soon be concluded and the chief returned home. His message may have been meant to avert violence, but he and Shinguacouse likely believed a treaty was imminent. Bonner never reported this incident to the company or the government. Peau-de-Chat's unilateral actions clearly indicated that the First Nations, and not Macdonell or other non-Aboriginal people, were in control.[18] Thus, a clash at Mica Bay was only narrowly avoided in July 1849, before the commissioners were sent out. The Fort William and Garden River First Nations had demanded a treaty and believed they would get one; instead they got Vidal and Anderson. For various reasons, neither one was a particularly prudent choice.

During the fall, Vidal and Anderson met most of the chiefs regarding their claims. Both before and after their meetings, the commissioners made extensive tours of the mines and water-power sites on the south and north shores of the upper lakes. Vidal and Anderson were not well received at Fort William. Peau-de-Chat did not trust them and they did not want to recognize him as chief. Later, Peau-de-Chat made a speech expressing his concern for the future and demanding thirty dollars for each man, woman, and child in perpetuity. After some discussion the following day, the chief revised his opinion and agreed to make a treaty. Although the commissioners reported that the meeting ended on friendly terms, it is clear they antagonized the Fort William First Nation with blatant threats. For example, a journalist from the *British Colonist* reported:

> these Commissioners then informed the Indians that their presents should be stopped, and that they should receive no pay for their lands; and when this last mentioned threat was held out by Mr Vidal before he left the Sault for Garden River; the reply to which was if we will not receive pay for our lands we will take them and keep them ourselves....Can there be anything more disgraceful or dishonest in a government, then [sic] instructing its servants to hold out threats like the above, and particularly so when it had actually received in cash, for these very lands, near ten thousand pounds. What has become of that money, or how has it been accounted for?[19]

Not only does this account indicate that the commissioners viewed the use of threats as acceptable, it also, and most significantly, indicates that they purposely falsified at least some of the events in their "report."

The Garden River First Nation met the commissioners, who refused to recognize Macdonell as their speaker. Shinguacouse, asked whether he would agree to a treaty, said he had not made a final decision and wished for another day to consider it. The chief, however, did discuss several areas of leased land, which were to be recognized in any future treaty.[20]

The Ojibwa selected reserves based on proximity to traditional fisheries, hunting and trapping territories and their gardens. But the area retained by Shinguacouse was problematic, encompassing nineteen mining locations. The commissioners informed the Ojibwa that the government would not recognize their independent land deals. At this moment

Macdonell interrupted, so angering the commissioners that they ended the meeting and the Ojibwa held their own council overnight.[21]

The second day had a similar tenor and outcome according to a journalist from the *British Colonist* who reported Shinguacouse's speech: that the minerals in their lands were for their own benefit; that two deputations to the governor had failed to bring justice; and that Macdonell had authority to conclude a bargain with the Crown on their behalf. Macdonell rose and began to speak but, according to the journalist, he was interrupted by Vidal who threatened to end the meeting and derail the treaty. When the Ojibwa refused to deal directly with the commissioners, Vidal walked out and Anderson remained as a "spectator."[22] Later, Macdonell reported that Vidal had threatened that the government would take Anishinabe land without compensation and that the Metis would receive nothing; that presents would be stopped and that the head chiefs would be deposed.[23] Threats were the basis of the negotiating style for Vidal and Anderson.

It is difficult to determine the aftermath of this stalemate. The silence between the Ojibwa and the commissioners at the Sault was not overcome. Instead, lines of communication reopened at Garden River in October 1849, where Shinguacouse's son, Augustin, and other young men sought out the commissioners, promising their nation would forego its hostility and negotiate a settlement with government representatives. The following morning, the commissioners talked one last time with Augustin and the young men who agreed to have no more dealings with Shinguacouse while he was taking advice from Macdonell. Vidal and Anderson did not use this situation to renew talks with Shinguacouse. Using the tactic of "divide and conquer," they left the matter unfinished and proceeded to meet the remaining First Nations. Vidal and Anderson mistakenly believed they could use the apparently compliant attitude of the young men to bypass the traditional leadership and the issues at stake. Augustin was likely sent by his father to keep the dialogue open in spite of the failed meeting at the Sault. When the commissioners declined to use this opportunity to rekindle talks with Shinguacouse, believing they had bypassed him, they continued to alienate him and his followers, thereby inflaming an already explosive situation.[24]

In their report, Vidal and Anderson claimed Ojibwa opposition could be easily overcome if it was impressed upon intransigent First Nations that they would be shut out of the treaty. Although the commissioners urged the Crown to negotiate quickly so that Ojibwa "attachment and confidence" would not dissipate, they had left the Anishinabe on both lakes on bad terms. So bad, in fact, that five or six days after they left, several hundred Ojibwa and Metis, led by Shinguacouse and Nabenagoching, landed at Mica Bay and forcibly shut down the operations of the Quebec Mining Company.[25]

Press accounts of the action varied widely. Bonner claimed the Ojibwa were in full war-paint brandishing "scalping" knives and ordering him to shut down the mine. But, according to Macdonell, Bonner answered the door and expressed relief that Macdonell and Metcalfe had accompanied the Ojibwa. Bonner already knew the Ojibwa were coming and believed Macdonell's presence would hamper the outbreak of violence. Macdonell introduced the chiefs to Bonner and told him that they were there to exercise their rights and reclaim their land and minerals. At a breakfast meeting with Bonner the next morning, he proposed to return the mine if Bonner signed a lease with the chiefs, acknowledging their rights and paying them rent. Macdonell left to secure the chiefs' agreement, but returned to find Bonner claiming he had no authority to agree. Bonner later declared that Macdonell warned him if a lease was not signed, between fifteen hundred and two thousand Ojibwa would join them immediately. Macdonell denied this, claiming what he had said was that such a force would come in the spring to "maintain their rights."[26]

Vidal and Anderson's report was submitted to the government on 5 December 1849—almost one month *after* the Mica Bay incident occurred. This uncharacteristically long delay was doubtless a result of the mine takeover. Their "report" was used to represent Shinguacouse and Macdonell as "trouble makers" prior to Mica Bay, thus setting them up to take responsibility for what had already happened. Anderson knew of the incident seven days after it had occurred. On 16 November 1849, he wrote to Robert Baldwin: "if immediate steps are not taken…to intimidate the Indians and half-breeds, they will…suppose Mr MacDonell has overawed the Government and the consequences may be most lamentable."[27]

Colonial reaction was swift. Elgin dispatched troops and erroneously identified "blackguard whites" as ringleaders and "American Indians" as major participants. Elgin claimed to have been arranging compensation for the Ojibwa since 1847. In reality, since coming to the colony in January 1847, Elgin had done nothing to arrest the chain of

events that led to Mica Bay.[28] Warrants were issued for the most prominent Anishinabe, Metis, and white leaders. Allan Macdonell was heard
at the residence of Chief Justice J.B. Robinson in Toronto (a close friend
of his family) on charges of "forcible possession" of the mine. Robinson
rejected the validity of the charge and a new deposition was filed.[29]

In December 1849, the Commissioner of Crown Lands received a letter from Mr. Cockburn, the secretary of the Montreal Mining Company,
which enjoyed good relations with Chief Kee-wa-konce at Bruce Mines.
Cockburn was afraid that if the government did not make a treaty "on
Lake Superior before Spring, there [would]…be a gathering of several
thousand…[Ojibwa], which might have the effect of making the Chief
(Kee-wa-konce) change his mind and attempt to recover his lands by
force, which might, and probably would be, attended with a melan-
choly loss of life and property."[30] Thus, colonial authorities had been
warned that if they did not act quickly, *a second* "Mica Bay" would occur
on Lake Superior, with possible ramifications for the Bruce Mines.

Shinguacouse and Nabenagoching were transported to Toronto, but
pardoned in May 1851. While detained, they demanded compensation
for mineral revenue collected by the government. MacDonell's connections to the Robinsons enabled both him and his Ojibwa friends to
avoid lengthy punishment. W.B. Robinson, the Chief Justice's brother,
recommended that Bruce send the Ojibwa home and that Robinson
himself be sent to settle their claims, because the former superintendent in charge of the affairs of the Montreal Mining Company, Bruce,
was not the best choice.[31] The executive council agreed and directed
Robinson to acquire by treaty that portion of Anishinabe land "required
for mining purposes." Compensation was to remain low because the
Crown conveniently viewed the Ojibwa as hunters without knowledge
of or use for the minerals.[32] Two weeks later, the Crown Land Department received a second letter from Cockburn of the Montreal Company warning of impending danger in the spring if no treaty was
made. Shortly thereafter, Robinson met Shinguacouse and Nabenagoching, promising a treaty would soon be made and warning them
to cause no further disturbances.[33]

Anishinabe from both lakes participated in the treaty negotiations.
On more than one occasion, Robinson made excuses for the low
amount of compensation offered and argued that "the lands now
ceded are notoriously barren and sterile, and will in all probability
never be settled except in a few localities by mining companies." He

assured the Ojibwa they would retain hunting and fishing rights in the shared area and that miners would buy Aboriginal goods. Robinson stated the government would pay a one-time amount of $32,000, or half of this with an annuity of $4,000. Neither Shinguacouse nor Nabenagoching viewed this as satisfactory and demanded an additional annuity of $10 per head.[34]

Robinson made *two* treaties with the Ojibwa, alleging that the Superior chiefs had wanted a separate treaty. Although this was a "divide and conquer" tactic, it also reflected the fact that Robinson could not initially obtain the consent of the Huron chiefs. Shinguacouse and Nabenagoching continued to demand more than Robinson was willing to agree to, including an annuity of $10 per head and land for the Metis.[35] Robinson's account of the negotiations is brief and does not explain why two treaties emerged. Shinguacouse and Nabenagoching, the former from Lake Huron, the latter from Lake Superior, both signed the Robinson *Huron* Treaty. Not only did they not agree to the terms of the Robinson Superior Treaty at the time it was hived off and signed, they also had very real interests in the minerals at Mica Bay. It was, no doubt, imperative for Robinson to separate these chiefs from the mining locations on Lake Superior.

The issue of minerals compensation did not disappear. The sum of $32,000 was too low. It was nowhere near what the government had already collected (at least $60,000) or what it was supposed to collect according to the terms of the original leases (at least $400,000). The injustice was apparent to Shinguacouse and Nabenagoching who continued to demand higher annuities. In the end, Robinson inserted an escalator clause in the treaty, which would bring increased annuity payments from the proceeds of future mining development.[36] It was an extra provision that Robinson had not been authorized to make. Such a concession must have been forced from Robinson by the chiefs *before* the treaty was signed. It is similar to the demand they had made in August 1848; namely, to be paid for every piece of mineral removed from their land in the past *and for* the future. The escalator clause, appearing in both treaties, reflected the persistence of the principal chiefs in safeguarding the rights and future of their people. By this promise, the Crown admitted First Nation ownership of and beneficial interest in the minerals of the shared treaty area, outside their reserves.

According to Elder Fred Pine, part of the Ojibwa understanding of the treaty was that it could be changed later in ways which brought additional gain to the signatories.[37] This was not reflected in the written treaty text. Although the settler government and its successors viewed the treaty as a closed document, they had added parts which were never discussed at the negotiations and would not have been agreed to. These additions rendered the document internally inconsistent.

According to Alexander Morris, a government commissioner, negotiating the Robinson Treaties was due to "the discovery of minerals."[38] These treaties differ from all others because they provided compensation for unauthorized mining activities. This compensation, amounting to $16,000 and an annuity of about $4,000 for four years, was to abrogate government responsibility for paying out the actual monies that were collected.[39] This did not work and disputes ensued because the Anishinabe claimed all of the revenues as their property. There is also the issue of breach of fiduciary obligation since the colonial authorities did not dispose of the pre- or post-treaty mining locations in such a manner that the greatest revenues would be generated.[40]

The Anishinabe always had beneficial interest in their mining locations which pre-dated the interest of the government and the mining companies. This fact was clear to the Ojibwa who had been asserting their rights to the minerals against outsiders since 1845. The north shore Ojibwa forced Vidal, Anderson, Robinson, the government, and the mining companies to recognize their subsurface interests and this recognition was reflected in the text of the treaties. However, the treaties also claim that the Ojibwa "fully and voluntarily surrender[ed]...all their rights, title and interest" in their lands. This claim is at variance with the kind of language used by the Ojibwa themselves in their previous transactions, and the language used by various Europeans to describe Ojibwa land and resource agreements, such as "granted," "leased," or "lent." None of these words mean a permanent release of First Nation title to land or resources. That is, land and resources were not being "sold" to non-Aboriginal people; they were being shared. When the Ojibwa "lent" land to be used for a railroad and demanded payment of a "toll" by all users, they were not selling the land and thereby gaining a right to compensation. They were allowing others to use the land for a stated purpose; the very fact that others passed on their land created their right to collect a toll. Herein lies the fundamental difference between what the Europeans meant to gain by the treaty and what the Ojibwa meant to exchange: the Europeans wanted ownership, the Ojibwa wanted to share but expected rent.

According to the treaty, the Anishinabe retained their reserves as exclusive and unceded territories and could sell the minerals or other valuable resources for the Anishinabe's sole benefit. However, another clause stated that the government could perfect its previous mining sales in their reserves if the developers fulfilled the conditions of sale. Revenue from these transactions were to accrue to the First Nations. This clause was not discussed in the negotiations. It was added without the knowledge or consent of the Ojibwa and it contradicted other terms in the treaty. It was possible for the government to implement this clause only by extending the payment period of the original "conditions of sale."[41] Robinson noted how the escalator clause showed the commitment of the Crown "to deal liberally and justly with all her subjects." Both treaties stated that in the "future period" if the shared lands should

> produce such an amount as will enable the government of this Province [Ontario], without incurring loss to increase the annuity hereby secured to them...the same shall be augmented from time to time, provided that the amount paid to such individuals *shall not exceed the sum of one pound Provincial currency in any one year*, or such further sum as Her Majesty may be graciously pleased to order.[42] [emphasis added]

Robinson did not mention a limit on the escalator clause in his account of the negotiations. It was added later without Aboriginal knowledge or consent. Nevertheless, the Ojibwa were to have a share in the beneficial interest in the shared lands.

The First Nations retained "full and free privilege to hunt over the territories now ceded by them, and to fish in the waters thereof." This unrestricted right was qualified by the phrase "excepting such portions of the said territory as may from time to time be sold or leased to individuals or companies...with the consent of the provincial government."[43] This qualification was also not discussed in the negotiations, nor would the Ojibwa have agreed to it. It was added afterwards and should not be a binding part of the treaty. According to the negotiations, the Crown intended hunting and fishing rights to continue for a very long time, since Robinson described the land as "barren and sterile," so much so that it would "in all probability never be settled."[44]

The Ojibwa did not relinquish mineral rights in the shared area. The treaty says they agreed merely not to molest miners. Because minerals were not expressly surrendered, they did not pass to the Crown.

In terms of mineral development, both treaties provided broad and open-ended possibilities. These, however, were shortly curtailed by the colonial government which almost immediately started to break the promises made and continued to allow the mining companies to abuse the Ojibwa.

It is quite clear the Ojibwa were unhappy with the treaty; discontent centred on the great distance they had to travel to collect their presents (which were independent of the treaty) and the amount of the annuity payments. Robinson did not address these complaints and felt if the Ojibwa were reminded of the escalator clause, troubles would subside. But dissatisfaction continued.[45]

Minerals were the most explosive pre- and post-treaty issue. Shinguacouse continued to be dispossessed of mineral resources and was angry that several mining locations in his village had not been closed.[46] His anger was a sure sign that he never agreed to allow the government to confirm the pre-treaty mining locations it sold as the treaty document alleged.

Some of the surveyors dispatched by the Crown to run the lines of the Indian reserves were personally interested in the minerals and timber in and adjacent to them. Thus it was no surprise that many of the reserve boundaries were fixed so that these resources would fall to the surveyors and their business associates.[47]

Among other boundary manipulations at Garden River, one had a significant impact. Surveyor John Keating caused the north line to run south of the known iron and copper deposits, instead of "ten miles throughout the whole" as prescribed by the treaty, thus excluding these minerals from the reserve area. This allowed his associates, including Charles Rankin, to stake the northern copper area. His action deprived the Ojibwa of their land and minerals and ensured that Rankin would not have to compete with Allan Macdonell, who was now effectively shut out of the mining locations east of Mica Bay. Perhaps that is why Macdonell began to concentrate more attention on Michipicoten Island—an early present from Shinguacouse.[48]

Once the treaty was signed, the government consistently failed to deal with Ojibwa dissatisfaction. Indeed, it appears to have consciously allowed adverse mining interests to dispossess the Ojibwa of their mines so that Rankin's group would have a monopoly. All of this combined to raise Ojibwa anger to at least the level it had been in November 1849 when they closed down Mica Bay. Although Macdonell had been trying since 1847 to have the Crown Lands Department recognize his claim to Michipicoten, part of the island was patented to John Bonner Jr. in June 1854.[49] That October, the Anishinabe and Macdonell forcibly shut down Bonner's mining operations on the island. The following month, the *Lake Superior Journal* reported that an "Indian 'war' on Michipicoten Island broke out. Some Chippewa Indians attacked workers of the Quebec Mining Company and 'went so far as to fire at the miners and made a very hostile demonstration.' The miners abandoned the island and fled to Sault Ste. Marie, hoping for legal and military assistance."[50]

CONCLUSION

The north-shore Anishinabe viewed minerals as important, and powerful, sacred articles. Aboriginal people did not need to proclaim "ownership" of the subsurface until outsiders threatened their long-established spiritual and commercial relationships with minerals.[51] Twice in five years, the Anishinabe and their allies stopped mining operations on the north shore. On at least three other occasions, they threatened to do so, saying they would assemble about two thousand warriors from both lakes. This would have been a substantial gathering of Aboriginal peoples under any circumstances, and underlines the importance they attached to minerals, the subsurface, and the potential wealth to be generated from this source, as well as the unacceptable nature of white encroachments. The closure of the Mica Bay operations hastened the negotiation of treaties which recognized Aboriginal ownership of and beneficial interest in minerals inside and outside of their reserves. When the settler government attempted to implement the contradictory minerals and other clauses in the treaties and refused to run the reserve boundaries as they had been negotiated, the Anishinabe, especially those at Garden River and Batchewana Bay, became very angry and, once again, shut down mining operations on Michipicoten Island.

Barter, Bible, Bush

Strategies of Survival and Resistance among the Kingston/Bay of Quinte Mississauga, 1783-1836[1]

Chapter 8

BRIAN S. OSBORNE

THE PLACE OF RESISTANCE

Blockade, barricade, battlement, and parapet are all words that evoke physical resistance to dynamic and palpable forces. Figuratively, they bring to mind colourful images of heroic conflicts and dramatic confrontations. Often, they become sites of iconographic narratives that become integrated into remembered pasts and constructed histories as "landmarks" and "lieux de memoire."[2] But the threatening forces need not be belligerent. They may manifest themselves in political policies, social attitudes, and customary practices. Let me illustrate this with two images. More metaphor than data, they are nevertheless provocative.[3]

First, there is the Basil Hall sketch of the Mississauga (fig. 1). When viewed in the context of other contemporary European commentaries, it reinforces the prevailing attitudes that range from pernicious racism, through casual derision, to patronizing concern for moral transformation. In all of these gazes, the domi-

Notes on pages 247-51.

nant image was of the "Other."[4] Secondly, there is the power of abstraction found in the map (fig. 2). In its panoptical preoccupation with order, control, and assertion of property rights, the map elided a prior "ethnogeography" of place. Settlement sites, hunting grounds, burial places, and sacred sites were eliminated—except from a relict topography and the recollections and traditional practices of the displaced Aboriginal societies. In this way, the map became the amanuensis of the treaty in choreographiing Aboriginal absence.[5]

Figure 1. *Mississagua Indians in Canada,* by Capt. B. Hall.

Nevertheless, Canada's First Nations have survived into the twenty-first century by means of complex forms of resistance. In his two seminal works—*Weapons of the Weak* and *Domination and the Arts of Resistance*—James C. Scott directed attention to the "fugitive political conduct" of subordinate groups and their various strategies for resisting domination.[6] He speaks of the "patterns of disguising ideological insubordination" and the "infrapolitics of the powerless," that function "in the teeth of power."[7] The same point is made by Steve Pile and Michael Keith's *Geographies of Resistance*. They argue that resistance doesn't have to be glamorous or heroic in people's efforts to be "enduring, in refusing to be wiped off the map of history."[8] In his study of the geography of ideology and transgression, Tim Cresswell speaks of unintentional and intentional transgression of rules and expectations as "unhidden acts of resistance" that can range from gesture and posture to literature and other cultural forms.[9] More importantly for the purposes of this chapter, Pile makes the connection between agency

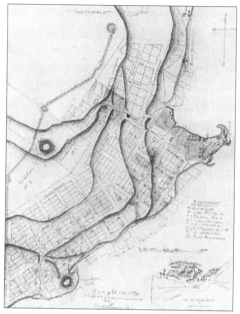

Figure 2. *The Town of Kingston and Its Fortifications, 1796*
(National Archives of Canada)

and place in his concern with the "geographies of resistance: "Thinking through geographies of resistance involves breaking assumptions as to what constitutes resistance. Now, this does not necessarily mean that resistance becomes "anything" or "everywhere," but precisely that resistance is understood where it takes place, and not through "abstract theories which outline insidious mechanisms, strategies and technologies of domination."[10]

What emerges from these ideas is that "spaces of resistance"—or places of contestation—are important locales for grounding various strategies. Not merely neutral containers, geography, locale, setting, place—whatever you wish to call them—are complicit in the actual strategies of survival and cultural continuity in several ways. They constitute the material basis for social and economic reproduction; they provide the action-space that is integrated into group identity; and they serve as the stage upon which power relationships with government and other institutions are acted out. That is, through all these modes of living—and dying—in particular places, the abstraction of space is socially transformed into a psychic geography that grounds a people's history and identity.

In this way, specific "ethnohistories" are integrated into specific "ethnogeographies." The continuous connection of peoples with their lived-in worlds reinforces their identification with time and place and each other. Dislocation from such places erodes the material and spiritual connectedness of peoples. Not surprisingly, the struggle to maintain a connection with such places—materially or abstractly—is therefore a central component of many strategies of survival.

THE CASE OF THE KINGSTON MISSISSAUGA

How do these issues relate to the Euro-Canadian contact with the Algonquian-speaking "Anishinabe" of the Lake Ontario region known as the Mississauga?[11] Originally located to the northwest of Lake Huron, in the early eighteenth century, the Mississauga expanded to the southeast, replacing the Iroquois as the primary occupants of the region lying to the north of Lake Ontario. Whether by a mythologized narrative of conflict and conquest, by a more prosaic demographic expansion into a vacuum, or by a combination of both, the Kingston Mississauga thus moved into Eastern Ontario along the line of ecological continuity known as the Frontenac Axis of the Canadian Shield.[12]

The new "homeland" of the Mississauga was located athwart the St. Lawrence/Great Lakes corridor of movement. For a century or more, the Mississauga constituted the dominant Aboriginal presence in this strategic region that was contested in British-French and British-American conflicts.[13] However, in fifty years, the Mississauga were rendered irrelevant to Britain's geopolitical design and military strategy by the elimination of the French political threat in 1763, the establishment of refugee British Loyalists in the region in 1783, and the cessation of hostilities with the United States following the War of 1812. Over the next decades, the Mississauga were confronted by a new political and cultural landscape. Deprived of their lands in 1783 and 1819-21, and converted to Methodism in the 1820s, they were ultimately confined to the restricted space "reserved" for them at Alderville in the township of Alnwick in 1836. In this way, the Mississauga became marginalized physically and symbolically in the expanding Euro-Canadian landscape.

Clearly, the years 1783-1836 constituted a period of significant social disruption and spatial dislocation for the Mississauga. It was a period that prompted the subtle exercise of several strategies of resistance and survival that reflected the Mississauga ethnohistory and ethnogeography. Although legally ceded to the Crown, throughout this period much of Kingston's hinterland continued as virtually unaltered wilderness that allowed the continuation of traditional patterns of hunting, fishing, and gathering. Further, all along the Bay of Quinte/Lake Ontario front, a series of rivers—the Trent, Moira, Salmon, Napanee, Cataraqui—served as well-known lines of movement into the interior network of rivers and lakes.[14] This ease of movement also facilitated easy contacts with the emerging small towns of Belleville, Napanee, and Kingston. It would appear, therefore, that it was not simply a matter of choosing between the two polarities of acculturation and traditionalism. The choices available to individuals and families were complicated by the proximity of alternative lifestyles in the mission, bush, and town. Ethnohistory was to be mediated by ethnogeography.

A REMEMBERED IDYLL

Increasingly, the "real" world in which the Mississauga functioned was dictated by the harsh realities of their interaction with, and dependence upon, Euro-Canadian society. But throughout this contact period, they sustained a connection with a "remembered world" of subsistence patterns and mythologies that tied them to their concept of homeland and their very identity.

From the eighteenth century, southeastern Ontario came to be the material setting for the sustenance of traditional Mississauga society and the homeland with which they identified.[15] Small groups subsisted on a routine cycle of hunting forest game, gathering maple sap in the spring, exploiting the seasonal runs of lake trout and whitefish, and harvesting wild rice in the fall. A detailed indigenous knowledge of the ecosystem and an extensive inventory of bush skills was an essential prerequisite for such a life. Also, the seasonality of this resource base was tied into a ritualization of time and space that impregnated individual and collective routines.

Time was marked by a repetitive cycle of years in which the social seasonal round mirrored the natural rhythms of the ecosystem: *seegwun* was the springtime season of the rising sap; *neebin* was the abundant summer; *tuhgwuhgin* marked the fall fading of the colours; and *peboon* was the season when the world was captured by the winter freeze. The finer lunar divisions of the year also reflected the people's close ties with nature:

> January...*Keche Munedoo keezis*...Great Spirit moon
> February...*Nuhmabene*...mullet fish moon
> March...*Neke keezis*...wild goose moon
> April...*Omuhkuhkee keezis*...frog moon
> May...*Wahbegwunee keezis*...blooming moon
> June...*Odoemin keezis*...strawberry moon
> July...*Mesquemene keezis*...red raspberry moon
> August...*Meen keezis*...huckleberry moon
> September...*Ahtabuhgah keezis*...fading leaf moon
> October...*Penaqueewene keezis*...falling leaf moon
> November...*Kuhskhuhdene keezis*...freezing moon
> December...*Munedoo keezis*...spirit moon[16]

Similarly, the indigenous knowledge of their habitat bound them to specific activity sites that Aboriginal toponymy transformed into a named and lived-in place: for example, *Machickning*, a fishing place; *Panituscotiyank*, a place for rendering fish products. And in all of this, the supernatural realm pervaded the material world because mythological stories were grounded in actual sites. Even people's own names reflected personal identification with the animistic totems of their patrilineal clans which demarcated familial relationships and the bonding of individuals with nature.[17] It was a communal society in which cohesion relied upon the individual's ties with family, clans, and the wisdom of the elders.

It was this "remembered world" that has always served as the core of Mississauga identity. Moreover, the traditional beliefs and skill sets provided the basis for their shifting strategies of adjustment—if not resistance—to subsequent encounters with their "real world." Throughout the 1783-1837 period, the Mississauga encountered the trauma of a collapsing system, an ineffective Indian Department, and a hostile society. Accordingly, as individuals and in groups, they seem to have deployed three apparent survival strategies: a dependent—even parasitic—relationship with the Euro-Canadian host society; the adoption of an alternative way of life offered by Methodism; and a return to traditional values and practices. But in all three strategies, the ties with the traditional way of life and traditional place were, to varying degrees, sustained.

BARTER AND DEPENDENCE

The traditional way of life of the Mississauga featured a detailed knowledge of the ecosystem, a grounded knowledge of place in terms of routes, skills in hunting, and tracking, and a familiarity with a range of weapons—traditional and modern. This skill set was of use to Euro-Canadians in three realms: the fur trade, provisioning local markets, and war. All of these activities allowed the Mississauga to exercise their indigenous skills in return for material benefits.

A major fact in Mississauga cultural history was their alliance with the British in the French-British conflict (1756-63), the American Revolutionary War, and the War of 1812. Throughout this period, a relationship developed—at first at Carleton Island and later with the garrison settlement of Kingston—whereby the Mississauga came to depend upon the British for supplies of various commodities. The provision of rum, arms, ammunition, clothing, and food in return for services created a dependence that eroded their former land-based systems of sustenance. This dependence was furthered by the loss of their lands. By the Crawford Treaty of 1783, the British acquired sufficient land from the Mississauga to lay out two ranges of townships behind Kingston, a further three million acres being "purchased" in 1819 and 1822 along the line of the Rideau Corridor.[18]

Increasingly, many Mississauga developed a survival strategy that is best described as barter—and at worst, as a symbiotic parasitism. Kingston was the locus for the distribution of gifts and allowances; the garrison paid them bounties for the return of deserters; and the market relied on them for such supplementary products as fish, game meats, and wild rice.[19] Depending on the activity, some Mississauga may have lived in or near Kingston while others must have continued to follow their traditional lifestyle in their homeland, occasionally travelling to Kingston to trade their commodities.

Despite the Mississauga's utility, contemporary observers described them in the clichéd racist tropes of the day, without differentiating between individuals or groups. For La Rouchfoucault-Liancourt, the Mississauga were "the filthiest of all the Indians…have the most stupid appearance…[are] wicked and thievish, and men, women and children all given to drinking."[20] Mrs. Simcoe's account of her visit to Kingston repeated the refrain, complaining that the Mississauga were "an unwarlike, idle, drunken dirty tribe."[21] Finally, a letter written in 1816 by Marshall S. Bidwell provides a choleric view of "this delectable town" and its inhabitants:

> You should have a sight of its streets knee deep in mud, its log houses, its red coats & its tawny visitors from every dirty tribe of Aborigines within five hundred miles. In one corner of a street, your eyes would be saluted with two happy lovers, perhaps a soldier & a squaw, extended in the mud & with heart felt devotion praying their adorations to the Cyprian Goddess.[22]

Such commentaries focused their jaundiced gaze on the Aboriginals' behaviours at a time when the number of Kingston's taverns and inns suggested that many Euro-Canadians were not immune to the allure of the "Cyprian Goddess." But even when allowance is made for the racism and bigotry of the day, some Mississauga do appear to have fallen into the social pathologies of a marginalized people. They had been reduced to a survival strategy in which the streets of Kingston became their host environment. With the final loss of their lands in 1822, at least some of the Kingston Mississauga appear to have also lost much of their self-identity and self-worth—and were available as visible prompts for the contemporary racist stereotyping of the "Indian."

Peter Jacobs—a convert to Methodism and a member of the Bay of Quinte community of Mississauga—corroborated the social and cultural disintegration of his people at this time:

> In about the year 1818 there were a great many hundreds of Indians of Kingston, Upper Canada, and at Belleville and Rice Lake. And they were all unhappy drunkards. I was well acquainted with these tribes of Indians. And in 1829 I do not think there were more than half the number; for they were dying very fast every year. Some of them were stabbed, some were shot, some were tomahawked, some were drowned, some were burned, and some were frozen to death. And thus we were going to destruction at a great rate.[23]

The numbers tell the story: in 1820, there were 315 Mississauga throughout Kingston and the Bay of Quinte; by 1827, that number had decreased to 223.[24]

Certainly not all of this attrition may be attributed to Jacobs's grim litany. Faced with the circumstances he described, some Mississauga may have turned their back on Kingston and retreated further into their homeland—beyond the surveillance of the Indian Agent and his census. Although it had been ceded to government and surveyed into some forty-six townships, most of the lands throughout the Frontenac Axis would never be settled and thus remained suited to the continued practice of the traditional Mississauga way of life—especially by small groups. Some people, however, sought another solution. They resorted to the spiritual enthusiasm and disciplined personal regimen offered by the radical evangelicalism of American Methodism.

REFUGE IN THE BIBLE—AND AN ISLAND

The reason the Methodists turned their attentions to the Mississauga is explained by contemporary theology and political history. The reasons why some Mississauga were receptive to the Methodists can be sought only in the trauma of the time and the succour afforded by a comprehensive mission-experience.[25] In many ways, the Methodists were well suited to take up their mission to the Aboriginal peoples of North America. From its origins in the ministry of John Wesley in the 1730s, the message of Methodism was aimed at those whose social or cultural situation rendered them outside the realm of established society: the poor, the sick, the dispirited, and the working class.[26] The Methodists' zeal to spread their message among the lower classes drove them to ignore parish boundaries, orthodox preaching styles, and formal accreditation of their clergy.[27] Viewed as a radical movement that threatened established social order, Methodism attracted the ire of the established state church, the Church of England.

A combination of evangelical zeal and social concern unencumbered by establishment prejudices of the day directed the Methodists to the Mississauga. Although saving Euro-Canadian souls was their priority, Methodists viewed the Aboriginal peoples as also being a ready field for missionary work. Their very survival was seen to require European intervention, conversion to Christianity, and its associated acculturation. At the centre of the Methodist mission was a discursive core that neatly fused Christianity, individualism, and productive labour. For the Methodists, therefore, the salvation of Aboriginals' souls also meant "raising" them to European standards of civilization.[28]

By the 1820s, some Mississauga had been exposed to Methodism through the preaching of one of their own, Peter Jones, a member of the American Methodist Church, and the son of a Mississauga mother and Welsh father. In 1823, Jones converted Peter Jacobs and John Sunday ("Shawindais"), the latter entering the ministry in 1837 and retaining his role as chief of the Mississaugas until his death in 1875. Further, in 1826, many of the Kingston/Bay of Quinte Mississauga were relocated to Grape Island in the Bay of Quinte, to the west of Kingston.[29] Their new home was intended to be an agricultural village and religious retreat, a refuge from a hostile and alien world. The church and its school were to be the central institutions, with the Mississauga gathered together in a community of well-constructed houses, set amidst well-tended fields, and dedicated to the cultivation of crops and raising livestock. By December 1828, the experimental settlement boasted twenty-six buildings, consisting of "twenty three dwellings, a meeting house, a school house, a house for the mill and stores."[30]

The agricultural model imposed upon the Mississauga by the Methodists introduced changes which affected all aspects of life and spatial and temporal routines. The annual regimen was now dictated by the seasonal demands of fall ploughing, spring sowing, and summer harvesting. Daily tasks involved maintaining clean homes, productive kitchen gardens, and caring for the livestock, as well as activities associated with lumbering and the community's workshop. Gone were the routines of their former life of hunting and gathering that had been dictated by the rhythms of nature. The Methodists imposed, instead, a rigorous regiment of time discipline and routine activities.

Time and space were now organized around worship. There were six required gatherings for prayer, preaching, and instruction on the Sabbath, worship three times a day throughout the week, with supplementary evening prayer meetings on Tuesday and Friday evenings.[31] A well-regimented secular schedule of labour and mealtimes was syncopated by the daily sounding of horns and bells.[32] Together, these regulated the time and places of community activities, along with frequent lectures on the merits of industry, reliability, and the work ethic. So comprehensive was the imposition of routine work and worship into the daily life of the Mississauga that little time and few places were left for the expression of individualism. Entire days, seasons, and years were carefully choreographed into regulated activity. This constant surveillance was an important part of the agenda of "civilization," with production being inspected regularly, good work being rewarded, and poor performance criticized.[33]

The new material landscape that surrounded them, the new time disciplines that regulated their lives, and the new spatialization of their lives, were accompanied by changes in the social organization of the Mississauga community. All aspects of family and social life were required to become compatible with the new way of life imposed by Methodism.

Mississauga gender roles rapidly came to resemble those of their Euro-American leaders. Men were responsible for most of the farm work, some becoming skilled in lumbering, carpentry, and smithing. They were also placed at the spiritual head of the family, some devout men even being sent on mission assignments to unconverted bands.[34] Male children were socialized into these roles, and their education emphasized arithmetic, grammar, reading, writing, geography, natural history, principles of astronomy, and sacred history.[35]

Women's roles were radically transformed by conversion to Christianity. The Methodists were appalled by the work required of women in their "traditional" way of life, and they strove to emancipate women from menial and degrading tasks, and to elevate them to equal status with Mississauga men—at least in the eyes of God! They were assigned the responsibility for the upkeep of homes and were instructed in the appropriate domestic skills. Few other tasks were assigned to Mississauga women: two worked in the hospital; some were involved in missionary work, though restricted to the making of clothes and goods for sale for support of mission work, or else the writing of letters of encouragement to other mission fields. Predictably, girls' schooling reflected these priorities. They were separated from the boys and their education focused on the domestic arts.[36] Some were even taken into the mission house to be instructed "more perfectly in the economy of the house, than could be otherwise done while living with parents."[37] Clearly, Mississauga women were required to abandon their former vital role in the family and group and become delicate, gentle, and efficient homemakers in the image of their Euro-American mentors.

Missionaries and teachers approached their acculturation agenda through the contemporary binary categories of paganism/salvation, dirt/hygiene, suffering/domesticity, and disorder/regulation. One convert, William Beaver, while using the discomforting idioms of his time, exposes the overt objectives of conversion:

> I tell 'em they must all turn away from sin; that the Great Spirit
> will give 'em new eyes to see, new ears to hear good things, new

heart to understand, and sing, and pray—all new! I tell 'em
squaws they must wash 'em blankets clean; must cook 'em vict-
uals clean, like white woman. They must live in peace, worship
God, and love one another. Then the Holy Spirit make the ground
all smooth before you![38]

The frequent references to filthiness and cleanliness in mission
records suggests that the introduction of Euro-Canadian ideals of personal hygiene was another key component in the acculturation of the
Mississauga. It was through such detailed attention to matters of style
of dress, standards of domestic upkeep, and emphasis on personal
cleanliness and modesty that the Methodists pursued assimilation
while at the same time "othering" the Mississauga.

Family roles also changed. In pre-conversion Mississauga society,
the extended family had played an important part in the socialization
of family members. Grandparents were revered sources of knowledge.
Male children were taught to hunt and fish by their fathers and uncles.
Girls learned their skills from their mothers and aunts. And most
importantly, extended families meant that family members spent much
time in each others' company.[39] All of this changed at Grape Island as
individuals were streamlined into segregated roles and activities that
took them beyond the home and family. Fathers and mothers were
required to be at their separate workplaces. Children were sent to
school where the responsibility for their education was appropriated
by Euro-American teachers. The wisdom of elders became redundant,
and respect for parents and older relatives was eroded. In place of the
communal wigwam and public social space, homes became segregated
private places occupied by one, or sometimes two, nuclear families.
And both communal public spaces and individual private spaces came
under the surveillance of the mission authorities.

In fact, the original social hierarchy of the Mississauga was
reordered. Obviously, the Methodist missionaries and teachers
assumed the leadership role in the settlement and took responsibility
for the religious instruction, planning of economic activities, education,
and community health and well-being. Although they did little without the consent of the Mississauga, they led the community and
replaced the long-standing Mississauga hierarchical system by a Euro-
American one. Furthermore, beneath the authority of the missionary
and teacher, Mississauga society was restructured. Former chiefs were

assigned the responsibility of being religious leaders and the community as a whole was divided into six religious classes, each overseen by an appointed Mississauga leader. The leaders were required to "watch over and instruct" their group; anyone failing to attend these mandatory meetings was liable to expulsion from the community. Others demonstrating exceptional progress in the eyes of the leaders and mission authorities were chosen to receive further instruction and become interpreters, teachers, or exhorters.[40]

As may be expected, conversion to Christianity also had a profound effect on Mississauga cosmography with its blurring of the corporeal and spiritual worlds. While the conversion-cum-civilization project revolved around complex metaphysical questions, its praxis concentrated on the reconstruction of the individual as corporeal subject. Henceforth, individuals would be assigned names that associated them with the pedigree of Christianity and the format of Euro-Canadian usages.[41] The new names were not innocent constructions, therefore, but another element of the acculturation process that reinforced Christian values, patrilineal descent, and replaced foreign sounds and meanings by familiar and useable identifiers. Also, the education provided by the Methodists emphasized a scientific view of an externalized nature and knowledge of a remote world. It too served to weaken the relevance and authority of shamans whose belief systems had been based upon revelations that reinforced local identities and local knowledge.

Given the extent and intensity of the required transformation, why did so many of the Mississauga turn to Methodism? The motivation behind the strategy is far from clear. Conversion was not a simple matter of rejecting one faith and accepting another. Nor is some simplistic assumption of syncretism acceptable. The arrival of the Methodists occurred at a crucial juncture for the Mississauga. Social hierarchies were crumbling, land and resource bases had been seriously eroded, and there had been significant social and cultural disruption. Their own religion appeared to be unable to cope with the social upheavals, the increasing abuse of alcohol, and the new health problems that affected Aboriginal communities.[42]

The Mississauga may have realized that their ability to depend upon a subsistence way of life of hunting, fishing, and gathering of produce had been greatly diminished and that acceptance of Christianity would give them enhanced access to other sources such as government aid, missionaries, and other benevolent agencies.[43] Certainly, the Methodists

placed emphasis upon the promise of material benefits and their combined secular and spiritual package was proselytized through a "rheto-
ric of contrast."[44] That is, the differences between the material and
spiritual advantages of the Euro-Canadian and Mississauga cultures
became an important part of the discourse of conversion. "In the wigwam I was cold and hungry," exhorted an eight-year-old Mississauga,
"Now we have plenty to eat, and live in good houses like our white
friends."[45] Similarly, another convert rhapsodized the material, cultural,
and spiritual transformations that ensued from the conversion of the
Mississauga to Christianity:

> And now they live the life of a Christian. And the man that knew
> nothing more than to kill the beaver and the deer, has since he
> embraced religion, become a husbandman, and can plough up his
> field, and plant his potatoes and his corn like an old farmer. And
> the Indian woman, that knew not how to keep her wigwam clean,
> and who only knew how to skin the deer, and dress the skin, has
> become a good housekeeper, and makes her floors glisten again.
> Dear sir, in sending the gospel among us it has made us to become
> men and women in society.[46]

Thus, Christianity was seen to be part and parcel of the European
lifestyles, and a means by which the Mississauga enhanced their status
and even equality with all men—at least in the eyes of God. This was
the message presented to the Mississauga by the Reverend Case at
Grape Island:

> That we are all brothers by creation, that God was our Father, that
> he made man at the first, and that all nations sprung from him;
> that the difference in our colour arose from the circumstances, such
> as our climate and our mode of living; and that the Great Spirit
> who made our first parents, was no respecter of persons, and that
> whatever he promised to one person he said to all nations; that all
> had a right to share in his love, and the blessings of His Gospel.[47]

Finally, there were similarities between traditional Ojibwa religion
and Christianity. Honesty and forthrightness were important parts of
both belief systems, and the Europeans' God protected the settlers and
their lands in much the same way the Mississauga's own spiritual
guardians had assisted in hunting and gathering.[48] Also, evangelical
Christianity's use of the devices of personal testimonies and exhorta-
tions were compatible with the Mississauga experience, as was the

collective enthusiasm of worship. The fact that Peter Jones was one of them, and that several other of their number became leaders and preachers, must have reinforced their commitment to Methodism.

It would appear, therefore, that for a decade or so, the ideals and praxis of Methodism saved at least some Mississauga from destitution, if at the cost of an increased acculturation and dependency. But ironically, what brought the Grape Island venture to a close was a combination of the very factors that had initially promised success. One of the main advantages of Grape Island had been its isolation, but it was too small for a self-sustaining community. As early as 1828, therefore, John Sunday, the chief at the Grape Island settlement, petitioned the government for more land:

> Our desire is now to change our former habits and become cultivators of the soil in order that our Children may have something substantial to rely on, and We therefore beg Our Great Father to allot us a small portion of land for that purpose. We have been obliged to adopt this change on account of increasing difficulties of our hunting in consequence of the settling of inhabitants throughout all parts of the country.[49]

The total story of the Mississauga contact experience was encapsulated in this statement: the loss of traditional lands; the inability to pursue a traditional way of life because of expanding Euro-Canadian settlement; and the willingness to adopt a sedentary life and become "cultivators of the soil." Ironically, it was their association with those who had expedited their conversion and acculturation, the American Wesleyan Methodists, that was the impediment to the government's co-operation. Indeed, colonial administrators threatened to cut government aid, annuities, and presents unless the Mississauga severed their relationship with their "radical" co-religionists.[50] Despite these threats, the Grape Island Mississauga remained faithful to the Methodists, and continued to press for more land.

LIFE IN THE BUSH—RESISTING ACCULTURATION

Not all of the Kingston/Bay of Quinte Mississauga had been attracted to the new life promised by conversion to Methodism. Some remained in the still unsettled backcountry where they sustained the values of the old way of life. Beyond the surveillance of the Crown or the

Methodists, these lands served as a reservoir of traditional lifestyles and an alternative to the Methodist acculturation agenda.

Thus, even after conversion, the acculturation of the Mississauga was impeded by the easy connections between the Grape Island community and the backcountry. Some of the Grape Island Mississauga practised a benign integration of Methodism and traditional lifestyles. While accepting the spiritual and secular regimen when at Grape Island, individuals and families availed themselves of the local bush resources by seasonal excursions to their fishing, hunting, and gathering grounds. In these ways, they retained important indigenous skills and practices without severing their connection with the new faith.

Others, however, were apparently unable to adjust to the new way of life at the mission and either fled from—or were expelled by—the Methodists and returned permanently to the bush. Given the recentness and trauma of their conversion and acculturation, the experience of such groups was predictably tortuous. One such group found wandering in a drunken state in the streets of Kingston was persuaded to return to Grape Island, only to leave again complaining—in what are, for us, theoretically loaded terms—that "they had no home there." This time, they sought seclusion in the backcountry where they were reported to have held prayer-meetings.[51] Groups like this, while living beyond the pale of mission life, were said to be "sober and orderly."[52] Certainly, a petition from some Mississaugas "residing in the vicinity of the Gananoque River, Lakes, Marshes and Woods" supports this view. What they complained of was "American citizens coming across the lines annually with great numbers of traps, spears, rifle guns, Dogs etc. to destroy the deer, furred game and fish (without regard to the season of the year)" and that they were "not able to provide food and the necessaries of life for themselves and families."[53] But in support of their petition they also argued that while they had renounced "the awful consequences and wickedness of many of their past habits," and while they were "now using their utmost endeavours to follow the example set them by their Lord and Saviour Jesus Christ," nevertheless, "the call of nature and their means of support are the same." What a clear statement of their position: converted but traditional; adherents to Christ but still subject to "the call of nature"! It would appear that groups such as this were willing to adopt Methodism's spirituality, but found the constant surveillance and close control at the mission to be incompatible with their individualism, sense of community, and ties to the land.

For others, however, the preferred strategy was somewhat less independent. Rather, they preferred the parasitic relationship with the local government agency, despite being viewed with disfavour by government authorities. In 1828, Major Darling referred to the eighty or so Kingston and Gananoque Mississauga as "the most worthless and depraved Tribe in the Canadas."[54] Four years later, another official noted that the "Kingston Indians" had been joined by a "band of worthless Indians from the Lower Province"[55] and that they had "sunk into excessive habits of idleness and intemperance."[56] The Methodists considered their presence to be a challenge and continued to proselytize among the "roving bands" of Mississauga in an attempt to bring them into the fold.[57] However, they had to contend with other countervailing influences. Thus, when Lieutenant Colonel By made the first voyage along the route of the newly completed Rideau on 24-29 May 1832 on the *Pumper*, he encountered "natives of the forest" living forty miles in the interior. A contemporary account describes the colourful scene that ensued:

> The reiterated shouts of the thunderstruck inhabitants rent the air....These natives of the forest were living on the banks of Indian Lake, distance forty miles in the interior and on the boat entering the lake, they formed themselves in front of their camp—number about forty or fifty men, women, and children, with an Indian Chief at their head—with two union jacks floating in the air, shaded with the dark green foliage of the clustering pines; they gave us three cheers, and fired a *feu de joie* that would not discredit a regularly organized corps. The boat by order of Col. By, sheered from her course about half a mile and took these sons of the wood on board—their canoes, about twelve or fifteen, towed astern.[58]

But a less romantic Methodist account of that encounter with the "sons of the forest" casts light on the social attitudes and practices of the day:

> We heard last year that when the first boat was ascending the Rideau canal, in the neighbourhood of Brewer's mills [sic], they fell in with this party of Indians—the novelty of the scene excited their curiosity, they were invited on board and solicited to drink brandy and other intoxicating liquor by the *gentlemen* who were in the boat, and who too fatally succeeded in their diabolical work, they got the Indians into a drunken frolic which continued several days at that time.[59]

The good Methodists attributed the subsequent presence of "drunken natives" in the streets of Kingston to the backsliding precipitated by this incident on the shores of the Rideau waterway that had penetrated the Mississauga homeland.

Faced with the visibility of the "Indian problem" in the streets of Kingston, and the knowledge of the continued presence of Mississauga throughout the ceded lands, the government attempted to settle them on a reservation on Wolfe Lake on the boundary between Bedford and North Crosby township.[60] By late in the summer of 1832, a reserve of nineteen lots containing 2,680 acres was established in Concessions 9, 10, and 11 of Bedford Township. Unlike the Methodist reserve at Grape Island, however, the Bedford reserve displayed none of the order of a centrally controlled community, nor were there any plans for establishing a school or church. Further, while each family was granted a 144-acre lot, their lands consisted of cedar swamps, granite outcrops, and lakes. Little of it was conducive to agriculture.[61]

The possible motive for the selection of these particular lands by the Mississauga raises questions about their overall strategy in the context of the options available to them. Having resisted the overtures of an acculturating Methodism, and being constantly threatened by a hostile dominant Euro-Canadian culture, Mississaugas might have seen the Bedford wilderness as a refuge. Certainly, they knew its qualities well, having been acquainted with it for some two centuries. Could it be that they hoped the intractability of the lands would render them unattractive to the ever-advancing settlers and thus ensure some isolation from Euro-Canadian influences? Is it possible that their declared interest in agriculture and sedentary life was but a strategy to curry favour with government, to get a secure title to lands for their community, and to use these as the base for the pursuit of their traditional lifestyles? The scheme is certainly suggested by their stated priorities for their annual gifts from the Indian Department. Whereas the Grape Island Mississauga had requested that guns, fire-steels, and axes were to be replaced by "articles of agriculture," the Bedford Mississauga were adamant that their presents continue to include rifles and traps.[62] So polarized had the two groups become in terms of these contrasting lifestyles and world views that they even refused to take their presents together.

It can only be speculated whether some of the Bedford Mississauga—unconverted and relapsed Methodist alike—were also attempting to retain their traditional social, political, and spiritual practices. If so, the strategy was doomed to be short-lived. In 1836, they were ordered to leave their lands in Bedford and join the Grape Island Mississauga in the new reservation being prepared for them on lots 12, 13, 14, and 15 on Concessions 1 and 2 of Alnwick Township. Eventually the majority did so. Others may have moved even further into the rear of the back-country. But all continued to maintain a seasonal contact with their traditional hunting territories throughout their homeland.

CONCLUSION: A NEW STAGE FOR RESISTANCE

Clearly, the new reservation at Alnwick did not come into being by the gathering in of a monolithic group. The 1783-1837 period had been traumatic for the Kingston/Bay of Quinte Mississauga because they lost both their lands and their independence. Their resort to several survival strategies meant that the new reservation incorporated several distinct groups with quite different recent histories and expectations.[63] Four core groups may be identified, although it must be recognized that over time, individuals and families frequently moved between the polarities of Methodist mission life, the traditional lifestyle of the homeland, and the opportunities—and social pathologies—of Euro-Canadian society. It is not a simple question of acceptance or rejection of acculturation. Nor is it a matter of varying degrees of syncretism along a continuum of traditional to modern. Rather, it appears that a more complex array of options may be deployed, depending on individual assessments of needs and situations.

First, there was the majority who had accepted and been transformed by Methodism—albeit in its local syncretic American-Mississauga form—and who lived at Grape Island. Nevertheless, they often had seasonal recourse to the resources—and freedom?—of the back-country. Second, there were those who had accepted Methodism, but rejected the strictures and rigours of mission life and attempted to sustain themselves by traditional skills throughout the homeland. But these groups appear to have suffered from occasional "backsliding" in the eyes of the Methodists in their interactions with Euro-Canadian society. Third, there were others who had resisted conversion, retained traditional Mississauga values and social organization, and retreated into the homeland beyond the surveillance of survey and census. And, finally, some lacked the support of either Methodism or traditional Mississauga life and—like Euro-Canadian peoples who had also been marginalized—resorted to the degradation and social pathologies of life around the margins of society. But even these Mississauga appear to have exercised some of their remembered skill sets to provide the commodities to barter for the means of their town-based survival strategy.

For all four groups, however, it would appear that, to varying degrees, the trauma of accommodating the "real" world was always negotiated by reference to their "remembered world" of traditional subsistence patterns and mythologies. It was this "remembered world" that bound them to place and their essential identity. Their remembered world was to constitute the core of their identity as they adjusted to—and resisted—the assimilation threatened by a century and a half of reservation life that was to follow.

Intentional Resistance or Just "Bad Behaviour"

Reading for Everyday Resistance at the Alderville First Nation, 1837-76

Chapter 9

MICHAEL RIPMEESTER

In 1862, under orders from his superiors, the Indian Agent responsible for the community of Mississauga First Nation peoples at Alderville conducted a survey of the population. Remarkable not only for the implication of power/knowledge in which such documents are necessarily implicated, this census is doubly remarkable in that it also contains moral judgments concerning each person enumerated. People were deemed temperate or not, of good character or not, and literate or not. Such descriptors and designations would seem to stand the test of time. One could surmise with relative surety that a drunk then would likely be a drunk now since the category of drunkard has remained relatively stable. For this chapter, however, I would like to destabilize and offer alternative readings of the "bad behaviour" identified by the Indian Agent and others like him. More specifically, I want to suggest that documentary evidence belies hidden, and sometimes not so hidden, tactics of resistance. In order to accomplish this, I will make use of a conceptual tool kit that critiques an event-based history.

Notes on pages 251-57.

When I began to think about and research Native issues in the mid-1990s, I was not at all sure of how to approach them. Serendipity and good advising through my doctoral program led me into a deep appreciation for anthropology and, especially, ethnohistory. A basic tenet of these disciplines is that the writing of history is a reflection of the values and assumptions of the society producing it.[1] This resonates closely with Foucault's contention that history functions as a will to power. That is, the production of history, read as a form of discourse, is also an exercise of power meant, in large part, to validate the present.[2] Similarly, Fogelson contends that those events that fill historical narrative are chosen by how well they fit the storyline the author/manufacturer/synthesizer is constructing.[3] Thus, mainstream history becomes, as Sahlins remarks, "the only game in town. It [a certain historiography] is prepared to assume that history is made by the colonial masters, and that all that needs to be known about the people's own social dispositions, or even their "subjectivity," is the external disciplines imposed upon them: the colonial policies of classification, enumeration, taxation, education and sanitation."[4] Those who cannot contribute to this validation are banished to history's shadows, save for those small moments when its path intersects with their own. History, then, acts upon the marginal; the marginal do not act upon history.

If mainstream history's events are seen to be the "only game in town," history's non-events are also subject to power. Fogelson identified five ways to describe what might seem uneventful, two of which are germane here. First, there must be some agreement that an event occurred at all. And second, even in the eventuality that a particular event is recognized as such by all concerned, there may be considerable variance attached to both its significance and the view of its consequences. My point here is to get between the spots where the histories of the Mississaugas and a visible history merge to explore the silences that at once connect and separate them.[5] Such a task may seem overwhelming in the face of the oppression and repression faced by the Mississaugas, and all Native groups, in the nineteenth century when colonial, and later federal, administrators tinkered with assimilative and civilizing policies. A thoroughly Eurocentric documentary record also frustrates access to these gaps.

However, as many authors have made plain, there can be no exercise of power without at least the potential for acts of resistance. And Scott suggests that it may be enough to read inference from the behaviours of subordinate peoples.[6] This assertion forms the basis of what I will try to do in this chapter. That being said, there are at least two caveats that seem pertinent here. The first concerns the political efficacy of exploring seemingly minor or trivial acts of resistance, those to which Scott refers as the "weapons of the weak."[7] That is, can the study of "everyday forms of resistance" help the weak to make a more significant claim to a place in historical narratives? Similarly, one could question whether or not focus on an actor-centred resistance potentially leads to uncritical acceptance of conscious intentionality on the part of the oppressed.[8]

Though this is not the place to rehearse the benefits of a particular theorizing of resistance, a couple of comments may be beneficial. Foucault suggests that "to make visible the unseen can also mean a change of level, addressing oneself to a layer of material which has hitherto had no pertinence for history and which had not been recognized as having any moral aesthetic or historical value."[9] I believe that searching the documentary record for micro-events, those that seem to have no purchase in the manufacture of dominant history, can be a way to prod the gaps left by mainstream histories. Their study can illustrate that Native peoples acted and were not merely the subjects of colonizers' agendas. Non-events, the small acts of resistance, of deviance, of transgression, point to a remarkable account of survival. One might wonder at the linkages between these dots of resistance.[10] The acts of "bad behaviour," that caught the eyes of Indian Agents and others like them were likely not part of a grand design of insurrection and ultimate liberty. But there was likely connective tissue that held them together. Minor acts of resistance (i.e., minor only in the eyes of the dominant and later academics) can serve at least two functions. First, their continued practice can prevent enabling limits from congealing into overly constraining limits. Second, their successful practice can provide some evidence, albeit fleeting, that resistance was possible and might be so again.[11] Examined in this context, attention to everyday forms of resistance may provide access to the institutions and practices of the oppressed that divert and/or facilitate the connections between seemingly diverse actions in an array of social spaces.[12] Thus, as I hope to show, the seemingly random reportage of social pathologies emerging from Alderville may be viewed as glimpses of a constellation of resistance and, ultimately, as cultural survival.

A second, and perhaps more significant, caveat concerns the ability of western academics to speak for and/or about a repressed Other. Spivak's provocative discussion of transparent scholars reconstructing peoples' lives in heliotropic arcs around the rising and falling suns of particular theoretical strategies clearly points to the dangers of academic gaming.[13] Such concern makes itself manifest in the creation of manufactured discourses, one of which may be based in the world of abstract theory and another which may be based in the lives of the people who form the subject of research. Simply put, and to paraphrase Clifford Geertz: How do we know we know?[14] In discussing resistance to power, for example, how can we be sure that what we are observing is actually resistant behaviour?[15] Similarly, questions based upon Ockhams's razor and Popper's net also seem appropriate here. Such concerns also raise the concern that well-intentioned research may fail to be accessible to those it purports to engage. That is, the very devices that are meant to liberate Other histories have become the very devices by which they are once again incarcerated.[16]

But where does this leave us in terms of research and the means to accomplish it? Not only must one question whether or not such work is ethically or morally feasible, but there's the related question of whether or not cross-cultural interpretation is possible at all.[17] I take as instructive the words of Inga Clendinnan, who, in the introduction to her work on colonial Guatemala, writes: "to offer interpretation without acknowledging their uncertain ground would be less than candid, while to state only what is surely known would be to leave unexplored what matters most."[18] That said, my purpose here is not to supply a consciousness, agonal or otherwise, to the people who lived at Alderville during the nineteenth century. Rather, I hope to contribute to the disruption or destabilization of the persistent categories into which Native peoples are slotted as drunkard, indolent, and backward peoples and to provide spaces for the exploration of those moments when conventional history bypasses that of the Mississaugas. Without definitive answers, I can only aspire to create space for discussion.[19]

THE BROKERS OF CULTURAL CHANGE

In the mid-1830s, the Mississauga Indians residing at a Methodist-sponsored mission on Grape Island applied for, and had purchased for them, a new reserve in Alnwick Township (see fig. 1). For more than a decade, the new reserve functioned as the mission had: Methodist missionaries and teachers led the Mississaugas through a process of largely

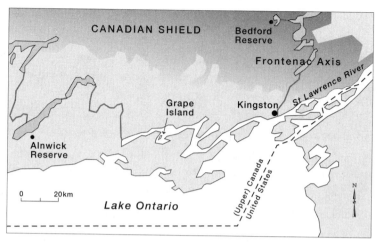

Figure 1. Southeastern Ontario. Source: Brian Osborne and Michael Ripmeester, "The Mississaugas between Two Worlds: Strategic Adjustments to Landscapes of Power," *Canadian Journal of Native Studies* 17, no. 2 (1997): 273.

voluntary cultural change.[20] However, in the mid-1840s, and in response to detailed investigations into what was becoming a serious "Indian problem," Indian visitors or agents were assigned as overseers of Native settlements. For the Indian Agent, and for the institution he represented, the reserve became a laboratory for experiments in the civilization and assimilation of Native peoples. Armed with evermore intrusive policy, the Indian Agent controlled almost every facet of life within the iron grip of bureaucracy. There is not the space here to deal adequately with the multi-layered and variously textured net of power in which the reserve at Alnwick was cast. Though it would be a mistake to elide or essentialize these sources of power in terms of content and/or goals, there were common agendas: both the Methodists and the government as represented by the Indian Agent were part of general civilizing project aimed at Canada's Native peoples.

The civilizing project, first named as policy in Upper Canada in the late-1820s, centred on the tight reorganization and careful monitoring of the landscapes of everyday life. The vehicle for this project would be the model agricultural village.[21] Its functioning would depend upon the breakdown and careful choreography of the everyday lives of its residents.[22] Indeed, its success depended upon the premise that a repetitive and carefully supervised regimen of economic, social, and cultural activities would eventually lead to the internalization of associated values and assumptions.[23] Formed around a core of church, school, domestic space, and farms and associated industries, each site of the model reserve had implicit in it a series of relationships involving specific people and particular tasks. In other words, lives were reduced into discrete functions syncopated around the rhythms of hours, days, weeks, months, seasons, years, and lives (see fig. 2). The model village also offered the means by which colonial and missionary agendas could be reconciled: although there was some small disagreement over whether Christianity or "civilization" should be the priority in rescuing Native peoples, the material and symbolic means by which this "rescue" was to be accomplished varied little.

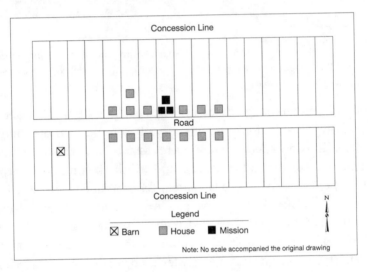

Figure 2. Alnwick Village. Source: National Archives of Canada, RG10, vol. 414, p. 657, C-9618.

Native peoples were deemed wards of the state and the reserve remained Crown Land. Because the Indian Agent served as the arm of the Crown, he became the dominant force in the community. Eventually, the Mississaugas became virtually helpless to act on their own accord. Anything beyond everyday decision-making required permission from Toronto and ultimately London, or later Ottawa. For example, the Indian Agent controlled access to the reserved lands and the resources found upon them. His role was ostensibly to protect the Mississaugas' interests and to prevent neighbouring settlers from plundering resources. But this protection was in fact a two-edged sword: in this context it often meant protecting the Mississaugas from themselves. This "protection" rendered them almost powerless to use the resources of their reserve land for either profit or for personal use.

The protection of land and resources became an almost continual bane to the Mississaugas. Though they had chosen the Alnwick site because there were few Euro-Canadians in the immediate vicinity, neighbouring settlers began to trespass continually on the reserve. For example, in 1844, one of the community's leaders wrote to the head of the Indian Department complaining that drunken men were frequenting the village and taking possession of the houses of absent Mississaugas.[24] Several Mississaugas wrote to the Indian Agent demanding the regulation of alcohol on the reserve. In one case, a man who regularly brought liquor into the village was finally apprehended after being caught under a bed. The important part of this report, however, is a barely legible postscript that suggests that the Mississaugas were powerless to expel the intruder by themselves.[25] This dramatic, albeit isolated, incident may be taken as indicative of the day-to-day power relations affecting the interaction of the Mississaugas: nothing could be taken for granted, nothing was ever easily accomplished, and everything (including requests for vaccines, a cattle pound, and the hiring of a doctor) required the filing of appropriate forms in triplicate.

MEASURING MISSISSAUGA RESPONSES

The efforts of policy makers, resident agents, and missionaries were geared to remaking the Mississaugas into models of Euro-Canadians. The documentary evidence suggests that Mississauga responses to this enterprise were varied. Some members of the community seemed to have accepted Methodism, to have worked hard at agriculture, and to have supported the Indian Department and the missionaries' efforts in running the community. Others, however, resisted, to varying degrees, the civilization package.

Christian Farmers

There was one group of Mississaugas who appear to have, at least at one level, accepted the agricultural, Christian model offered by the Methodists and the colonial administration. For instance, analysis of the state of agriculture on the Alnwick reserve between its establishment and 1876 seems to suggest that there was some progress made in

Table 1. Alnwick Reservation Agricultural Statistics

Category	1842	1851c	1857	1861c	1871	1874	1875
Value of Property						78,000	
No. of Dwellings							
Frame	22		22		34	22	23
Log	14		18			18	18
No. of Barns							
Frame	6		11		19		
Log			16				
Area of Reserve (acres)	3600					3669	3669
Acres under Cultivation	400 cleared	337	491	417	821	1088	1088
Acres of Pasture		62	103	206	185	117	117
Acres of Wood						2464	2464
No. of Ploughs	8		26		12	13	13
Harrows	6		22			13	13
Horses	2		7	6	6	11	11
Cows	11		12	9	17d	11	12
Sheep			5	9	9	7	8
Pigs			42	26	40	54	55
Oxen	8 yoke		33	12	10	16	16
Young Stock	21		8	7		4	6
Corn (bushels)		124	58	116	65	222	250
Wheat (bushels)		570	918b	484b	603b	971	1000
Peas (bushels)		463	305		270	380	400
Potatoes (bushels)		801	1370	1220	1561	1875	1900
Oats (bushels)		339	259	939	525	560	550
Hay (tons)		35a	50		46	19	20
Turnips (bushels)				200			
Timber (dollars)						1284	
Sugar (lbs)		625			70	1051	
Butter (lbs)				440	160		
Wool (lbs)				27	20		
Pork barrels (200 lbs)				12			
Beef barrels (200 lbs)				2			

a — measured in bundles not tons.
b — includes both fall and spring wheat
c — includes the only households enumerated in the agricultural census
d — includes milk cows and other cattle

Sources: Canada, *Journals of the Legislative Assembly*, 1847, Section 3, Appendix 41 (here-after cited as *JLAC*); Agricultural Census, Alnwick Township, County of Northumber-land, 1851; *Royal Commission* 1858, Appendix 29, 278-79; *Personal and Agricultural Census*, Enumeration District no. 1, of the Township of Alnwick of the County of North Umber-land, 1861; *Schedules* 1, 3, 4, 5, *Census*, District 54, West Northumberland, Subdistrict of Township of Alnwick no. 2, 1871; Canada, *Sessional Papers*, no. 8, 8(7), 1875, 21-22; no. 9, 9(7), 1876 (hereafter cited as *SP*).

creating an agricultural community (see table 1). There were improvements in the number of acres brought under cultivation and in the production of many crops, particularly wheat, potatoes, and oats, but production of other crops such as peas, hay, and corn remained at relatively low levels. Likewise, there was little increase in the numbers of livestock kept by the Mississaugas. The numbers of horses and pigs slowly expanded, the numbers of cows and sheep remained somewhat constant, while the number of oxen showed a marked decrease. The decrease in the number of oxen, the primary draught animal on the reserve, is perhaps the most significant because it suggests that clearing and cultivation became less of a priority. Similarly, the numbers of agricultural implements such as ploughs and harrows had also declined by the 1870s. It appears, then, that there was a general lack of enthusiasm for an agricultural lifestyle. Indeed, one commentator suggests that little beyond that required for subsistence was produced.[26]

These aggregate statistics belie the actual place of agriculture on the reserve. Closer examination reveals that agricultural production was not evenly spread through the community. Although each family was given a fifty-acre lot to start upon, it appears that a relatively small number of them accounted for most of the agricultural production of the reserve. Indeed, the national agricultural censuses taken in 1851 and 1861 record that only a handful of Mississauga families (sixteen and thirteen respectively) engaged in farming to a degree that warranted enumeration.[27] Statistics on agricultural production at Alnwick presented in a 1858 Royal Commission bear this out.[28] Of a total of forty-nine families who were reported as being in possession of at least twenty-five acres of land in 1856, only fourteen had cleared as much as twenty acres (28.6 percent) and only thirteen (26.5 percent) had twenty or more acres actually under cultivation. These thirteen households, in fact, accounted for almost 65 percent of the land under cultivation on the reserve. It is not surprising, therefore, that these families also accounted for a large proportion of the community's production of potatoes (43 percent), hay (72 percent), oats (71 percent), peas (64 percent), Indian corn (67 percent), spring wheat (74 percent), and fall wheat (45 percent). They also owned all of the horses and sheep, a third of the oxen, half the cows, and over 80 percent of the pigs.

By the 1870s, then, agricultural production had become concentrated and only a few families were assembling comparatively large farms. One family, for example, controlled 150 acres, of which 65 were improved. Another had acquired 175 acres and had improved 120. And yet another worked 200 acres, 58 of which were under cultivation. Out of the thirty-two families enumerated in the agricultural census of 1871, only seventeen accounted for over half of the cultivated land on the reserve (53 percent) and reported as much as twenty acres of improved lands. These families also accounted for much of the production of spring wheat (68 percent), fall wheat (100 percent), oats (100 percent), peas (100 percent), corn (53 percent), and potatoes (72 percent) and much of the livestock (all of the horses, cows, and sheep and all but two of the oxen and pigs). Furthermore, it is perhaps no coincidence that most of the spriritual leadership (meaning the leading members of the Methodist church) were also part of this group. Without going into too much more detail, it could be argued that this group of Mississaugas acquiesced with assimilative goals.

The apparent accommodation of these Mississaugas, however, must not be interpreted simply. Their acceptance of the agricultural model belies strategies which suggest the active manipulation of social and power relationships by the Mississaugas' leaders. There are, for example, many occasions where the Mississaugas refuse outright to do the bidding of either the Indian Agent or the Methodists. Over and over the Mississaugas declined to allow the department to grant licenses to cut timber on the reserve and alienate reserve lands.[29] Indeed, the Mississaugas constantly challenged the way that the reserved lands as a whole were controlled from afar.

A particularly significant instance of refusal involved the planned removal of the Mississaugas to a new reserve two hundred kilometres to the north.[30] Euro-Canadian settlement pressure had led to requests that the reserve be included in alienable Crown lands. Again, however, the Mississaugas ultimately refused to buckle under pressure. But in this case the refusal is much subtler and demonstrates active manipulation of power structures. As the Mississauga leaders saw it, a removal would solve nothing. In addition to losing the work that some had put into their farms, a more northerly position would hamper further agricultural development and would cost the Mississaugas a great deal of money (as they pointed out to the Indian Agent).[31] In addition, the petition suggested that a removal would not preclude future problems concerning the incursions of Euro-Canadians on their lands. The Mississaugas wrote,

> We opened a settlement here in the year 1836 when there was only one small house in this township....We still think the desire for our removal exist mainly in the minds of moneyed men to afford them the opportunity of increasing their wealth by investing their money in our lands. We have always relied upon the friendship and kindly feeling of the British Government and we have been fostered and protected by the Government. We have ever been faithfully and loyally attached to the Kings and Queens of England—We have shed our blood when the War cloud covers the land of the British Lion for the defense of British rights and possessions and we are always ready to take up arms and defend our beloved Sovereign Queen Victoria.[32]

This might read as a standard, formal request for aid, but petitions like this may also represent an alternative defensive strategy.[33] At first glance it seems very little like an act of resistance. It is certainly not an outright refusal to comply with the wishes of superiors. Rather, the petition is couched in terms that restate the relative positions of the Mississaugas in a power hierarchy. By using this strategy, the Mississauga leaders contributed to the perpetuation of dominant discourses concerning the relationship between Natives and Euro-Canadians. But such subservience cost them relatively little and can ultimately be viewed as a political weapon. By acknowledging a subordinate role, by stating a need for protection, and by recounting their continued loyalty and service to Britain, the Mississaugas are, in effect, both reminding the Indian department of a long-standing relationship and requesting that the government continue to uphold it. Negation of this role would potentially have long-standing repercussions and perhaps would undercut the very assertions of continued protection by which the government claimed authority over the Indians. In this case, it appears their strategy was successful. Letters from the Indian Agent to various Indian department officials suggest that the department eventually accepted further refusals.

Alternative Lifestyles

There were others among the Mississaugas who accommodated civilization strategies to a far lesser degree. For them, one of the most obvious forms of resistance was to leave the community permanently, or for months at a time. This strategy struck deep chords among government officials, missionaries, and the pro-acculturation Mississaugas. Its potency derives from the fact that mobility existed in binary opposition to the devices of assimilation and civilization the reserve represented. As table 2 shows, the overall population was relatively stable. But there are hints that there was considerable turnover of individuals.

Table 2. Population of the Alnwick Reserve, 1869-75

Year	1860	1861	1862	1863	1864	1865	1866	1867
Population	223	216	217	225	225	216	184	184
Emigrated	1		2	2		1	35	14
Immigrated			11	4			10	27
Net +/-	+1	-7	+1	+8	0	-9	-32	0

Year	1868	1869	1870	1871	1872	1873	1874	1875
Population	198	207	203	205	194	205	201	196
Emigrated								
Immigrated								
Net +/-	+14	+9	-4	+2	-11	+11	-4	-5

Source: Census Return of Indians under the Superintendence of W.R. Bartlett made on 9 August 1860, NAC, RG10, vol. 545, 123-24, C-13358; Census Return of Indians under the Superintendence of W.R. Bartlett made on the 10th day of July 1862, NAC, RG10, vol. 546, 404-405, C-13358; Census Return of Indians under the Superintendence of W.R. Bartlett made on 10 day of July, 1863, NAC, RG10, vol. 547, 410-11, C-13359; W.R. Bartlett to W. Spragge, Toronto, 22 August 1866, NAC, RG10, vol. 549, 401, C-13360; Census Return of Indians under the Superintendence of W.R. Bartlett made of the 1st day of July 1867, NAC, RG10, vol. 550, 404, C-13360; Census of the Indians under the Superintendence of W.R. Bartlett on the 1st July 1868, NAC, RG10, vol. 551, 520, C-13360; SP, no. 17, 3(5), 1870, 25; no. 23, 4(5), 1871, 23; no. 22, 5(7), 1872, 58; no. 23, 6(5), 1873, 61; no. 17, 7(6), 1874, 30; no. 8, 8(7), 1875, 107, no. 9, 9(7), 1876, 83.

Leaving the reserve may have accomplished a number of different goals for those who chose this tactic. A nomadic lifestyle may have allowed people to make a living without working their farms to any real extent. Indeed, hunting and fishing seemed to offer a viable economic alternative to farming. Statistics from the 1871 census, for example, suggest that a fur trade seems to have constituted a significant proportion of the reserve's annual income.[34] This is not to say that the Mississaugas who chose this strategy completely rejected agriculture. By 1871 many had given up most of their original allotments of land, but most retained a small portion upon which to cultivate a kitchen garden. These gardens were often small. Fifteen families, for example, had no more than an acre under cultivation and many of these planted only a quarter- or a half-acre of potatoes. Potatoes, in particular, yield a high food value and a high product per unit of land. In fact, all but seven of the households enumerated grew at least some potatoes. Much the same could be said for wheat production. Although the large farms on the reserve produced most of the wheat, there were a few families who cultivated a couple acres of wheat. The combination of a couple of acres in wheat and perhaps an acre or two sown with potatoes or other vegetables would likely provide support for a family of four.[35]

Leaving the reserve may also have represented a withdrawal from the omnipresent gaze of government and church officials. This veil of distance was likely useful in diffusing the effects of civilizing agendas in a number of ways. For one, secrecy can aid in the defence of a particular way of life.[36] A secret identity conceals information, particularly information which would draw the disapproval of dominant or mainstream groups or individuals.[37] This was likely true in the case of the Mississaugas. A nomadic lifestyle, hunting and gathering, a "traditional" cosmography, and the sites where these things were practised (the backcountry in the vicinity of a closed reserve in Bedford Township—see fig. 1) were certainly anathema to the civilizing desires of both the Methodists and the government.[38] But secrecy can also perform quite another function. The use of stories, myths, and place names, among other things, served as mnemonic devices through which the Mississaugas could maintain "traditional" social memories.[39] Secrecy and continued reproduction of social memory create and naturalize systems of meaning that describe and explain difference.[40] That is, by creating and maintaining exclusionary boundaries to the civilized world and its agents, this group of Mississaugas were creating, maintaining, and protecting their own ontologies, solidarities, and praxis that set them apart from those who chose to stay on the reserve. And this difference may have had a double benefit. Not only was a sociocultural divide erected, but "exclusionary practices that cloak and constitute the manufacture and safe-guarding of ideological differences have the potential to promote…a sense of superiority to the outside world. And in the context of the siege-like state of 'traditional' Mississauga culture, there is no doubt that commitment to pre-reserve values would have been valued as a superior goal." [41] The preservation and clandestine practice of socio-cultural traits can, then, be viewed as a reaction against the radical reordering of life-worlds. In other words, it can be viewed as a productive form of resistance.

Besides leaving, there was also at least one other way in which negative responses to cultural and social change were articulated: chronic "bad" conduct. Like seasonal mobility, indolence, drunkenness, immorality, religious "backsliding," and prostitution obviously ran counter to the ideological functioning of the reserve. After all, the reserve was based on Euro-Canadian, Christian work ethics and morals. Behaviour that challenged these expectations was immediately identified as being out of place. And because these socially peripheral activities were so symbolically charged, they became a common feature of reports from the reserve.

But how can this behaviour be interpreted? Research among displaced peoples has demonstrated that coerced relocation can lead to feelings of trauma and stress associated with the diminishment of ontological security—the loss of confidence that the natural and social worlds are as they appear to be. New places can come to be associated with the stigmas of ambiguous control.[42] Such negative associations and commensurate feelings of dependency and lack of self-worth lead to attempts at escape through substance abuse and other social pathologies.[43] Yet it seems possible to take this analysis deeper. There is a growing literature that emphasizes the strong links between the body and the socio-cultural milieu in which it circulates.[44] Some tentative links may, therefore, be drawn between the Mississaugas' "bad" behaviour and the purposeful symbolic inversion of deeply rooted Euro-Canadian norms and values. The negation of the values of a "mainstream" world may, therefore, not represent weakness or personal failure, as it was surely interpreted by government and church officials. Instead, deviance or transgression may indicate the adoption of a particular identity when no other alternatives present themselves.[45] In other words, in a world in which there seems to be nothing but chaos, a deviant persona and lifestyle (the two are by nature mutually inclusive) may be a way of ordering the disorder.

In fact, the rejection of standards of cleanliness, temperance, chastity, and industry can be interpreted as a powerful renunciation of the civilization package. For though there was little that could be done about the material conditions of life at Alnwick, each individual ultimately held control over their own bodies. Taken alone, these acts of defiance may not amount to much. But taken together, excessive alcoholism, wandering, unsanctioned barter, and prostitution threatened the continued "progress" of the reserve. Indeed, in asserting particular deviant lifestyles, these resistors were actively disavowing another. It is in this instance that the "bad" behaviours of the Mississaugas described by the Indian Agents and missionaries can be treated as resistance.

Furthermore, it appears that there was an active manipulation of the public transcript that suggests the actions of the dissenting Mississaugas engendered more than random acts of defiance. For example, there are many letters emanating from the reserve which suggest that those engaged in "wrongdoing" sought to take advantage of the promiscuity of public space to recruit others, especially from among the young.[46] It is also perhaps telling that occupation returns for 1851 and 1861 show that the number of farmers remained constant, while the number of labourers markedly decreased and the numbers of hunters and basket makers increased (see table 3). This turnover may be linked to a movement away from the "civilized" world of the reserve and a reassertion of older life ways. There was also an ongoing testing of the limits of acceptable behaviour. It appears as though many of the offenders recognized that the band council was relatively powerless, the Indian Agent was often in distant Toronto, and that the Methodist missionaries seemed to wield little control over the functioning of the reserve.

Table 3. Occupations among the Mississaugas, 1851 and 1861

Occupation	1851	1861
Missionary	1	2
Servant	0	2
Labourer	42	5
Basket Maker	0	7
Farmer	16	17
Hunter	0	17
Doctor	0	1
Shoemaker	0	1

Source: Manuscript Census of Canada, 1851, 1861.

It is also clear that this group was no less politically astute than their acculturating neighbours. For example, they often used the means installed by the Indian department in attempts to overthrow the pro-acculturation band council. And, in the instance of the forced removal to the north in 1868, the openly resistant Mississaugas were enthusiastic supporters of the proposed move—supporting the Indian department and opposing a greater proportion of their community. Support of the department was, however, tangential to institutional agendas. Removal had important benefits for this group. First, the new reserve occupied an ecological niche that was ill-suited for agriculture, was very thinly settled by Euro-Canadians, was contiguous to lands containing an abundance of fish and game, and which, ostensibly, would allow for relative freedom from constant surveillance. Second, removal would also provide the means to rid themselves of the pro-acculturation Mississaugas. New Indian policy was even providing the means to do so. Making use of the knowledge that many of the farming Mississaugas had no desire to move, and of the highly unpopular legislation designed to promote assimilation, the dissenting Mississaugas tried to effect the enfranchisement of these individuals, a move that would force them to remain behind on the lands they would receive from the government.[47]

GROUNDING RESISTANCE

It seems clear, then, that there was no monolithic or essential response to the exercise of power wielded by government agents and missionaries. Rather, each group seemed to work within the specific contexts of power relations and the material and symbolic processes that sustained them. Indeed, there seems to be a growing consensus that resistance does not emerge from a romanticized free space. Instead, in negotiating lives in the context of overlapping realms of power, oppressed people make use of resources available to them.[48] De Certeau, for example, contends that subordinates tactically use, or poach, the conditions and/or contexts of the exercise of power to their own ends.[49] Put simply, "people make do with what they have."[50] In this light, resistance need not so much refute or fly in the face of existing domains of power as they might hybridize them and/or introduce points or shadows of instability or ambiguity among them.[51]

As a geographer, thinking about resistance has led me to reconsider the ways in which space is conceptualized in power/resistance relationships. It would be tempting, for instance, to view the Alderville reserve as roughly the equivalent of Bentham's panopticon, a prison designed to have the inmates monitor their own behaviour under the threat of potentially ceaseless surveillance.[52] However, the power implicit in the plan of the reserve and in its physical manifestation could not have been complete. Because the organization of space and human relationships are inextricably combined, it seems trivial to suggest that the mutuality of oppressed peoples is bound to particular landscapes: spaces can be tamed, inverted, poached and/or hybridized in the same manner as socio-cultural relationships. The site of the reserve, then, may have to be viewed as being less of an instrument of power, and more of a site of discontinuity, of negotiation, and of ambiguity.[53] Indeed, oppressed peoples often nurture this ambiguity in order to circumvent safely, and continually, oppressive exercises of power and to ameliorate untenable circumstances. And again, knowing that such disruption is feasible and that the creation of these muddied spaces is likewise possible may give reason enough to resist again. As de Certeau argues:

> Innumerable ways of playing and foiling the other's games...that is, the space instituted by others, characterize the subtle, stubborn, resistant activity of groups which, since they lack their own space, have to get along in a netw ork of already established forces and representations....In these combatants' stratagems, there is a certain art of placing one's blows, a pleasure in getting around the rules of constraining space.[54]

It seems clear that the landscapes of the reserve became the focus of struggles over meaning. In essence, the reserve became a space whereupon colonial agents sought to make improvement discourses materially manifest. But unlike the Grape Island experience, where the intention was to isolate the Mississaugas from the evils of white society, by the 1860s assimilation was seen to depend upon the good example of industrious neighbours. The order of public spaces then became an important facet of social control on the reserve. For example, the mission school building was rented after it failed. A resident missionary wrote to the deputy superintendent:

> In my opinion it would be for the advantage of the Indians that a sober and an industrious white man should be placed on the farm who would be bound to build a good substantial house, Barn, and keep the premises in good order for if the place were allowed to remain unoccupied and uncultivated it would fall into a state of neglect and the Indians would lose all the benefit to be derived from the leasing of it.[55]

Clearly, the leaders of the Mississaugas saw the same advantages and many of their requests to the department concerning leases echoed these terms. But just as importantly, they recognized that negative examples were equally potent. Mississauga leaders were especially keen, therefore, that people of poor morals and character be prevented from making public displays of bad behaviour.

Yet it is also clear that some of these offenders understood the importance of public space. For instance, they tested the limits of control with public displays of drunkenness, clandestine dealings with Euro-Canadian neighbours, and periodic retreats from the reserve. In attempts to discredit the leadership of the community, dissenting groups used exactly the same devices employed by their opponents. For example, a group of Mississaugas wrote, "The tribe of Alnwick having mett this day for the purpiss of stoping the payments of John Simpson and John Rice which is paid to them by the Tribe of Alnwick we dont wish to be ruled by any person that drinks we have enuff of them without the Chiefs and secretary geting drunk which is a very bad example to our young people in our vilage."[56] These, in essence, became a public display of refusal to comply with the values and norms of those in control.[57]

Struggles over lifestyle and subsistence were wound up in specific material and symbolic landscapes of the reserve. This is particularly true of the primary sites of socialization: the church and the school. Though it was one of the two key locales associated with acculturation, there is little documentation concerning the role of the church at Alnwick. However, something clearly happened to the church community. Through the early 1840s, reports regarding church attendance and the religious progress of the Mississaugas were overwhelmingly positive. In 1841, for example, there was this report:

> In every respect it is believed that the Mission is advancing in religious knowledge and domestic habits. Fewer instances of intemperance, less roving in their habits, more settled and industrious, and of course, their wants are better supplied. During the last summer and autumn a blessed work of grace prevailed which brought into society several valuable members, among these are aged men, some of whom were deemed hopeless, are now very pious and promising, one is our useful & interesting school Teacher. Prayer is heard in most of the families in the village & there is a general attendance on Public Service.[58]

But by the late 1840s, the sanguinity of these reports declined markedly. In the report for 1846, for example, the author complains,

> We continue to suffer loss from the wandering habits of a part of the Indians. While scattered abroad the classes are not met, prayer meetings are not attended, and the wanderers are exposed to temptations and sometimes fall into the sin of intoxication. Some of these have been cut off and others, put back on trial.[59]

By the 1860s and 1870s, records suggest that church membership had undergone a precipitous decline, reaching a low of between thirty and fifty individuals (in comparison to a membership of 85 to 170 on Grape Island).[60] Apathy towards the church reached such a degree that the author of the report for 1865-66 wrote, "we sorrowfully record the opinion that the moral and social character of the Band is not in harmony with the labours bestowed upon them."[61] Indeed, though the details are sketchy, reportage of church discipline became a regular feature of the Methodist's *Annual Reports.*

Unlike the church, reactions to the school are well documented. Although there is little evidence regarding the conditions under which children laboured at the school, it seems likely that there are similarities between this school and other residential and day schools for Native peoples in Canada.[62] Certainly, Native ways were dismissed and devalued and the old stories were likely not mentioned at all.

The records also indicate that the children and their parents often resisted the socialization efforts of the school in many ways. One of the most obvious forms of resistance was absenteeism. Despite the increases in the number of students suggested by the annual reports during the 1860s and early 1870s, it is probable that these statistics enumerate the total number of scholars who were to attend the school. Table 4, a quarterly report, illustrates that total enrolment and the numbers of children actually attending school were often entirely different figures. An 1852 report outlines the obstacles:

> The naturally indolent habits of the Indians, and their taste for rambling and hunting, exercise a baneful influence on the minds of the children when at home. Averse as they have been, before their conversion to Christianity, to fixed habits of labour and industry, and influenced in a measure as they still are by their former habits, they naturally take part with their children in complaints about being "made to work." The less intercourse, therefore, the children are allowed with idlers, the better: those who are the farthest removed from their being more steady at school, they make the best improvement, both in science and labour.[63]

The problem became severe. In 1858 the Indian Agent wrote in his report for the Royal Commission that though there were forty school-age children among the Mississaugas, on average only ten were attending.[64] Indeed, one commentator observed that many children stayed only a short time and seemingly left as soon as they received new clothes.[65] But there were other factors that may apply to this endemic truancy. One was the unwillingness of parents to send their children to the school. Commenting on the schools at Alnwick and Mt. Elgin, a department official wrote, "The chief impediment to the satisfactory working of the Schools seems to be first, the unwillingness of the Northern Tribes to send their children to Alnwick—Second the irregular and as I regret to learn the gradual diminishing attendance of the Day Scholars, I trust however, that experience may suggest remedies for these evils."[66] Again there are several reasons why this may have been so. In one of his reports, the agent responsible for the reserve wrote to explain that there were several times during the year in which attendance was particularly poor. These, he reasoned, were during the hunting season, the time for gathering wild berries, the fishing season, and the time for making sugar.[67] In fact, in another letter, he suggests that the school was continuously open for only a small portion of the year.[68] Furthermore, many bands, including the Alnwick Mississaugas, balked at having to pay a quarter of their annuity for an institution "which in every case is spoken of as a useless expenditure of their money as the Indians derive no benefit from it."[69]

Table 4. Statement of the Attendance of the Scholars at the Alnwick Industrial School from 31 March 1852

Period	Total Number of Scholars per Quarter by Return	Number of Scholars in the Institution throughout the Quarter	Average Number of Scholars Maintained throughout the Quarter	Average Deficiency
31 March to 30 June 1852	33	31	32	18
1 July to 30 Sept. 1852	52	39	45	5
1 Oct. to 31 Dec. 1852	47	38	42	8

Source: Statement of the Attendance of the Scholars at the Alnwick Industrial School from 31 March 1852, NAC, RG10, vol. 411, 274, C-9616.

But there were also other reasons for not supporting the school. A missionary explained it this way: "many of the parents have strong prejudices against the school."[70] Two years later, the same man wrote to explain that the low average attendance for one quarter was due to the continued attempts of parents to steal their children away.[71] Indeed, it appears that in the same way that school officials sought to keep children from their parents, parents may have attempted to keep their children from the school. The school may have represented a real threat to those who desired to maintain some elements of Mississauga culture. Exposure to two different worlds in the same day may have led to friction in the home and, certainly, to internal conflicts within the children.[72] As Native peoples, they were imbued with a discourse of Euro-Canadian superiority and at the same time they returned each night to homes where they interacted with families who may have spoken Mississauga and who did not measure up to Euro-Canadian standards of order. It is perhaps no surprise, therefore, that one of the missionaries wrote with some exasperation "if we could have them entirely under our own control, apart from any influence of Indian examples, we could do much better."[73]As he suspected, the school was only one part of the socialization process. Indeed the other important locale for socialization was the home. Especially among those Mississauga children who periodically left the reserve with their parents, the home environment may have nurtured an anti-reserve, anti-school attitude. That such socialization was going on was clearly recognized by all parties concerned.

CONCLUSION

Expectations for the reserve were, then, rarely realized. Although the Methodists and the Indian department were largely able to impose their version of civility upon the Mississaugas through the implementation of a strict regime of time and space disciplines, gendered divisions of labour, and participation in a market economy, they could not force the internalization of associated values and assumptions. Some of the community attempted to work within this acculturation framework, but it is clear that they did so on their own terms. There was a point beyond which they would not accommodate the wishes of the government: the diminishment or relocation of the reserve. They had simply put too much effort into this endeavour to react passively to seemingly arbitrary exercises of power. Others openly resisted any acculturation at all. They refused, or were unable, to accept the discursive package of improvement through agriculture. Many of this group spent portions of the year away from the reserve. Others quite openly defied the socio-cultural mores of Methodism and government policy.

In many cases, these individuals sought to publicly demonstrate their rejection of acculturation through the only medium left to them: their own bodies. For them, the reserve stood only for the inappropriateness of the agricultural village and the unwanted external control of the Methodists, the Indian Department, and their assimilating neighbours.

It is here in the seemingly small events, letters sent to Indian Department officials, the symbolic inversion of public spaces to offer alternative discourses (or, at least, to destabilize dominant discourses), and the political astuteness of various groups in facing up to oppressive exercises of power that the historical geography of the Mississaugas lies. These are the records of cultural survival and of purposeful individuals. This is not to say that there has been some kind of ahistorical or pan-Native reaction to oppression. Reactions and resistances have developed in specific and evolving contexts. And resistance almost always drew countermeasures on the part of governments, government agents, and missionaries. Certainly, the story told here does not end in 1876: the Mississaugas of Alderville are still there and continue to strive to retain a grasp of their culture and identity and continue to resist.[74]

ACKNOWLEDGEMENTS

I wish to thank Brian Osborne, David Butz, and David McNab for their comments on various drafts of this chapter. I also gratefully acknowledge the support of SSHRC and Brock University. Finally, I offer my appreciation to Loris Gasparotto for his efforts in constructing the map.

"White Gold" versus Aboriginal Rights

A Longlac Ojibwa Claim against Damages Caused by the 1937 Diversion of the Kenogami River into Lake Superior

SUSAN CAMPBELL

Ginoogaming First Nation, located approximately two hundred miles northeast of Thunder Bay and until 1988 known as Long Lake Reserve No. 77, is part of the Nishnawbe-Aski Nation covered by Treaty 9, the 1905-06 "James Bay Treaty." During the summer of 1990, although residents did not organize their own barricades in solidarity with Aboriginal people surrounded by QPP/Canadian Army forces at Kanehsatke (Oka), some did help block the Canadian National Railway's main east-west line where it crosses neighbouring Long Lake No. 58 First Nation, just west of the town of Longlac.[1] Ginoogaming people demonstrated not only in solidarity with Mohawks in Quebec but also their "frustration over the unwillingness of authorities to find just resolutions to aboriginal land issues" that were both long-standing and intensely local.[2]

With nearly half of its residents under the age of twenty, Ginoogaming is a highly typical reserve in terms of its young, vulnerable population. But it is also atypical of Treaty 9 communities

Notes on pages 257-61.

127

for its low ratio of "on reserve" to "off reserve" band members.[3] One reason for this low residency rate is that, because of Ginoogaming's relatively large size, many formerly non-Status Aboriginal people, who are known after the 1985 amendment of the Indian Act as "C-31s," have been assigned to it.[4] Ginoogaming and its neighbour, Long Lake No. 58, are at the north end of Long Lake, a narrow north-south body of water some 170 miles in circumference lying just north of the height of land that divides Ontario's two great watersheds. A remnant of the southwestern extremity of glacial Lake Ojibwa-Barlow which covered the region approximately six thousand years ago, Long Lake in its natural state formed the most southerly headwater of the Kenogami River. The Kenogami and the Ogoki are tributary to the Albany, the largest river lying entirely within Ontario. In turn, the Albany and the Moose are the two main rivers that, from the Ontario side, empty into James Bay, Hudson Bay, and ultimately the Arctic Ocean.

Ginoogaming was established through adherence, as of 9 August 1906, to Treaty 9. This was the last signing prior to the "adhesions" (subsequent treaty arrangements with groups who had not signed the initial treaty) of 1929-30. In 1905-06 the main signatory for the Crown was poet and former accountant Duncan Campbell Scott, who from 1913 until 1932 would be Deputy Superintendent General of the Department of Indian Affairs. In accepting Treaty 9, the Ojibwa and Cree communities covered by it were, according to Scott,

> to make certain promises and we were to make certain promises, but our purpose and our reasons were alike unknowable. What could they grasp of the pronouncements on the Indian tenure...delivered by the law lords of the Crown, what of the elaborate negotiations between a dominion and a province which had made the treaty possible...?Nothing. So there was no basis for argument. The simple facts had to be stated and the parental idea developed that the King is the great father of the Indians, watchful over their interests, and ever compassionate.[5]

In reality the motives of the two sides were not so incomprehensible. What Aboriginal people wanted was "above all else...a form of influx control" against Euro-Canadian trappers, prospectors, railway-builders, settlers, and liquor-traders.[6] For its part, the Canadian government intended to rid itself of the "burden" of Aboriginal title, or as much of it as was considered to have survived *St. Catherine's Milling.*

The latter was a landmark case on federal-provincial jurisdiction according to which the British House of Lords Privy Council ruled *for* Ontario and *against* the federal government (and thus Aboriginal rights as a federal responsibility), leaving Aboriginal rights regarded as no more than "personal and usufructuary" (that is, the mere use[s] of land rather than ownership) and furthermore dependent, not on prior occupancy, but merely "the good will of the Sovereign."[7]

While treaties have never been known for their generosity, Treaty 9 (the only "numbered treaty" to which a provincial government was party) was "distinctly parsimonious"; "Scott's penny-pinching attitude and the need to persuade a reluctant Ontario government to contribute to the anticipated costs resulted in its niggardly provisions."[8] The federal government was to pay the treaty commission's expenses while Ontario reimbursed federal authorities the eight-dollar "present" given to every individual who "took treaty"[9] plus the four-dollar annuity ("lower than those under the [previous] western treaties") each was to receive thereafter.[10] In keeping with Ontario's requirements, reserves were to be assigned so that their boundaries enclosed "no valuable water-powers." They were laid out on the basis of one square mile per family of five. This, the commissioners conveniently purported, rather than depriving Aboriginal people of their way of life, would confer "a secure and permanent interest in the land which the indeterminate possession of a large tract could never carry."[11] The result of such thinking has been that, "south of 60" (the latitude which divides the provinces from the Yukon, the Northwest Territories, and Nunavut), 6.5 million acres of reserve land are fragmented into 2,242 tracts that, on average, measure only 2,899 acres. Whereas in the USA entire "tribes," sometimes several, tended to be concentrated on single reservations, in Canada the opposite has been customary.[12] This makes Ginoogaming's twenty-seven-square-mile landbase almost six times the national average.[13]

Under Treaty 9, the 1,617 people who "took treaty" during the 1905 season collectively received $12,936. Since around 40,000 square miles were affected, the land was relinquished for slightly less than $4 per square mile. Overall, Treaty 9 achieved the cession of about 90,000 square miles of territory. The land "loaned back" to Aboriginal people as reserves covered 524 square miles, only about 1 percent of their former territory.[14] In 1910, Ginoogaming's land borders were surveyed as straight lines, its other boundaries being provided by the Making

Ground River and four miles of the northeastern shore of Long Lake. Land loss began almost immediately: in 1915 just over forty-one acres were ceded (at $5 per acre) to the Northern Ontario Railway as right-of-way for a line cutting across the northeast quarter of the reserve toward Longlac.[15] This trackage is now part of the Canadian National Railway's trans-continental route.[16] Forcing treaties was thus vital to advancing the "frontier." Negotiation of Treaty 9 corresponded with the 1906 birth of the Hydro-Electric Power Commission of Ontario (HEPC) as the world's first such government-owned utility for the generation of "white gold."[17] Hydro-power installations being heavily capital-intensive, "additions to capacity tend to take place in a series of discontinuous steps."[18] For most of its first decade, HEPC thus distributed electricity bought from relatively small privately owned hydro-power facilities. As Jean Manore's analysis of the industry shows in her book, *Cross-Currents*, this pattern was typical across northern Ontario. By 1913, however, HEPC was ready to begin construction of its first installation on the Severn River at Wesdell Falls, near the Ontario-Manitoba border.[19]

HEPC was still in its infancy when plans were drawn to divert water from the James Bay watershed into the Great Lakes. As a 1910 study produced by the federal Department of Mines put it, "The Nipigon river...in its descent to Lake Superior...affords one of the most magnificent water-powers in central Canada."[20] That use of Ontario water had already developed not only provincial and national but even continental dimensions was emphasized by the 1909 signing of the US-Canadian Boundary Waters Treaty and by the establishment of the International Joint Commission.[21] Activity sped up during the 1920s, when HEPC engineers formulated plans to force water from the two main tributaries of the Albany, the Ogoki, and the Kenogami, south into Lake Superior. The attitude was that rather than allowing these rivers to "waste" themselves in "unfruitful companionship with the arctic-minded Albany River," they should give their "by no means insignificant support to the Great Lakes-St. Lawrence system, the mighty feeder of the power pools of the south."[22] During the late 1920s, a flurry of correspondence discussing how best to exploit the resources of "new Ontario" flew between various branches of the federal and provincial governments.[23]

The Depression of the 1930s hit resource-extraction sectors of the economy particularly hard. While in the mid-1920s approximately 880,500 tons of wood pulp annually were being exported to the US, by the worst point in the Depression the amount had fallen by more than half.[24] To the extent they had become dependent on commercial fur trading and wage labour (for example in railway construction and maintenance, mining, and the lumber industry), Aboriginal people were very much affected.[25] In May 1937 the Ontario government's executive council authorized HEPC to "store water in Long Lac and the river flowing thereout including tributaries thereto...control the water of the said lake and rivers...[and] use said water to raise and lower the level of water, flood, dry and overflow land." Engineers were to "enlarge and change the boundaries and course of streams and generally improve, develop, divert, alter and use the said lake and rivers."[26] Properly speaking, this was illegal—it was not until nearly five years later that the federal government gave Ontario formal permission to begin engineering the Kenogami-Long Lake diversion.[27] The project got underway in mid-1937 with construction, some fifteen miles north of Long Lake, of a 300-foot wide by 50-foot high concrete dam. At the lake's south end, 50 to 100 cubic feet of water per second (over 80 percent more than previously) were made to pass, via a five and a half-mile channel, through the height of land into the Aguasabon River. This permitted logs to be floated directly from Long Lake into Lake Superior.[28] Apparently no thought was given to any harmful effects likely to result from the project, nor did the Department of Indian Affairs seem ever to have encouraged the federal government to intervene on behalf of its Aboriginal "wards." In a "Specific Claim" land rights action launched by Ginoogaming in March 1996, it was asserted that residents were not advised "about the project or its potential impacts on...[their] lands [nor were they] party to any agreement with respect to these impacts" (para. 14). This paralleled contemporary American Indian experience south of "the medicine line," where huge projects undertaken by the US Army's corps of engineers, primarily in Montana and the Dakotas, severely affected people living along impounded sections of rivers; "Land belonging to seven Indian reservations was flooded."[29]

The financial cost of diverting the south Kenogami River and Long Lake was just over $1,277,200, of which $877,215 was paid by HEPC, the rest by the government of Ontario.[30] In early 1937, before construction had even begun, pronouncing it "wise and in the public interest...to ensure unto the Crown a sufficiently large cut of pulpwood...to justify the expenditure involved in the development of the said water-course," and conditional on the Pulpwood Supply Company "harvesting" at least 100,000 cords of wood annually, the provincial government had granted a twenty-one-year lease to clear-cut Crown land surrounding Ginoogaming.[31] By the end of the 1939-40 fiscal year, this arrangement had earned the province slightly under $94,000, with revenue for 1940-41 anticipated at $87,000.[32]

According to Ginoogaming elders, one environmental cost of diversion was raising the Kenogami River north of Long Lake by as much, at certain times, as thirty feet. Another was that the lake was engineered to rise or fall according to the extent of flow required in the southern reaches of the system. Its maximum level rose by up to eight and a half feet (almost triple the three feet conservatively estimated) as it became a reservoir for some 287,300 acre/feet of water.[33] Whenever flows were deemed excessive, Long Lake was made, "at the whim of man," to empty northward, redisturbing its ecological functions and continuously preventing them from restabilizing.[34] The entire Kenogami River was affected because such alteration of flows and "capture of their hydraulic energies" profoundly alters aquatic ecosystems and landscapes.[35] Even the short-term consequences of works such as the Kenogami diversion have increasingly been recognized as intrinsically unpredictable.[36]

In early 1938, a lengthy collection of *Correspondence and Documents relating to the St. Lawrence Deep Waterway Treaty 1932* was tabled in the House of Commons. A few weeks later, relating to the Kenogami section of the project regarding exports of electrical power, it was supplemented by a booklet of *Correspondence* which included a US State Department paper complaining that "successive governments in Canada [had] been traditionally reluctant to permit the long term exportation of power." Franklin D. Roosevelt's Secretary of State, Cordell Hull, rejected Canadian notions that it had exclusive rights to the water it diverted into the Great Lakes. Conveying "renewed assurances of [his] highest consideration," Hull concluded that despite the US Senate's 1934 refusal to ratify the *St. Lawrence Deep Waterway Treaty*, his government was nonetheless ready and eager "to push to a speedy conclusion negotiations looking towards a mutually satisfactory agreement dealing with the varied and important problems of the Great Lakes-Saint Lawrence River Basin."[37] In 1941, in the context of World War II, Canada and the US signed a major agreement on both the engineering of waterways navigable by ocean-going ships and the development of electrical power generation throughout the St. Lawrence/Great Lakes basin. Although this wartime agreement was also subsequently rejected by the US Senate,[38] the

Canadian government had already informed the State Department that it and Ontario were ready to proceed with diversion of the Albany River's second major tributary, the Ogoki.[39] Completed by mid-1943, the Ogoki project engineered North Summit Lake, South Summit Lake, and the Little Jackfish River, redirecting water from a huge area south across the height of land into Lake Nipigon. This increased the velocity of the Nipigon River by about 50 percent, allowing for construction or enlargement of generating stations at Pine Portage, Cameron Falls, and Alexander.[40]

During World War II, HEPC began using Kenogami/Long Lake water to generate electricity near the mouth of the Aguasabon River.[41] After the war, at a cost of $12.8 million, this generating station was enlarged with the construction of a 1,400-foot wide by 120-foot-high dam. In 1946 HEPC contracted to supply Longlac Pulp and Paper/the Pulpwood Supply Company (a subsidiary of Wisconsin-based Kimberly-Clark, active in Québec since 1920) with the electricity needed by its new bleaching kraft pulp mill at Terrace Bay.[42] This had an initial capacity of 270 tons of wood pulp daily.[43] Decades later Kimberly-Clark would acknowledge that, during the early years of its operations in Ontario, the Kenogami-Long Lake/Aguasabon River/Terrace Bay route had "provided an economical method of delivering wood from the Long Lake watershed to Lake Superior, making delivery to the USA a viable proposition."[44] It is worth noting that it was not until the late 1960s that Ginoogaming itself began to receive electricity.[45]

In 1949 Longlac Pulp and Paper/Kimberly-Clark and the Department of Indian Affairs negotiated a logging lease over all twenty-seven square miles of Ginoogaming. Since the lease was for eighteen years at $230 per year, logging was to be carried out for $10.84 per square mile annually. In 1951 Kimberly-Clark leased 22.9 acres of Ginoogaming land near the northwest corner of the reserve, where most of its people live, as the site for a sawmill. Within a short time, however, the company found itself obliged to take action to prevent erosion from turning its mill site into an island. A dike was built and the enclosed space filled with mill-waste topped with gravel.[46] When the company applied to have this acreage added to its lease, a bureaucrat in Ontario's Department of Lands and Forests actually suggested this tiny scrap of land, although entirely surrounded by Ginoogaming and Long Lake, rightfully belonged to the province. The head of the Department of Indian Affairs' Reserves and Trusts division sardonically responded that "It would be very difficult to explain to the Indians...why this property is not considered part of the Indian Reserve," especially as "considerable acreage was lost without compensation by the flooding of the foreshore."[47] In 1961, 3.21 acres designated "Water Lot D.R. 23" were officially added to Ginoogaming's landbase.[48]

In 1968-69 Ontario's Ministry of Natural Resources (MNR) carried out an aquatic habitat inventory of Long Lake. The study was done at Halfway Road Landing and Birch Bay, well south of Longlac and on the opposite side of the water from Ginoogaming. The inventory found various pollutants present, notably seepage from nearby mines,[49] pulp-log bark, effluent from Kimberly-Clark's Weldwood plant, and sewage from Longlac. Whitefish (*Coregonus clupeaformis*) were plentiful, but infested with *Triaenophorus crassus*.[50] By the 1980s, people would be warned against eating fish caught in Long Lake because the fish were found to be accumulating mercury.[51] (By now, Ginoogaming people have accepted as fact that their lake is unsafe even for swimming.)[52] The situation of Long Lake's Ojibwa people thus prefigured that of the Cree in northern Québec, where within six years of water impoundment in reservoirs by the first phase of the James Bay Project, walleye and northern pike were found to contain four to five times their normal levels of mercury. No one had predicted such an ecological and thus human disaster.[53]

In the meantime, in 1975 Ginoogaming's chief, Gabriel Echum, had informed the MNR of the need to halt erosion by rip-rapping or shoring up artificially, part of the Ginoogaming shoreline.[54] Chief Echum pointed out that fugitive logs from the numerous booming grounds around the north end of Long Lake often prevented reserve residents from safely launching boats and canoes. The MNR referred the problem to HEPC's successor, Ontario Hydro, one of whose maintenance engineers reported that helicopter inspection of Ginoogaming's shoreline revealed "very little signs of erosion"; also that, when the dam was constructed, since it hadn't been anticipated that "proposed operating water levels would...exceed...pre 1938 lake level maximums," no water power lease had been obtained.[55] In 1981 Ontario Hydro reiterated to Chief Echum's successor, Victor Chapais, its assertion that erosion had been negligible.[56] In 1983, and again in 1986, Ginoogaming appealed to the Department of Indian Affairs to arrange to have the erosion of its shoreline properly documented.[57] In 1987 it was at last established that, as of 1983, erosion had indeed cost Ginoogaming 31.8 acres of its landbase.[58]

A decade elapsed before, in January 1993, Ginoogaming presented the Department of Indian Affairs with its first specific claim for compensation. Because it was put forth for "fast track" consideration, the amount at issue was by definition not to exceed $500,000. Rejecting Ginoogaming's case, Indian Affairs contended that the flooding and erosion the reserve had suffered "was the result of the Kenogami diversion project...undertaken as a provincial project in conjunction with the Hydro Electric Power Commission." Since the federal government's involvement had been limited to "authorization under the Navigable Waters Protection Act and the Boundary Waters Treaty of 1905 [actually, 1909]"—neither of which "authorized the flooding of reserve lands"—it claimed it was in no way responsible for damages.[59] This rejection was a blessing (albeit well-disguised) in that, had it been accepted, opportunities for further recourse would likely have been extinguished.

In March 1996, Ginoogaming advanced a more ambitious second claim which contended that, relative to long-term consequences of the diversion of the southern Kenogami River and Long Lake, the Canadian government had neglected to protect the Aboriginal rights of the people of Ginoogaming. The claim called for compensation from the federal government for its breach of Treaty 9, its failure to adhere to the provisions of the Indian Act, and for "the initial and ongoing breach of its fiduciary duties and responsibilities." The main distinguishing feature of fiduciary relationships is that "the relative legal positions [of parties to them] are such that one...is at the mercy of the other's discretion."[60] The people of Long Lake were in an unequal bargaining position with Ottawa.

Unlike the first claim, the second claim was not submitted to the "fast track" process; thus fair compensation was expected to exceed $500,000. Like its predecessor, claim 2 presented no estimate of the amount of land and financial compensation the community would regard as just. Although unfortunate, this was unavoidable because the ecological status of Long Lake and the condition of Ginoogaming's streams, creeks, and low-lying areas had not been adequately assessed. In brief, then, whereas in 1993 claim 1 had emphasized the narrower issue of land loss due to erosion, three years later claim 2 called for compensation on wider bases related to considerations of "loss of use" and indeed "deprivation of way of life."

Claim 2 emphasized that, as of 1983, Ginoogaming had already lost 31.8 acres of its land base through erosion of its shoreline and that land loss was continuing. A burial ground had been destroyed and pollution and siltation had damaged fish-spawning grounds which "from time immemorial" had flourished in Long Lake. Unnaturally high water levels in the lake, combined with their sharp fluctuation, had adversely affected the Making Ground River and its tributaries, Rockyshore and Phipps creeks. This, in turn, had damaged plant and animal habitat. Parts of Ginoogaming territory had become "swampy or permanently wet, thus resulting in their loss of use." Particularly grievous was the drowning of *manomin* (wild rice) beds, both within the reserve and around it. In claim 2 Ginoogaming thus contended that the federal government's failure to prevent the flooding and erosion, together with its "past and ongoing failure to seek appropriate compensation" for affected lands, amounted to "a breach of its obligations...compensable under the Specific Claims Policy."

Specific Claims policy required that communities claiming compensation for "loss of use" show direct financial loss of *either* "the foregone net income that the claimant band would have obtained from the use of the asset, plus the lost opportunity to save and reinvest at least part of the net income" *or* "the opportunity to sell the asset and invest some or all of the proceeds to earn a steady stream of income."[61] Such a quantitative approach was highly problematic, not least in that it is hard to estimate lost earnings from a resource which, in the very nature of things, was not assessed before it was damaged. For example, we lack written records for how plentiful and healthy moose were around Long Lake's outlet into the Kenogami River some seventy years ago, or exactly where and in what quantities wild rice was being harvested. A partial solution is to rely on the knowledge of elders, for "if there are any experts on the impact of a dam, they are the people...who conduct 'research' almost every day of the year."[62]

It is extremely difficult to determine the exact causes of ecological damage. Not only are such causes multiple and mutually reinforcing, but those seeking to document them still lack the conceptual tools to do so. At Ginoogaming some "loss of use" has undoubtedly been related to Ontario government-authorized logging of surrounding Crown land and DIA-brokered logging of the reserve, rather than to water diversion. Finally, the valuation system being used (known as Shaller/DIA) fails to take into account the cultural and spiritual significance of what the dominant society persists in regarding as no more than exploitable resources. A good example is provided by the importance of wild rice to the Ojibwa: "wild rice harvesting is not just a part of our economy, it is also part of our spiritual and cultural life. The customs surrounding this harvest are as sacred and symbolic to us as is the breaking of bread in the Christian churches."[63] Similarly, what justice can there be in treating a burial ground as of no greater significance than any other piece of rural "real estate"?

What basis is there for the view that the federal government ought ultimately to be held responsible for the damage Ginoogaming suffered, and continues to suffer, as a result of the diversion of the south Kenogami River and the "reservoirization" of Long Lake? Section 91(24) of the 1867 Constitution Act—in what was significantly its only mention of Aboriginal people—stated that the federal government is responsible for "Indians, and lands reserved for the Indians." A few years later, section 88 of the Indian Act made clear that when, on reserves, provincial law conflicted with treaty rights, Indian Act provisions were to prevail. In the early twentieth century, under Treaty 9, Canada undertook to protect the people covered by it in pursuit of "their usual vocations of hunting, trapping and fishing throughout the tract surrendered." At the first signing of Treaty 9, at Osnaburgh on 12 July 1905, Chief Missabay had expressed misgivings about accepting the treaty, saying "We will have to give up our hunting and live on the land you give us, and how can we live without hunting?" Treaty commissioners assured him that the people's "present manner of making their livelihood would in no way be interfered with."[64] Almost a century later, all sides agree that the federal government *did not* directly cause the damage suffered by Ginoogaming consequent to the Kenogami/Long Lake diversion. Furthermore, given that in 1937 the federal government had not given its formal permission, the Ontario government was *ultra vires* in authorizing HEPC to begin work on the project. However, in 1943 the Canadian government *did*, as noted above, belatedly give the province permission to go ahead.

In 1982, section 35(1) of the Constitution Act stated the "existing Aboriginal and treaty rights of the Aboriginal peoples of Canada are hereby recognized and affirmed." In 1984, in *Guerin*, the Supreme Court ruled that a fiduciary's duty "is that of utmost loyalty to his principal."[65] In 1990, in *R. v. Sparrow*, it clarified how "existing" and "recognized and affirmed" were to be construed. Also in 1990, in *R. v. Sioui*, Justice J.J. Lamer ruled that "treaties and statutes relating to Indians should be liberally construed and uncertainties resolved in favour of the Indians."[66] Yet in its dealing with Aboriginal people, the Canadian government continues, in practice, to be adversarial: "The St. Lawrence Seaway, in the form finally approved in 1953...was essentially the realization in physical form of an idea which had shaped Canadian economic development from its earliest years."[67] Hydro mega-projects are unfortunately far from being "history." Ontario Hydro has long-range plans to further dam Hudson Bay's western tributaries, particularly the Moose River. Worse, in the context of globalization combined with US profligate use of its water resources—several continental schemes similar to the plan advanced in the early 1960s by the North American Water and Power Alliance (NAWAPA)—continue to cast covetous eyes on continental waters.[68] With a history of contravening its fiduciary responsibilities and thus "the rule of law," the Canadian government cannot be trusted to safeguard water or any other kind of Aboriginal rights.

POSTSCRIPT

On 15 August 1998 Ginoogaming Chief Gabriel Echum signed a $4.9 million agreement settling the reserve's over sixty-year-old grievance against HEPC/Ontario Hydro. The agreement covered

> compensation for damage to land from flooding and erosion, compensation for economic losses, compensation for cultural losses by constructing a cultural/healing centre, a monetary sum to protect the reserve shoreline from further erosion, post-secondary scholarships for 16 years, monitoring the impact on the environment for 15 years, compensation for damage to graves and other sites on Long Lake, a lease payment over 10 years to be renegotiated every decade, and an agreement with Ontario Hydro to manage the water levels of the like to more closely mimic nature.[69]

The most visible result has been Ginoogaming's Keemeshomnishnanak Monument, a turtle-shaped earth mound some 180 feet in diameter dedicated to the memory of community ancestors. Planned by Ontario Hydro and built by the reserve's Making Ground River Development

Corporation,[70] its sacred space is entered by way of three totem door-ways, each topped by a rainbow-painted arch. On the monument's north and south sides are patterns—honouring, respectively, the bear and wolf clans—outlined in stones and filled with fine gravel. At its centre is a large teepee frame covering a six-foot stone. This is sur-rounded by a ring of twelve smaller rocks, each with plaques giving the names (some in English, many in Ojibwa) of grandmothers and grand-fathers who have departed for the spirit world.

Although this is very touching, one may feel that the delaying and deflecting tactics deployed for so long by Indian Affairs have succeeded and that, at least as far as damages to Ginoogaming are concerned, Ontario Hydro has gotten off rather lightly. Certainly according to some young reserve residents, the supposed settlement is "only the beginning." The struggle continues.

ACKNOWLEDGEMENT

Meegwetch to Charlton Thompson, Ginoogaming band manager at the time of my July 1999 visit. Charlton facilitated this work in sev-eral ways, not least by taking me miles north of Longlac to see the "damn dam."

BIBLIOGRAPHY

American Society of Civil Engineers. "Diversion of Water from the Albany River Watershed to the Great Lakes Basin: Ogoki Diver-sion/ Long Lake Diversion." N.p.: mimeo., 1946.

Berkes, Fikret. "The Intrinsic Difficulty of Predicting Impacts: Lessons from the James Bay Hydro Project." *Environmental Impact Assess-ment Reports* 8, no. 3 (1988): 207-208.

Bryce, J.B. "The Long Lake and Ogoki Diversions: Their History, Bene-fits, and Estimated Effects." Toronto: Ontario Hydro, mimeo., 1973.

Canada. Department of Indian Affairs and Northern Development. *Outstanding Business: A Native Claims Policy, Specific Claims.* Ottawa: DIA and ND, 1982.

———. International Joint Commission. *Correspondence and Documents Relating to the St. Lawrence Deep Waterway Treaty 1932, Niagara Con-vention 1929, and Ogoki River and Kenogami River (Long Lake) Projects and Export of Electrical Power.* Ottawa: J.O. Patenaude, 1938.

————. International Joint Commission. *Correspondence Relating to Kenogami River (Long Lake) Project and Export of Electrical Power.* Ottawa: J.O, Patenaude, 1938.

————. International Joint Commission. *Correspondence and Documents Relating to the Great Lakes-St. Lawrence Basin Development, 1938-1941.* Ottawa: Edmond Cloutier, 1941.

————. International Joint Commission. *Correspondence and Documents Relating to the Great Lakes-St. Lawrence Basin Development, Supplement No. 1.* Ottawa: Edmond Cloutier, 1941.

————. *The James Bay Treaty.* Ottawa: Queen's Printer, 1964.

————. Royal Commission on Aboriginal Peoples. *Report.* Ottawa: Minister of Supply and Services, 1996.

————. *Schedule of Indian Bands, Reserves and Settlements.* Ottawa: INAC, 1992.

————. Task Force to Review Comprehensive Claims Policy. *Living Treaties: Lasting Agreements.* Ottawa: DIA and ND, 1986.

Clatworthy, Stewart, and A.H. Smith. "Population Implications of the 1985 Amendments to the Indian Act: Final Report." Winnipeg and Perth: Four Directions Consulting and Living Dimensions, 1992.

Di Matteo, Livio. *The Government of Ontario and Its North: 1871-1911.* Thunder Bay: Lakehead University, Centre for Northern Studies, Research Report no. 33, 1992.

Douglas, Dan. *Northern Algoma: A People's History.* Toronto: Dundurn, 1995.

Driben, Paul. *Aroland Is Our Home: An Incomplete Victory in Applied Anthropology.* New York: AMS Press, 1986.

Driben, Paul, and R.S. Trudeau. *When Freedom Is Lost: The Dark Side of the Relationship between Government and the Fort Hope Band.* Toronto: University of Toronto Press, 1983.

Driben, Paul, and D. Auger. *The Generation of Power and Fear: The Little Jackfish River Hydroelectric Project and Whitesand Indian Band.* Thunder Bay: Lakehead University, Centre for Northern Studies, Research Report no. 3, 1989.

Easterbrook, W.T., and H.G.J. Aitken. *Canadian Economic History.* Toronto: University of Toronto Press, 1958.

Froschauer, Karl. *White Gold: Hydroelectric Power in Canada.* Vancouver: UBC Press, 1999.

Ginoogaming First Nation: Community Information Book, 1998. Longlac: Ginoogaming First Nation, 1998.

Hall, Anthony J. "The St. Catherine's Milling and Lumber Company versus the Queen: Indian Land Rights as a Factor in Federal-Provincial Relations in Nineteenth-Century Canada." In *Aboriginal Resource Use in Canada*, edited by Kerry Abel and Jean Friesen. Winnipeg: University of Manitoba Press, 1991.

————. "Treaties, Trains, and Troubled National Dreams: Reflections on the Indian Summer in North Ontario, 1990." In *Law, Society, and the State: Essays in Modern Legal History*, edited by L.A. Knafla and S. Binnie. Toronto: University of Toronto Press, 1995.

Hamilton, A.C. *Canada and Aboriginal Peoples: A New Partnership*. Ottawa: Public Works and Government Services Canada, 1995.

Hartt, Patrick E. *Interim Report and Recommendations*. Toronto: Royal Commission on the Northern Environment, 1977.

Healey, M.C., and R.R. Wallace, eds. *Canadian Aquatic Resources*. Ottawa: Fisheries and Oceans Canada, 1987.

Hedican, Edward. "Some Implications of Contemporary Economic Activity among the Ojibwa of Northern Ontario." In *Papers of the Thirteenth Algonquian Conference*, edited by William Cowan. Ottawa: University of Ottawa Press, 1982.

G.W. Kyte. *Organization and Work of the International Joint Commission*. Ottawa: J.O. Patenaude, 1937.

Knight, Rolf. *Indians At Work*. Vancouver: New Star, 1978.

Kresz, D.U., and B. Zayachivsky. *Precambrian Geology: Northern Long Lake Area*. Toronto: Ministry of Northern Development and Mines. OGS Report 273, 1991.

Kulchyski, Peter, ed. *Unjust Relations: Aboriginal Rights in Canadian Courts*. Toronto: Oxford University Press, 1994.

Long, John S. "'No Basis for Argument': The Signing of Treaty 9 in Northern Ontario, 1905-06." *Native Studies Review* 5, no. 2 (1989): 19-54.

Manore, Jean L. *Cross-Currents: Hydroelectricity and the Engineering of Northern Ontario*. Waterloo: Wilfrid Laurier University Press, 1999.

McPherson, Dennis H., and J.D. Rabb. *Indian from the Inside: A Study in Ethno-Metaphysics*. Thunder Bay: Lakehead University, Centre for Northern Studies, Occasional Paper no. 14, 1993.

Morrison, James. *Treaty Research Report: Treaty 9 (1905-06), the James Bay Treaty*. Ottawa: Indian and Northern Affairs Canada (INAC) Treaties and Historical Research Centre, 1986.

Muller, R.A., and P.J. George. *Evaluating the Environmental Impact of Hydroelectric Development in Northern Ontario: A Preliminary Report*. Hamilton: McMaster University, Program for Quantitative Studies in Economics and Population Research, Report no. 55, 1982.

Nelles, H.V. *The Politics of Development: Forests, Mines, and Hydro-Electric Power in Ontario, 1849-1941*. Hamden, CN: Archon Books, 1974.

Ontario. *Department of Lands and Forests Report for 1938*. Toronto: Government Printer, 1939.

———. Hydro Electric Power Commission of Ontario. *31st Annual Report*. Toronto: HEPC, 1938.

Ontario Hydro. *The Gifts of Nature: The Story of Electricity at Work in the Province of Ontario*. Toronto: Ontario Hydro, 1961.

———. *Hydro in the Northwest*. Toronto: Ontario Hydro, n.d. (1975).

Primus, C.L., and L. Paul. *Water Diversion Proposals of North America*. Edmonton: Department of Agriculture, Water Resources Division, 1969.

Quimby, G.I. *Indian Life in the Upper Great Lakes: 11,000 B.C. to A.D. 1800*. Chicago: University of Chicago Press, 1960.

Ray, Arthur J. "The Hudson's Bay Company and Native People." In *Handbook of North American Indians*. Vol. 4, *History of Indian-White Relations*, edited by Wilcomb Washburn. Washington, DC: Smithsonian Institution, 1988.

Sanders, Douglas. "Pre-existing Rights: The Aboriginal People of Canada." In *A Commentary on the Canadian Charter of Rights and Freedoms*, 2nd ed., edited by G. Beaudoin and E. Ratushney. Toronto: Carswell, 1989.

Schaller, Huntley. *Loss of Use Considerations in Determining Compensation for Specific Claims*. Ottawa: INAC Research and Analysis Directorate, 1992.

Scott, D.C. "The Last of the Indian Treaties." *Scribner's* 40, no. 5 (November 1906): 573-83.

Surtees, R.J. "Canadian Indian Treaties." In *Handbook of North American Indians: History of Indian-White Relations*. Vol. 4, edited by W. Washburn. Washington: Smithsonian Institution, 1988.

Titley, E.B. *A Narrow Vision: Duncan Campbell Scott and the Administration of Indian Affairs in Canada*. Vancouver: UBC Press, 1986.

Waldram, James B. *Cumberland House and the E.B. Campbell Dam: An Economic Impact Study*. Thunder Bay: Lakehead University, Centre for Northern Studies, Research Report no. 24, 1991.

Weinrib, Ernest J. "The Fiduciary Obligation." *University of Toronto Law Journal* 25, no. 1 (1975): 7.

White-Harvey, Robert. "Reservation Geography and the Restoration of Native Self-Government." *Dalhousie Law Journal* 17, no. 2 (1994).

Wilson, A.W.G. *Geology of the Nipigon Basin, Ontario.* Ottawa: Department of Mines, Geological Survey Branch, Memoir no. 1, 1910.

Zaslow, Morris. *The Northward Expansion of Canada, 1914-67.* Toronto: McClelland and Stewart, 1988.

———. *The Opening of the Canadian North, 1870-1914.* Toronto: McClelland and Stewart, 1971.

Varieties of Contemporary Resistance

Aboriginal Title on the Ground

Establishing and Protecting Occupation of Land

KENT MCNEIL

The Aboriginal peoples of Canada have long been acknowledged as having some kind of interest in the lands that were occupied by them at the time of European colonization.[1] This interest has been variously described by the judiciary as "a personal and usufructuary right,"[2] a burden on the (provincial) Crown's underlying or radical title,[3] and a *sui generis* interest that is inalienable other than by surrender to the Crown.[4] However, the precise nature of this interest, which is generally called Aboriginal title, remained undefined until 1997 when the Supreme Court of Canada handed down its landmark decision in *Delgamuukw v. British Columbia*.[5]

The *Delgamuukw* case involved a claim by the Gitksan (also spelled Gitxsan) and Wet'suwet'en nations to Aboriginal title and self-government over the territories they traditionally occupied and controlled in northwestern British Columbia.[6] The trial was the longest and most complex litigation in Canadian legal history, taking 374 court days and involving 76 witnesses and 9,200

Notes on pages 261-67.

147

exhibits. The claims were substantially dismissed by the trial judge, but the Supreme Court of Canada overturned this judgment and ordered a new trial, in part because the trial judge had erred in his treatment of the Gitksan and Wet'suwet'en's oral histories, especially by not giving them independent weight.[7] In rendering its decision, the Supreme Court avoided the issue of self-government entirely, but provided a detailed description of Aboriginal title and outlined how it can be proven. The court also made clear that Aboriginal title is under exclusive federal jurisdiction,[8] and commented on how the title could have been extinguished in the past and could be infringed in the present.[9]

While the *Delgamuukw* decision did lay down important principles and guidelines for courts to apply in future Aboriginal title litigation and for parties to take into account in land claims negotiations, it did not resolve the claims of the Gitksan and Wet'suwet'en.[10] As a result, the government of British Columbia has taken the position that no Aboriginal title to land exists in the province unless actually proven. It tries to justify this position by relying on the fact that the Supreme Court placed the onus of proving Aboriginal title on the Aboriginal peoples. In the absence of such proof, provided either in court or, presumably, during land claims negotiations, the provincial government has been ignoring Aboriginal title, and continuing to issue permits or licences authorizing forestry companies, for example, to cut timber on lands that are claimed by Aboriginal title.[11] The Aboriginal peoples who are asserting that they have Aboriginal title are distressed by the province's attitude, and are seeking ways of protecting their lands from these provincially authorized intrusions.

This chapter aims to suggest ways in which the Aboriginal peoples of British Columbia, and elsewhere in Canada, can assert their Aboriginal title on the ground without first having to prove it in court. Starting with a brief overview of the Supreme Court's treatment of the issues of content and proof of Aboriginal title in *Delgamuukw*, it then examines legal arguments to support assertions of Aboriginal title. Finally, it offers advice on how these assertions might be strengthened on the ground. The strategies presented here are intended to provide lawful alternatives to the kinds of direct action and resistance that might be described, from the perspective of non-Aboriginal governments, as civil disobedience. My intention is therefore to suggest ways for Aboriginal peoples to use the Canadian legal system to their own advantage.

CONTENT AND PROOF OF ABORIGINAL TITLE

Prior to the Supreme Court's decision in *Delgamuukw*, it was uncertain whether Aboriginal title was limited to the traditional uses that had been made of the land by the Aboriginal people in question, or also included such things as standing timber and underground minerals, even if unused by the people in the past. The court resolved this uncertainty by deciding that Aboriginal title is not limited to traditional uses. In the words of Chief Justice Lamer,[12] it is "a right in land" that "confers the right to use the land for a variety of activities, not all of which need to be aspects of practices, customs and traditions which are integral to the distinctive cultures of Aboriginal societies."[13] Aboriginal title "encompasses the right to exclusive use and occupation of the land," and includes resources on and under the land, such as minerals and oil and gas.[14]

However, the Chief Justice did place an inherent limit on the uses that Aboriginal peoples can make of their lands, as they "cannot be used in a manner that is irreconcilable with the nature of the attachment to the land which forms the basis of the group's claim to aboriginal title."[15] So, to use Lamer's own examples, if Native people prove their title by showing that the land was used as a hunting ground, they will not be able to strip-mine it, or if they prove title by establishing a special bond of a ceremonial or cultural nature, they probably will not be able to turn that land into a parking lot.[16] But subject to this inherent limit, which is designed to preserve the land for future generations of Aboriginal people, they have "*the right to choose* to what uses [the] land can be put."[17] Moreover, because their title includes the right to *exclusive* use and occupation, no one else has a right to come onto their land for the purpose of engaging in uses that the inherent limit prevents them from pursuing themselves. To allow others, including the Crown, to do so would be inconsistent with the justification for the inherent limit, namely preserving the land for future generations.

In addition to the inherent limit, Aboriginal title has certain *sui generis* characteristics that distinguish it from other common law interests in land. First of all, because it is based on occupation of land prior to the Crown's assertion of sovereignty, its source pre-dates Crown sovereignty and involves "the relationship between common law and pre-existing systems of aboriginal law."[18] Second, Aboriginal title is held communally, whereas other common law interests are held by individual persons, either natural or corporate. Finally, unlike other common law interests, Aboriginal title is inalienable other than by surrender to the Crown.[19] In addition to these *sui generis* characteristics, Aboriginal title was accorded constitutional status by the 1982 Constitution Act,[20] whereas other property rights were not.[21] However, this status does not provide it with absolute protection, as it can still be legislatively infringed as long as the test for justification of infringements of Aboriginal rights laid down in *R. v. Sparrow*, and embellished in *R. v. Gladstone*, can be met.[22]

In order to prove Aboriginal title, the people claiming it must establish that they were in exclusive occupation of the land at the time the Crown asserted sovereignty. Occupation can be shown by physical presence on the land, taking into account "the group's size, manner of life, material resources, and technological abilities, and the character of the land claimed."[23] As the Aboriginal perspective is relevant to proving title, occupation can also be shown by proof of Aboriginal customs or laws in relation to the land. Examples given by Chief Justice Lamer are a land tenure system, laws governing land use, and trespass laws.[24] The occupation must have been exclusive because Aboriginal title results in a right of exclusive use and occupation. However, in this context the concept of exclusivity must also include Aboriginal perspectives. Moreover, shared exclusivity, involving the sharing of occupation by two or more Aboriginal groups, would result in a joint Aboriginal title.[25]

The time for establishing exclusive occupation is the time the Crown "asserted" sovereignty over the territory in question. The reasons Lamer gave for choosing this date are, first, that Aboriginal title is a burden on the Crown's underlying title, and "it does not make sense to speak of a burden on the underlying title before that title existed."[26] But as the Crown's underlying title would have vested only upon Crown *acquisition* of Crown sovereignty, I think Lamer intended to use the word "asserted" to mean "acquired" in this context.[27] Lamer also said that, because Aboriginal title is grounded in occupation, it "does not raise the problem of distinguishing between distinctive, integral aboriginal practices, customs and traditions and those influenced or introduced by European contact."[28] In this way, he was able to distinguish the time for proof of other Aboriginal rights, that had been set in the *Van der Peet* decision as the time of European contact.[29] He also said that, "from a practical standpoint, it appears that the date of sovereignty is more certain than the date of first contact."[30]

Chief Justice Lamer recognized that proving Aboriginal title at the time of Crown assertion of sovereignty might present insurmountable evidentiary hurdles for some Aboriginal claimants. He therefore gave them the option of relying on present occupation as proof of pre-sovereignty occupation, provided that they could show continuity between the two. When this approach is taken, he said "there is no need to establish 'an unbroken chain of continuity' (*Van der Peet*, at para. 65) between present and prior occupation," as the "occupation and use of lands may have been disrupted for a time, perhaps as a result of the unwillingness of European colonizers to recognize aboriginal title."[31] Instead, he said that a "substantial maintenance of the connection" would suffice.[32] Moreover, changes in the nature of the occupation would not preclude a claim, "as long as a substantial connection between the people and the land is maintained."[33]

By allowing Aboriginal peoples to rely on present occupation, the Chief Justice evidently meant to make the task of proving their Aboriginal title easier. But how can they prove continuity between present occupation and occupation at the time of Crown assertion of sovereignty without having to prove occupation at the earlier date, thereby defeating the purpose of relying on present occupation in the first place? What Lamer must have had in mind here was proof of present occupation and of a connection with the land for a long enough period back in time to infer that the lands were in fact occupied by the Aboriginal people in question at the time of Crown assertion of sovereignty. But even interpreted in this way, his requirement of proof of continuity is inconsistent with common law presumptions arising from occupation of land. I will now outline these presumptions, and present a legal strategy that should enable Aboriginal peoples to rely on them to their advantage.

PRESUMING ABORIGINAL TITLE FROM PRESENT OR PAST POSSESSION

In laying down the requirements for establishing Aboriginal title, the Chief Justice clearly placed the onus of proof on the Aboriginal peoples.[34] But while the relevant date for proving occupation is the time of assertion of Crown sovereignty, we have seen that present occupation can be relied on to prove pre-sovereignty occupation. This is very much in keeping with fundamental common law principles, by which a *prima facie* title to land can be established by proving present occupation.[35] However, one will search in vain in the judgments that have established and applied these principles for Chief Justice Lamer's further requirement of proof of *continuity*, which he said is necessary where Aboriginal people rely on present occupation to prove their title.

At common law, a person who is in factual occupation of land is presumed to have possession of it.[36] From this possession another presumption arises, namely that the possessor also has a good title, or, to put it the other way around, title is presumed from possession.[37] This presumption of title can of course be disputed by anyone who can show that he or she has a better title. So, for example, if A is in possession of Blackacre, and B can prove that A entered as a trespasser and the land actually belongs to B, B will be able to recover possession from A, either by re-entering the land or by bringing a legal action. However, unless acting on behalf of B, C will not be able to recover the land from A by pointing out that A is a trespasser and the land belongs to B. The reason is that, as between B who has possession and C who has neither possession nor title, the common law favours B.[38] Another way of explaining this is that anyone who seeks to acquire possession must rely on the strength of his or her own title, not on the weakness of the title of the person currently in possession.[39] Moreover, these presumptions apply against the Crown. So where the Crown, or its grantee, seeks to acquire land from whoever is in possession, the Crown's title generally has to be proven.[40]

As I have argued in detail elsewhere, these common law presumptions should apply where Aboriginal people are presently occupying lands in Canada.[41] Proof of present-day occupation would then raise a presumption of Aboriginal title, which the Crown would be able to rebut if it could prove that the lands were in fact unoccupied at the time it asserted sovereignty.[42] Proof that the lands were then unoccupied, and hence unowned by Aboriginal peoples, would also establish the Crown's title because, when the Crown acquired sovereignty over a territory, any lands that were unoccupied and unowned at the time would automatically have become Crown lands.[43] So while the initial onus of proof would still be on the Aboriginal people, with this approach they could discharge the onus of proof by proving their present occupation, and thereby shift the burden of proof onto the Crown.

In *Delgamuukw*, Chief Justice Lamer did acknowledge that "the fact of physical occupation is proof of possession at law, which in turn will ground title to the land."[44] However, while correctly applying these common law principles to decide that the Aboriginal peoples had title to the lands they occupied at the time of Crown assertion of sovereignty, with all due respect I think he failed to appreciate their relevance in the context of present-day Aboriginal occupation. In particular, his requirement that Aboriginal peoples who rely on present-day occupation must prove continuity with pre-sovereignty occupation is inconsistent with eight centuries of common law, and so should be re-assessed by the Supreme Court.

While application of the common law principles that possession is presumed from occupation, and title is presumed from possession, would make it easier for Aboriginal peoples who are presently in occupation of lands to prove their Aboriginal title, the fact remains that many Aboriginal peoples have been dispossessed, either partially or completely, of their traditional lands. Are these common law principles of any use where this has happened? The answer must be yes, because any occupation of lands, including past occupation, gives rise to the presumptions that the occupiers had possession and hence title at the time.[45] So if an Aboriginal people can show that they occupied lands at any time after Crown assertion of sovereignty, the presumption should be that they had possession and title.[46] As pointed out, the Crown could then try to rebut this presumption of Aboriginal title by proving that the lands were unoccupied when it asserted sovereignty. Failing that, the Crown might present evidence to show that Aboriginal title had been surrendered or extinguished in the meantime, either by treaty or by legislative taking. But once again, the burden of proving surrender or extinguishment would be on the Crown because Aboriginal title, once proven to exist, is presumed to continue until shown to have been surrendered or extinguished.[47] Moreover, a grantee of the Crown would have the same burden of proof as the Crown itself because, if the Crown at the time the grant was issued did not have more than the underlying title that it has to all Aboriginal title lands,[48] the grant would be either null and void, or subject to the Aboriginal title and hence to the Aboriginal titleholders' right to exclusive use and occupation.[49]

ASSERTING ABORIGINAL TITLE ON THE GROUND

Aboriginal peoples who are presently occupying their Aboriginal-title lands do not need to go to court for a declaration of their title. Like any other landholders, they are entitled to use their lands in accordance with their own needs and desires, subject to the inherent limit described above and any applicable common law or statutory restrictions.[50] However, in case they ever do need to go to court, it would be prudent for them to affirm their occupation in as many ways as are practical. This could be done by continuing, or renewing, their traditional uses of the land, which might include hunting, fishing, trapping, gathering, and horticulture, and maintaining trails, roads, shelters, cabins, dams, weirs, snares, fences, and the like for these purposes. But the uses need not be limited to uses made of the land historically, because any acts on or in relation to the land, whether traditional or not, would support their occupation. Of particular importance would be acts that demonstrate Aboriginal peoples' intention to occupy and control the lands for their own purposes, and to exclude others. Putting up signs advising outsiders that the land belongs to the Aboriginal people in question, and telling intruders that they are trespassing and need to either ask permission to come onto the land or leave, would be a way of doing this. Moreover, as Chief Justice Lamer said in *Delgamuukw* that the occupation necessary for establishing Aboriginal title can be proven by reference to Aboriginal customs and laws, an Aboriginal people could support their occupation further by reaffirming their customs and laws in relation to the land. This might be particularly important where the lands are not physically occupied, but have spiritual or cultural significance for them. Identifying these areas, and indeed their lands generally, by maintaining place names and including them on maps, which could then be posted on a web site, would be a further way of informing the world that such land belongs to them.

While it is not possible to list all the potential activities that might be engaged in to establish occupation, I hope that the suggestions here will provide a sufficient indication of what is generally required. It is important that the occupation be shown and maintained over as much of the land and in as many ways as possible, taking into account the character of land involved and the resources of the people concerned. Moreover, since the occupation sought to be established is communal, this should be a community endeavour, with broad-based participation.

Now it is apparent that this strategy of asserting occupation can be pursued only where the lands in question are not presently occupied by others. If the lands are occupied by others, but the Aboriginal people who claim them are in a position to show earlier occupation, the Aboriginal claimants would have to initiate legal action if they want to recover them.[51] But even where no one else is currently occupying the lands, establishment of occupation by an Aboriginal people might not go unchallenged. The Crown, or a grantee of the Crown, might try to take the lands, either by bringing a legal action or by entry. What then?

If the Crown or its grantee brought a legal action to acquire possession of the lands, then as plaintiff it would generally have to prove its own title. As long as the Aboriginal people are in occupation, their possession and title should be presumed. If the Crown or its grantee bypassed the courts and simply entered, then the Aboriginal people would have to initiate legal proceedings to protect their occupation.[52] They could do so by initiating an action for declaration of their Aboriginal title, but in my opinion it would be simpler and probably more effective for them simply to bring an action of trespass, because a trespass action does not require the plaintiffs to prove title. Instead, they can rely on their occupation, and force the defendant to prove its own title, or at least a right to commit the acts of alleged trespass.[53] So provided the Aboriginal people could show that they occupied the lands at the time of the entry, by bringing a trespass action they would effectively be able to place the burden on the Crown or its grantee to prove its own title or some other right to enter.

CONCLUSIONS

The strategies outlined in this chapter are intended to make the onus of proof placed on Aboriginal peoples by the Supreme Court in *Delgamuukw* less burdensome. My suggestion is that Aboriginal peoples who can prove present or past occupation should be able to rely on the presumptions of possession and title that generally arise from common law. If they are able to prove present occupation, they should then be able to protect that occupation by an action of trespass against anyone who cannot prove that he or she has title or other right to enter. If they are not presently in occupation, but can show occupation at any time after the Crown asserted sovereignty, that occupation should raise the same presumptions of possession and title.[54] If they brought an action to recover the lands, the burden should then be on the current occupier to show either that the lands are not subject to Aboriginal title because they were unoccupied when the Crown asserted sovereignty, or that Aboriginal title has been validly surrendered or extinguished. Failing that, the Aboriginal claimants should be entitled to recover the lands.

These strategies, if successful, would not result in a judicial declaration of Aboriginal title because they rely on a *presumption* of title, and involve legal actions that are designed to protect or recover possession. But why should Aboriginal peoples be satisfied with this? One answer is that, from a practical standpoint, this is all they need: title is really irrelevant if a right of possession is affirmed. But at a more fundamental level, it may be more in keeping with Aboriginal autonomy and the inherent nature of Aboriginal rights to limit judicial intervention in the protection of Aboriginal lands from outside interference. Why should Aboriginal people require, or even desire, a declaration of title from a Canadian court to lands that were theirs long before Europeans ever appeared in North America? The position of certain Hopi chiefs on a similar matter was aptly put in a letter to President Truman in 1949: "We will not ask a white man, who came to us recently, for a piece of land that is already ours."[55] Likewise, the Aboriginal peoples of Canada do not need Canadian courts to recognize their title to lands that they know are theirs.

Space, Strategy, and Surprise

Thinking about Temagami Ten Years after the Blockades

Chapter 12

JAMES LAWSON

On the tenth anniversary of the 1988-89 Temagami blockades, nostalgia threatens, as with any anniversary. The impulse towards nostalgia is increased by subsequent history: a shattering internal dispute in the First Nation, on the apparent brink of a settlement; the First Nation's basic leverage from land cautions rejected at the Supreme Court (1991), and litigation to renew them rejected, that strategy abandoned for the less ample Robinson-Huron Treaty of 1850; and the titanic issue of re-engaging the current Ontario government.

There have been other disappointments. There were promising experiments that arose in multi-stakeholder and bi-national land-use planning notably the Wendaban Stewardship Authority (WSA) and the Comprehensive Planning Programme and Comprehensive Planning Council (CPP and CPC). But these experiments were exhausting, and divided and embittered environmental and Aboriginal leaders: hard-won compromises were threatened (in the case of the CPP) or ignored (in the case of the WSA), and the seemingly endless CPP/CPC process unified and emboldened local municipal leaders against Ontario. In 1995, the government closed the local Temagami MNR offices and centralized district offices in North Bay.

The fact remains that the blockades inspired many, including a generation of activists in several province-wide movements. Their memory alone is a resource for the future. The TAA's Vision of Coexistence, the exchanges and friendships that emerged across deep and bitter silences, the WSA and even the much discussed and often revised CPP/CPC, all contributed to a much wider provincial re-examination of Aboriginal law, of the MNR, and of environmental strategy. That subsequent developments brought much of this strategy into question, obliges those who remember fondly to reflect assiduously.

During the blockade experience, hopes were high for unity, or at least for an alliance for change, among environmentalists and the First Nation. Those hopes proved to be misplaced, or perhaps ill-timed. The tensions between environmentalists and the First Nation have received some quiet comment. But perhaps the greatest understated loss to the First Nation and the wilderness movement in the mid-1990s was the growing hostility of resource interests and municipal leaders.[1]

I suggest, building on the work of Jeremy Shute and others, that these hopes were frustrated by different, enduring visions for the place, and by the failure to build up enduring understandings among them. During and after the crisis, the boundaries and characteristics of recreationists' "Temagami country" remained distinct from those for "N'Daki Menan" within the First Nation, and the overlapping resource-driven "Temiskaming area."[2]

Moreover, the story offers us a key to the understandings that endure: those political visions developed experientially rest on the real occupation *and generation* of different spaces in the Temagami area. Both change and continuity are inherent to these visions, experiences, and even spaces. On the level of ethics, I suspect the violent disruption of any space necessarily implies loss, disorientation, and suffering. On the level of politics, much could be learned—and much accomplished—from experiencing, from studying, and where needed, from adapting these experiential bases.

If the legacy of the blockades illustrates this need to build understanding, the Temagami blockades were also strategic acts, rather than encounter sessions. However much one works towards a politics of consensus and understanding across differences, certain situations, including those specifically involving non-violent action, do require the political calculus of winning and losing.

This chapter does take sides, and is based on a couple of hopeful assumptions. The first is that there will be a new wave of protest and reform, in the name of sustainable ecological relations and conscionable settler-Aboriginal relations. Recent scholarship is building the intellectual base for such a development (e.g., Kent McNeil and David T. McNab). Second, that alliance will be based on a sounder dialogue among resource workers, ecologists, and First Nations' citizens. Activists and thinkers such as Laurie Adkin or Brennain Lloyd of Northwatch, and the Wilderness Society/CPAWS's work on jobs and the forest have strengthened these capacities. Strategic situations must be found and exploited which lessen the hostilities among potentially friendly forces. But third, flabbergasting the opponents that remain will remain a necessity for the foreseeable future. All this requires both a vocabulary that can successfully identify strategic situations of surprise, and an appropriate daily practice that begins to generate spaces of coexistence.

This chapter seeks to develop a language that strategically approaches the increasingly well-known story of Temagami with an eye to relationships in space. Space is a crucial dimension of social and political relations, in which forces may surprise one another to advance their own causes. I begin with a discussion of strategy, and the place of non-violence in strategic thinking. Then comes the theme of surprise, one critical basis for confrontational political acts that "work." Then I seek to develop a rather specific spatial language that appears to speak specifically to the actors who met at the Red Squirrel Road. I attempt to show that this theoretical excursion can help us to address questions about such moments of confrontation, and to learn from them.

AN "INDIRECT APPROACH" TO A STRATEGIC LANGUAGE

Although most groups and individuals who organized blockades at Red Squirrel Road thought through practicalities involved with non-violent resistance, not all reached the same conclusions. At many points, the possibility (and limits) of violence and intimidation were debated. Bridges have been burned in Temagami, apparently with the knowledge of dissident Aboriginal activists, environmentalists' tires

have been slashed, and trees spiked. Violence isn't unique to this blockade. In the wider North American scene, "monkey-wrenching," for
example, is a big part of some militant environmentalism; some forest
workers vent their anger physically or in threats; and the warrior societies are part of the wider Aboriginal movement. So Temagami has
been fortunate to have actors who chose both firmness and forbear-
ance as their strategic options.

The bounds separating violent from non-violent action constitute an
important theoretical question. Strategic thinking developed first and
most concretely in military contexts, both in Europe and in China.
Aspects of this military literature have entered non-violent and political
theory and practice. Metaphorical "campaigns," "strategic plans,"
"fronts," and so forth are part of virtually all strategic thinking, but so too
are some more elaborate concepts. Authors like B.H. Liddell Hart carried
strategic problems from wartime—such as the "indirect approach" discussed below—into peacetime.[3] Even Gandhi praised the military
virtues of discipline, obedience, and courage as practical necessities.[4]

The moral high ground and love for one's enemy are often presented
as central assets in non-violent resistance. But perhaps there is violence
in these metaphors and concepts? For instance, traditional military discipline places real limits on democracy, and it is a common assumption
in strategic thought that winning forces enjoy internal unity of command. Military strategy normally assumes that the sides are already
opposed and clearly defined. The first question turns on clear identification: Who are our friends? Who are our enemies? Can one build peace
with justice on such models? And yet to struggle without the benefit of
all the actual mental tools available also seems unwise.

For some classic practitioners, from Thoreau to Gandhi to King, non-
violence is effective only if the practitioners embrace love for the enemy
as a good in itself. Others see non-violent and violent action as pragmatic alternatives in the stark calculus of bodies broken and blood
shed. Gene Sharp, a key American pragmatist on this question, denies
that non-violent technique has absolute moral superiority over violence. Instead, he merely notes its relative effectiveness, how little
destruction it involves. He does not deny that practical differences
remain, but considers those differences a matter of investigation. I take
up that stance for a time as a learning device, but I do not renounce
Gandhi's challenge.

So, then, what can non-violent theorists learn from the art of war? There is, for example, the idea that an enemy's strength can be used against him. This central insight of Asian martial arts and strategy influenced Western thinkers in non-violence, just as much as it influenced the anti-colonial guerrilla.[5] In the first place, non-violence in particular is said to work precisely because enemy violence goes unanswered: the very disproportion of their own means shames the enemy and undermines morale. To Richard Gregg, this lies at the core of successful non-violent non-cooperation: a kind of moral ju-jitsu.[6]

In this use of the enemy's own strength, there is also the element of surprise. Gregg's ju-jitsu succeeds only if the enemy fails to recognize it or to act on its implications. Non-violent action succeeds where other techniques fail, because in a world organized around violent military actions, non-violence itself presents a surprise to an opposing army. In a colonial context, Gandhi similarly argues that the surprise lies in encountering any resistance at all.[7]

When non-violent practices surprise the violent, they are demoralizing and thus effective by their very nature. But Gandhi—like Martin Luther King Jr.—operated in settings rife with overt officially sanctioned, and vigilante violence against oppressed peoples. But how and why does non-violent action work? Above all, what happens in the fourth decade since the American peace and civil rights movements first put non-violent action on everyone's television and on many a political agenda? In an Ontario where even Bay Street management actually picketed the NDP's Queen's Park, does *violent* action not become the logical resort?

Note that I mean situations where violence would surprise the authorities and those in the dominant society. I do not forget Ipperwash, Kahnesetake, Allan Gardens, or Queen's Park.[8] In Canada, and perhaps especially Ontario, systemic violence against First Nations, against other disadvantaged groups, and against the environment is not much acknowledged. That is because it is generally organized under a different "regime" of violence. State coercion remains fundamentally surprising and unusual to members of the dominant society; and it is also different in character, because it is normally conducted by the police rather than the military. Such is the basis of the notion, if not exactly the fact, of a "Peaceable Kingdom." The "peace" of this peaceable kingdom is not morally trivial in itself. However low a standard it is, relative to the peace the oppressed require, it also has strategic sig-nificance: violent resistance generally generates surprise but little support, and indeed, may strengthen its enemies.

SURPRISE AND THE INDIRECT APPROACH

If Ontario's systemic violence against First Nations continues, it will leave only non-violent action in overtly non-violent settings. That is a relatively happy condition, at least for the general population, but even in the chill light of pure pragmatism, it is a strategic problem. Violent surprise may fail to demoralize the powerful and because non-violent techniques have become so common, they may fail to surprise or to startle the wider public to examine the routine violence of the status quo. But perhaps the problem is a false one, even without the obvious ethical problems with violence. Perhaps there's a problem in thinking of non-violence as the primary strategic basis for the surprise of non-violent actions. By contrast, Liddell Hart describes the strategic value of surprise as a separate conceptual problem that should concern both violent and non-violent strategy. And, perhaps because he is a military historian, he links surprise, not to non-violent technique and its politi-cal or moral implications, nor to the very emergence of resistance, but— if at all—to *manoeuvres in space*.[9]

The key to surprise is to organize a confrontation in which one knows what to do, but one's opponent does not. The present chapter has simply assumed this is strategically important. But it is worth point-ing out that the importance of the opponent's ignorance to strategy came as something of a surprise to classic European strategic thought. European traditions have tended to favour the direct application of overwhelming force: the strategy of grinding down the enemy. Liddell Hart quotes Clausewitz on this point, "to introduce into the philosophy of war a principle of moderation would be an absurdity—war is an act of violence pushed to its utmost bounds."[10] But Liddell Hart argued that this "direct approach" is feasible for very few powers, and the results remain fickle even for them. In the 1920s, he became an admirer of the classic craftiness of the Chinese military thinker, Sun Tzu, who took a different view of surprise.

Sun Tzu's *Art of War* turns on the relationship between normal, direct approaches to the enemy (*cheng*) and extraordinary, indirect (*ch'i*) ones.

In the words of Samuel Griffin, we "may define the *cheng* element as fixing and the *ch'i* as flanking or encircling, or, again, as the force of distraction and the force of decision....A *ch'i* operation is always unexpected, strange, or unorthodox; a *cheng*, more obvious."[11] The *ch'i* element and cunning in preparation essentially determine how little direct force is required. Distraction and deception are essential in the "economy of violence," an economy which, like all others, seeks to minimize costs.[12] For the pragmatic theorists of non-violence, this indirect approach forms common ground for both violent and non-violent strategy—common ground that would horrify rigorous Gandhians. But this common ground is ultimately intended to minimize violence when the time comes for a final, direct approach.

SURPRISES IN SPACE

Not all movements in space seem to involve surprise. Activists plan confrontations in real spaces. Sensible ones plan them in places where activists are in a strong position and their opponents are in a weak position; and they avoid spaces in which the opposite situation prevails. But generally, even in such cases, one seeks first to *be* in places where one is not expected, where preparations have not been made. To approach a confrontation strategically means surprise by the transgression of terrestrial boundaries or distances, that is, getting to, being in, and acting strategically in a place one is not expected to be. In the first place, this action implies knowledge of different types of terrain during strategic preparation. It also involves movement, the strategic actors' transgression of boundaries and distances.

In all this, Sun Tzu is especially helpful. As one commentator noted about Sun Tzu's words, "'Ground' includes both distances and *type of terrain*."[13] Sun Tzu explores both with indirection in mind. At the simplest level—"distances"—one could simply read strategic advantage from measurements on a map. For instance, the Red Squirrel Road extension's strategic advantages for ecologists and the Temagami people, and Owain Lake's strategic advantages for MNR in 1996, cannot be divorced from their relative proximity to particular concentrations and activities of "friendly" and "opposing" social forces. The Red Squirrel Road extension blockade could be supplied and publicized from the lake where tourists and the First Nation were concentrated, from the road itself, and from the First Nation's temporary base at Camp Wanapitei.[14] It affected lands that wilderness canoeists and members of the First Nation knew well or could visit readily. Few of these attributes applied to Owain Lake.

But relative proximity is not enough to know about space: as Sun Tzu knew, terrain is rarely a "level playing field," and there is little one can do about that in the course of normal strategic deliberations. He considered the character of already-given kinds of terrain, from the standpoint of crossing their boundaries and from the standpoint of conflict within them: "Ground may be classified according to its nature as accessible, entrapping, indecisive, constricted, precipitous, and distant," and in respect of troop deployment, "as dispersive, frontier, key, communicating, focal, serious, difficult, encircled, and death."[15]

This is not enough and we must think more deeply about Temagami. Landscape obviously appears to us as an already-given strategic reality, at least relative to immediate strategic actions; and this is how Sun Tzu approaches it. On any given blockade, on any given fall, a given landscape acquires relatively fixed social and strategic importance. But, in long-term strategic analysis, as ecological historians and political ecologists have emphasized, "natural" spaces are still dynamic and still partly *social* realities in their own right. The ultimate geo-strategic emphasis should embrace the natural and social processes that constitute the landscape as it is and as it can be, rather than on the apparent permanency that landscapes present to contending social forces.[16]

This "geo-strategy" would be irrelevant if such processes were confined to the very long term, in which conscious and particularly political action has little role. Fernand Braudel thought this way about nature, but Mike Davis does not, and in this, Mike Davis is right.[17] The intimacy of changes in the land to our own purposes is especially critical when strategic theory is applied to land-use politics. For those persons who were opposed to the routine clear-cutting of old-growth stands in Temagami, clear-cutting and the construction of logging roads are not merely the topics of the dispute, they are—consciously or not—part and parcel of the *conduct* of the dispute.[18] In the most cynical version, clear-cutting old-growth becomes a central strategic act—even a tactical act—of both the industry and the ministry that issues the industry cutting permits. But even where timber management is not executed with politics in mind, its apolitical acts have the immediate strategic effect of altering the physical and social terrain, and thereby the terms of political engagement. (As Antonio Gramsci pointed out, successful political strategy must flow out of the capacities and resources that different social forces forge in their day-to-day, seemingly apolitical activities, and hence, day-to-day activities cannot be ruled out of political strategy.[19]

To take another example, old growth has attracted and empowered Temagami ecotourist operators both economically and politically. Tourism without Temagami's old growth is economically possible, of course, but it would not emphasize the same services or have the same role in land-use politics. Equally, reducing this "over-mature" timber as part of the "normalization" of the forest would involve the political and geographic ascendency of the industry and professional foresters oriented to "sustained-yield" timber management; the introduction of alternative management techniques would empower different branches of government.[20]

These then are disputes *about* day-to-day land use that are prosecuted by surprise and other elements of strategy. But they are also prosecuted *through* day-to-day land use and on the basis of ideas that flow *from* land use. And disputes operate against the ever-changing web of life. We have from Sun Tzu the types of terrain that are directly tied to our immediate tactical purposes. By identifying distinct, meaningful kinds of social space, we acquire new basic principles for identifying and understanding the potential for certain indirect manoeuvres. But in the fluidity of terrain itself and in the breadth of historical and social vision that strategies of resistance imply, Sun Tzu seems less helpful than the TAA's vision of coexistence.

SPATIAL LANGUAGES IN RELATION TO THE INDIRECT APPROACH

We have learned that distinct spaces are intertwined with the fate of the various constituencies active in local land politics, as well as with natural processes. But we do not yet have a language for analyzing those types of space, even if we do have good texts to describe them in the Temagami case. In this section, I summarize an integrated spatial taxonomy different from Sun Tzu's. I begin by arguing that some manoeuvres are based on spatial displacement, some on changes of spatial scale, and others on the sudden transformation over time of a prevailing spatial order. (Later, I propose that a more specific typology of space arises from interaction with different social forces in the conduct of routine lives.)

Spatial displacement provides one of the most obvious spatial bases for surprise. If the current terrain is not working to one's own advantage, one may simply relocate. This surprises both those left behind and those encountered. For example, the government chose in 1996 to reopen logging in the Temagami area at remote Owain Lake, and Ontario environmental groups based in the south have occasionally insisted on consultation meetings in Toronto or Ottawa.

Spatial displacement may also be undertaken for non-strategic reasons. Heavy forest investments were displaced in the nineteenth and early twentieth centuries from the Ottawa Valley to richer timber locations on the shores of the Upper Great Lakes. As a partial consequence, Temagami avoided the clearances of similar areas further south. But conservation measures also dwindled as the resource-poor region's relative importance diminished. The upper great lakes and northwestern Ontario took the brunt of new clear-cutting practices.[21]

Secondly, different spatial scales may be constituted, such as the level of neighbourhood, town, region, nation, international region, or the entire globe. After an extensive period of organization on one level, a movement or other social force may achieve overwhelming surprise by rapidly shifting the scale of its operations. The achievements and activities of an opponent, which always must be organized at some scale, may be upset and the opponent caught unawares by a different scale of opposition. If size does matter, larger-scale resistance is not necessarily superior. David Harvey writes of "militant particularisms" to identify the highly localized community politics that became so important in Temagami.[22]

But how could such forces possibly matter? In the case of Temagami, the already-depressed forest industry in eastern and northeastern Ontario was side-swiped by the continental softwood lumber dispute in the mid- to late 1980s, weakening it and rendering it vulnerable to challenges in Temagami and elsewhere.[23] Surprised by continental competitors, regional operators were unable to take on central leadership tasks to defeat or divert the local critiques of environmentalists or the First Nations. Nor was industry in a position to oppose compromises that provincial agencies forged with the interests arrayed against the status quo. Harvey is useful here because he knows that strategic terrain changes along with the actors. He claims that the movement between different spatial scales should not assume anything about the permanence of those scales. In fact, movement in space creates and remakes spatial scales in its own right.

Harvey also finds that such movements are not equally possible at all times, and in this lies a third basis for surprises in space. In a period of crisis, particular spatial patterns break down, while others can be established in the absence of new fixed norms. As Storper and Walker have argued, old spatial patterns may be abandoned along with existing places.[24] New places may be *generated* in the process, not merely discovered or occupied.

For an example of such a historic crisis in spatial patterns, a historical detour is necessary. The past thirty years of Temagami history turns very much on the Lake Temagami Plan and the planned resort at Maple Mountain, and on the unprecedented opposition coming from environmentalists and the First Nation in 1971.[25] With these plans, normal provincial practice was being introduced. It was not being reinvented in Temagami: it was there to reinvent Temagami. Maple Mountain was a plan to restore Keynesian high employment levels to the northeast, as traditional resource industries ran short of raw material. The Lake Temagami Plan was also trying to intensify tourist and other industries without spoiling the recreational commons.

In the 1980s, the self-proclaimed correspondence of post war provincial economic management and Keynesian economic principles was effectively questioned.[26] But the post-war ambition to achieve comprehensive zoning of interests in land, coordinated by expert government planners, certainly had much to do with the Keynesian revolution in government responsibilities. In this respect, it resembles the ideology of sustained-yield forestry management, the allocation of carefully delineated timber limits and quotas, and the heavily mechanized clear-cut techniques.[27]

One political sign of a crisis is when a normal practice provokes a surprising response. What was abnormal and surprising in Temagami in 1971 was that such effective opposition arose to entrenched state-planning techniques. Tellingly, these opposing forces were rooted in increasingly rare spatial practices: the resource and later wilderness tourist activities that grew up around the water routes, portages, and hiking routes known collectively as *nastawgan*. The Aboriginal interest in particular was able to counterpose its own spatial interests through the strength of other branches of the state itself, as expressed in the cautions blocking land sales in N'Daki Menan through the provincial land registry. The aboriginal capacity to make N'Daki Menan matter in the daily life of other interests derived from renewed legal debate about the character of Aboriginal title. At the time it was an open question whether unextinguished Aboriginal title came under the registry's mandate to protect exclusive property rights.

The surprise unleashed by Aboriginal activists was interesting and effective, not so much in its "demoralizing" impact on the state, but in the new scale at which the state was disempowered: activism not only paralyzed some of the state's more important economic functions in the area to an extent that had hardly been expected, but in the process redrew the area itself. State actors were not structured to anticipate this spatial shift after decades of Keynesian-inspired practice, and having themselves been constituted on the basis of different scales of operation (MNR districts and geographic townships), they could not rapidly respond. The recreation of N'Daki Menan as a politically significant contemporary scale of social practices in space was crucial to the introduction of Aboriginal counter-narratives about the proper relation of human society to that land.

THE (LARGELY) DELEUZEAN VOCABULARY OF A STRATEGIC, SPATIAL LANGUAGE

We have examined questions of displacement, changes between scales, and periods in which changes of scale become possible. The entry of N'Daki Menan and the provincial state introduces a second step in developing the emerging spatial language: to be able to conceive of these spatial acts occurring among the distinctive spaces that correspond as far as possible to the entire political field of actors.

The problems of Temagami are normally analyzed using separate, unrelated social-scientific literature, or by political literature that in theoretical terms sets aside the social origins and characteristics of the various "groups." A settler/First Nation divide can draw on anthropological or postcolonial theories; a working-class/leisure-class divide on class analysis; a tourism-resource sectoral divide on analysis of sectoral interest;[28] a north-south regional divide on dependency or other regional theory: each is certainly evident in Temagami, and each involves distinctions in social space. But these approaches, if taken singly, would oversimplify the socio-political strategic situation. The convergence of so many radically distinct spatial practices in a single case is something that the social sciences in developed countries rarely need to address. As a partial consequence of the indictment of resource management since the 1960s, multi-stakeholder land-use planning has been discussed extensively and refined as a practical planning problem. But this institutional approach is little concerned with the social basis for different spaces.

The spatial taxonomy I find more adequate to this situation is developed from a critical appropriation of distinctions made in Deleuze and Guattari's *Thousand Plateaus*, especially the chapter "On Nomadology," with some supplementation from their sources and from the earlier *Anti-Oedipus*.[29] The result appears uniquely fitted to the strategic considerations in Temagami, and perhaps to other places in central and northern Canada.

Here I identify five distinct spaces and relate them to what Deleuze and Guattari call "social formations," by which they mean a social structure or complex which functions in a particular way on its surroundings. A surrounding is principally an environment of "flows," whether of people, goods, ideas, other species, or natural materials. The internal structures that account for these distinguishing functions are characterized as "machines" or "apparatuses." Their operations and relations are said to operate in their distinctive fashion without reference to scale, physical location, or period.

Deleuze and Guattari's writing is evocative rather than schematic, a fluid, shifting style they associate with "nomadic thought"—the act of summarizing does violence to it. But it is not my purpose to adhere to their theoretical project, least of all to accept the often racist or romantic overtones that enter into it. It is the "rational core" of their fundamental social and spatial distinctions that is helpful here, along with their sustained spatial treatment of the state and the varied forms of resistance to it. The fact that they define their social formations in terms of function, that is, on the formations' distinctive impacts on the endless flows of the environment, means their concept becomes a tool by which the critic can break out of the limitations of his seemingly unconscious Eurocentric world view. Happily, part of their own project is to invite fruitful departures from their text. Here, I propose to depart in the quite different direction of critical political economy, and treat the various social formations as distinct elements of social structure which may be "articulated" into larger complexes through an inherently political process.[30]

The first space is called the *ecumenon*. It is a global or ecumenical space generated by a machine of the same name. The ecumenical machine's distinctive function is not to homogenize the various other social formations and the spaces their machines generate, but to encompass them and make them compatible with its overarching purposes. Both capitalism and the Catholic church are identified by Deleuze and Guattari as ecumenical social formations. Highly diverse social forces are threaded together, but their diversity is not submerged. (Deleuze and Guattari tell us that truly assimilative and homogenizing forces at work in the world apparently originate elsewhere in their schema.)

The second space is striated, perhaps the most familiar experience of space for residents of highly developed agricultural and industrial settings. It is generated by the interplay of two social formations, and hence of two quite distinct "machines." The first social formation is the urban, the distinctive machine of which operates to "polarize" flow in its environment. In other words, it tends to direct flow from hinterlands to urban centres, and between centres through a network of roads and other instruments of communication. For students of Canadian political economy, one should emphasize that this conception of the urban emphasizes an interurban network of communication, not merely a hierarchical relation with the hinterland, which is a multipolar, web-like space.

The second social formation of striated space is the state, perhaps Deleuze and Guattari's central preoccupation. But this is not the narrow institutional state of Max Weber. It embraces all the manifestations of authoritarian command and obedience. Its distinctive machines are three concrete "apparatuses of capture": the payment of ground rent, the payment of tax in money, and the payment of labour in wages. Their impact on the flows in their environment is expansionary and homogenizing: "not only to vanquish nomadism but to control migrations and, more generally, to establish a zone of rights over an entire 'exterior,' over all the flows traversing the ecumenon."[31] In combination, these machines are a force of "territorialization," a force that fixes things and people to given points in space.

These then are the two major social formations generating striated space. After striated space itself, one thinks of a surveyor's map of rural Saskatchewan, the grid system of Toronto's downtown core, or metaphorically, the warp and weft of woven cloth. It is a space of lines, a space of zoning and property limits. It is organized hierarchically from a centre, and is therefore often called "arborescent," for the central taproot and trunk of many tree species. This is also a space organized according to the "royal sciences," a form of knowledge (such as Western natural sciences) whose very techniques and purposes rely on domination and control. The map is a classic tool of such science, for it imagines the land from the "eye of God," high above its object of study. It is a space imposed from above (both physically and hierarchically), and it is understood and generated in two dimensions.

The roads and other forms of communication in this space serve a specific purpose, worth noting in a book about blockade and resistance. That purpose is to allocate rights over land parcels to populations, rights that are indefinitely fixed, clearly bounded, and mapped. It is a space where characteristic "regimes of violence" are those of police repression and criminality, rather than the violence of war.[32] Finally, it is the space of "relative movement," that is, the movement from fixed point to fixed point within a self-contained space. The bodies that move are also clearly distinguished from their surroundings and internally unified.[33]

Smooth or nomadic space, on the other hand, is all heterogeneity, chaotic uncentredness, and inscrutable interconnections. Such space arises out of the nomadic social formation's "war machine," whose characteristic impact is to pulverize what it encounters, being inherently anti-state and consequently anti-"territorial." War itself is merely a symptom of this machine, the "regime of violence" that corresponds to this space. With respect to characteristic movement, this is the space of speed, which Deleuze and Guattari conceive of as "absolute movement."

In absolute movement, smooth space is occupied along a "line of flight." This is the prime contrast model in Deleuze and Guattari's own project for the allocating road of striated space. The line of flight is a vortex-like dispersion of human numbers speeding in a common direction. The movement of these hordes along a line of flight resembles the decentred rush of gas molecules released into a vacuum. The war machine neither "owns" nor "seeks" the points on its path (which is what the state or the urban apparatuses would do) but characteristically "occupies" them. Smooth space is therefore associated with deterritorialization, the interruption of all relationships between things or people and the land.

Holding together all these associations is the romantic European nightmare of mounted pastoralists: the "Mongol hordes" of the central Eurasian plains. Reading this nomadism with an anthropology of nomadic pastoralists, one can readily criticize it.[34] Yet Deleuze and Guattari make the important distinction between the nomadism of such peoples and other kinds of social formation that European thought has often confused. This is important, because literal nomadism is of little relevance to Temagami. But, metaphorically, the concept is more applicable. One should think less of woven cloth than of the entangled fibres of felt; less of a survey map than of a cyclone or vortex; less of a central taproot than of a tangled mass of fungal rhizomes. Nomadic space is where order or fixity of all kinds is vanquished. Yet its destructive force is paradoxically contained in modified form within most states themselves, in the form of the carefully separated armed forces but also elsewhere. Canada as a dominant society presents itself to its surroundings as an articulated amalgam of the state, the urban, and the war machine.

Deleuze and Guattari relate the generation of "holey space" to artisans and prospectors. This fourth kind of space is also characterized by movement, but in specific relation to "matter-movement": the extraction, movement, and the reworking of matter through chains of institutional and technological "assemblages." Social actors within it—miners and craftspeople—are necessarily "itinerant," not nomadic. That is, as the village of Temagami knows well in the wake of the Sherman mine, they follow matter-flows. Holey space is the space generated by the work process of the staples trades, from its source through secondary processing. Like an elaborate precapitalist mine, holey space is honeycombed, and is not readily mapped from above. Being in holey space does not lend itself to ready self-orientation or mutual communication.

Itinerants' form of knowledge is distinct, informed by the "minor sciences" of craft and work experience, rather than by the "royal sciences" of striated space. It is they who provide the knowledge base that operates in the generation of smooth space, having a special relationship to the war machine. In practical terms, this space and its inhabitants necessarily cuts across all other kinds of space and social formations, including the state and the urban. But their mobility links them particularly with the nomadic war machine.[35] Much more than holey space is involved in modern metropolitan-driven staples industries. But in the consideration of northern resource communities and their stout assertion of a lifestyle, a land ethic, and a set of economic problems different from those typical of southern Ontario, holey space provides for some useful reflection.

Finally, Deleuze and Guattari refer to a distinctive hunter-gatherer or "primitive" social formation. This social formation is offensively named, so its (relatively) inoffensive intent should first be explained. The term is based on an existing anthropological discussion of "stateless" societies. In his books called *Archaeology of Violence* and *Society against the State*, Pierre Clastres is specifically concerned to explore how some societies prevented a separate institution of obedience and command from emerging, given that other societies have had one for so long. Clastres argues that to see social formations as backward, ineffective, or unsophisticated for "want" of a state is to judge them by purposes they were not organized to realize. Of course, the dominant society presents its own institutions as universally desirable, and generally considers the state to be synonymous with any kind of sophisticated political order. Here, by contrast, the state is defined narrowly as the separate institutions that rest on command and obedience, and no normative weight is attached to having one.

Like many Deleuzean concepts, this state-preventive formation tends to overlap with others, such as the anti-state war machine. But the two terms are not used interchangeably. The former formation is set against the internal potential of a State and social inequality; Deleuze and Guattari set the war machine against the state as an existing external reality.[36] Some of the institutions common to stateless social formations illustrate this anticipation and prevention of hierarchy. For example, should a chief acquire authority beyond what relies on the people and speaks for them, or should a class structure begin, prophetic traditionalist movements have commonly emerged, dispersing them. Chiefly gift-giving prevents accumulated inequalities. A specific regime of violence organized around balanced reciprocity or "struggle," rather than "war" or "policing," similarly disperses rather than concentrates power.[37]

"Statelessness" still conceives of this difference from state societies only in negative terms. But the basic distinction between the two social formations may identify some of the stakes in the encounter between some First Nations with the Canadian state. For instance, certain aspects of the Anishnabai tradition seem comparable. In the Anishnabai tradition, institutionalized leadership certainly existed: this was no anarchy. But the consensus of elders or ultimately of the whole people was the decisive decision-making mechanism. Individual leadership relied more on exhortation, on example, and on articulating community consensus than on authoritative commands. Fission, gossip, teasing, and ostracism resolved conflict (and to some extent still do), not authoritative decision-makers, legal rulings, or police coercion.[38]

Deleuze and Guattari appear not to have discussed a space specific to this "primitive" social formation. Indeed, they viewed woodlands as naturally striated spaces, looking only at the vertical lines of the trees themselves. (I will address this shortly.) But they did theorize that this social formation was marked by a distinctive form of movement. There is a high level of routine movement, but it is not the vortical or "nomadic" movement of a war machine; nor is it the primarily passive "itinerancy," merely following matter movement in holey space. Instead, it is "transhumant" or "rotational" movement:

> Transhumants do not follow a flow, they draw a circuit; they only follow the part of the flow that enters into the circuit, even an ever-widening one. Transhumants are therefore itinerant only consequentially, or become itinerant only when their circuit of land or pasture has been exhausted or when the rotation has become so wide that the flows escape the circuit.[39]

Hence, while sharing relatively high routine movement with nomadic and itinerants, transhumants have strong, fixed ties to the land. The circuit operates seasonally for the harvesting of resources in times of abundance, and for allowing those resources time to recover.

This leads me to think that a specific kind of space may be theorized for state-preventing social formations, based on the Algonquian *nastawgan*. These are set networks of seasonal paths, portages, and canoe routes intersecting with the seasonal pathways of other species. Temagami still has especially dense networks of *nastawgan*, mentioned often in the early pro-wilderness literature of the 1970s.

Temagami has been a *locus classicus* for study of the Algonquian hunting territory system. I view that system as the social core of *nastawgan* space. Under this system, summers were meeting times; family territories, often based on watersheds, were the normal wintering places. Winter-time dispersion was a crucial survival strategy. The hunting territories were well understood and delineated, but were periodically redistributed; their stewardship transferred flexibly from generation to generation. The principles of the hunting territory system imply "a continuous inhabiting of place, an intimate understanding of the relationship between humans and the ecosystem."[40] Finally, unlike movement along a road in striated space, which is a separate action from both mapping and maintaining it, movement through *nastawgan*—for purposes inherent to the gathering and hunting territories—was central rather than incidental to understanding and reproducing the *nastawgan*. In sum, *nastawgan* space is of a piece with the transhumant social formation: it arises from a cyclical movement anticipating and preventing cumulative scarcities, surpluses, inequalities, and subordination within a set territory.

Working from what is known about the Algonquian First Nations, I also suggest that this social formation rests on a distinctive form of knowledge. The generators of *nastawgan* space developed and used a knowledge of wide, immensely complex ecological relationships. The *nastawgan* system was merely a means of access, but its character shaped that wider knowledge. This knowledge was transmitted predominantly by oral traditions, example, and experience. Such knowledge was effective, but unlike the "objectivity" of what Deleuze and Guattari call the royal sciences of striated space, or the minor sciences' artisanal appreciation of the ways of inanimate objects, it is grounded to a distinctive degree in the spiritual relationship with animate beings.[41] When one discusses relationships in an Anishnabai social formation, these relationships cannot be separated from human relationships as readily as they can be in settler society.

In total, then, there are at least five distinct spaces which differ in kind rather than in scale, location, or period. They may be related to distinct social forces, which operate on the flows that surround them in quite distinct ways. They round out the spatial strategic language I've set out to outline. In the final section of this chapter, I try to show that this spatial vocabulary can have strategic importance.

SOME KEY QUESTIONS AND PRELIMINARY ANSWERS

- *In Temagami, why were the land cautions of the early 1970s an effective and durable instrument of surprise and leverage against the government and against resource industry?*

Hodgins and Benidickson have noted that, until the 1970s, the activities in Temagami were effectively coordinated in pluralist fashion by the relative compatibility of holey and *nastawgan* space. Different pathways and travelways criss-crossed Temagami for different activities as part of different social formations, without normally producing more than intermittent and localized conflict. Mining and forest extraction in the twentieth century had significant but still quite localized impact. Settlement, as in most of northern Ontario, remained concentrated along transportation routes and at rich resource sites.[42] *Nastawgan* space not only survived severe local impacts from mines, logging, and settlement but its seasonal movements meshed adequately with the seasonal extraction needs of industry. Tourists could be escorted for money through the *nastawgan* system in summer and fall; other tourist services further supplemented and sustained the traditional rotation system. The coordination of these activities was ad hoc, and above all, seasonal.

Throughout the twentieth century, mining and logging were conducted clearly for metropolitan use, and the state (notably the Department of Lands and Forests, and its Temagami Forest Reserve) was surveyor, licensing agent, and manager. But the dual forces striating space, for all their cruel demands for exclusive rights to clearly fixed and bounded territories, were not thoroughgoing, and the First Nation never abandoned *nastawgan* spatial practices completely. Conscious coordination under state institutions like the 1901 Temagami Forest Reserve proved to be abortive. The province was unwilling to provide an adequate reserve to the First Nation, and therefore unable to use the worst rules of the Indian Act to confine the First Nation to a fixed territory. Nor did striation have the whole-hearted support of local miners and loggers. However much their work was linked to state activity, they had an understanding of Temagami that remained significantly at odds with the norms of southern-based bureaucracies.

A tendency towards striation was certainly afoot during this century. But comprehensive land-use planning involved a far more systematic striation of space. Existing activities in the area were themselves already becoming mutually exclusionary and fixed to particular territories, in a series of developments that Hodgins and Benidickson have noted and that I have called "spatialization."[43] Logging adopted heavy machinery, the clear-cutting regime as an exclusionary use of forestland, extraction by logging road rather than by river, and the striating ambitions of sustained-yield forestry. Logging was now conducted far more comprehensively, and its impacts displaced all other existing activities far more completely, for many years at a time. By the 1960s, Bear Island was shifting from an intercultural gathering place to a more uniform Aboriginal reserve community; provincial winter-schooling schedules were instituted for the First Nation, cutting young families off from the seasonal rounds. Alongside the traditional white-water youth camps, which had relied on the *nastawgan* and First Nation support staff, new camps arose that emphasized in-camp programs. Even the planned tourist resort at Maple Mountain represented an unprecedented scale of tourist operation centred on a fixed site; it conflicted with and interrupted the mountain's spiritual importance.

These competing demands for exclusive rights to bounded land increasingly required a coordinating principle that was neither ad hoc nor seasonal. The provocative 1973 Lake Temagami Plan (MNR) was the state's response. This represented a transition from de facto coordination by compatible seasonal schedules to coordination by zoning. It is a shift in emphasis that remains evident in the area's most recent land-use plan, the MNR's 1996 Comprehensive Planning Programme (MNR).

What then of the land cautions? Comprehensive land-use planning is in some ways entirely typical of striated space: it presents a comprehensive image of the land, promising "a place for everything, and everything in its place." But the strategic thinker is also attentive to the potential for counter developments, even if these are only the potential for ju-jitsu, the inversion of the very strength of the dominant system. In the Temagami case, strategic thinkers turned for example, to the land registry system, part of the state structure supporting the striation of space as private property.[44] The Temagami land cautions were an intervention in striated space that translated *nastawgan* space for the dominant social formation. Paradoxically, the limits of N'Daki Menan, the product of a social formation designed to frustrate the emergence of a state, were enforced by a State agency through a court order. But the whole system of land allocation and profit from the rents had been premised on the prior ownership of the land by the Crown. Striated space under the state cannot deal with overlapping rights of the same kind to the same land, and had ignored a critical right, namely Aboriginal title, as its foundational act in North America. Hence N'Daki Menan land cautions, beyond the manner in which they were executed, were confusing and a profound surprise by their very nature. Years would pass before the government could determine a course of action.

- *Why did non-Aboriginal wilderness activists and the TAA both come to blockade the same logging road in the fall of 1989 at about the same time? Why was this relatively effective in surprising and disadvantaging their opponents?*

The Temagami First Nation at Bear Island is not frozen in its pre-contact organization, any more than modern Ontario mirrors the Upper Canada of 1791. *Nastawgan* space and much associated with it remain a feature of the Temagami area, albeit in adapted form. *Nastawgan* routes are mapped, remembered, and used. Moreover, others have shared in appreciation of that space. In this century, recreational hikers, canoeists, and youth camps have all joined the rapidly changing First Nation in the evolution of *nastawgan* space. It is now the base of many wilderness canoeing and hiking routes. Tellingly, it is those new interests on the trail that have pursued the most spirited defences of Temagami's *nastawgan* space against state and urban forces.

This connection between the non-political spatial practices of two stakeholder groups and their political engagement is a critical factor in the background of the Temagami dispute. N'Daki Menan makes sense when viewed from a canoe; it makes little or no sense on a map of geographic townships or departmental districts. A logging road like the Red Squirrel, by contrast, makes eminent good sense on a ministry map or in a sawmill's business plan, but it makes little if any sense from the canoe routes it crosses. Moreover, the logging road as part of striating allocation of land serves a different purpose, and has different requirements and impacts from a canoe route within the *nastawgan*. It will interrupt hunting territories and build timber berths instead. In this respect, "N'Daki Menan" resembles "Temagami country" far more than it resembles the "Temiskaming area." Consequently, the wilderness tourist operators, camp directors, and former campers who knew the area through the *nastawgan,* understood the threat of the Red Squirrel Road. Or rather, they sensed the striating threat of *any* road. Moreover, through their non-political activities, they could publicize that threat in a way that provincial planners could not.[45]

- *Why were these two movements unable to maintain a stable alliance during the blockades of 1988-89? Why were they unable to maintain adequate internal unity in the land and land-use negotiations that followed?*

These questions enter sensitive territory, so some provisos are in order. Much romantic nonsense could be made linking particular individuals, communities, and spaces, especially between First Nations, *nastawgan* space, and the forest. Such nonsense can set up utopian cages for a whole people, and risks delegitimizing the difficult real decisions that must be made under the dual claims of lived heritage and the relentless assimilative pressures of the state. It can also limit the legitimate adaptation to new conditions that occurs in any tradition. I have no interest in contributing to such errors, particularly given the context of this book. Also, intercommunity or interorganizational disagreements in a relatively small human setting are, inevitably, also personal disagreements. As a second proviso, my interest here is on patterns of social life in space, and not about personalities.

The models just outlined should be understood as preliminary, but also as attempts to understand elements of social reality. Social structures and spaces are presented as having differential impacts on specific individuals, organizations, and communities. But they do so, articulated in different ways into larger social complexes; they can also emerge and die out, and people have the right to affect the course of that history by deliberate choices.

Temagami is rare in the extent to which certain non-Aboriginal vacationers, non-Aboriginal people providing certain kinds of services to them, and the First Nation all shared the *nastawgan* as the vantage point for their primary understandings of Temagami. But those involved in the politics of these constituencies repeatedly altered the level of trust and solidarity they had in one another.[46] On one level, as the second question implies, both Aboriginal and non-Aboriginal recreation interests were as internally complex as any human constituency. But on another, more interesting level, Aboriginal and non-Aboriginal people were still socialized into quite distinct spaces and social structures, and over time this complex of interests and ideas infused their collective view of viable and acceptable solutions.

In particular, people raised in a southern Ontario or heavily populated American setting are habituated over generations to landscapes and land-use solutions that rest on state structures. They will tend to assume that the centralized clarification and enforcement of boundaries through the policing of zoning laws, timber limits, or property lines will separate conflicting interests, and that this separation resolves disputes. Such a perception will be especially intense for those who have not lived much of their lives in the different spatial context of northern and central Ontario. By contrast, people raised on Bear Island are habituated over generations to spaces and land-use solutions that rest, at least in part, on state-preventative apparatuses. Many will tend to resist an approach that assigns parts of the community rights to portions of the land, in favour of holistic treatments of the whole land. It would make sense that, as some part of their experience, those using the land may come to a central agreement about its use, but those decisions would arise from some form of consensus, and the solutions would be ongoing adjustments. The latter pattern, if no longer the only active one in their lives, would be given greater legitimacy by the subsequent searing encounters with state agencies of the dominant society. In the course of the crisis period in Temagami, the two sides of the civilization divide repeatedly baffled and angered one another, often over what each considered fundamental or self-evident about the way Temagami ought to be.

This difference seems to be a useful way of thinking about environmental "preservationism" as it was introduced in Temagami land-use politics. In 1987, the Temagami Wilderness Society proposed a large wilderness reserve in the area, in addition to a large wilderness park that many of its members had worked hard to achieve. The quantities of land each activity would be assigned under this proposal certainly differed sharply from the preferences of the province, the industry, and the local population, and that difference contributed substantially to the hostility of local residents towards environmentalists and "canoeists." But the TWS and the state shared the assumption that conflicts could be resolved by having the state allocate particular plots exclusively to particular human interests—or to ecological processes. On this point, the First Nation broadly disagreed, especially if it was to be treated as an interest that would be assigned its own plot: the TAA insisted that it must have a role throughout N'Daki Menan.[47]

The spatial factor may have some bearing on the First Nation's own discussions about land talks and the basic institutions of self-government. Here was a people, forged in the logic of *nastawgan* space, planning their future in a setting dominated by state and urban forces, as well as by holey space: this paradox underlies many different positions within the First Nation. The TAA's innovative Vision of Coexistence insisted on having an ongoing role throughout N'Daki Menan. In negotiations over a comprehensive settlement of Aboriginal title, the province effectively shut down this approach. Those negotiations ultimately reverted to something closer in principle to traditional treaties:

zones would be created where the First Nation would have ongoing rights, and the rest would revert to the Crown in return for compensation to the TAA. The state never accepted the idea that, coming out of a transhumant or rotational tradition that gathered and dispersed seasonally, TAA spatial relationships to the land would have to be deeply compromised if any of the traditional lands were utterly transferred to other interests but that an approach closer to the TAA's could be compatible with other interests sharing access to the land.[48] Perhaps the state actors involved believed incorrectly that the TAA wanted to "own" everything. That clearly would have been an uncompromising position if the point were to allocate exclusive rights land parcels.

The differences within the First Nation over the package that finally emerged surely arose from the convergence of many different forces, some immediate, personal, or political. But some voices in Temagami have very publicly decried emerging hierarchies and the imposition of a "government" in connection with the proposed land settlement of 1993-94. This position has been linked emphatically to strong trapping and other commitments to the family hunting territories of *nastawgan* space at the Red Squirrel Road and elsewhere.[49]

As for the environmental or pro-wilderness movement, it seems more possible in the wake of the CPC findings and the 1996 events at Owain Lake to distinguish between a "northern" environmentalism and a "southern" one. "Northern" environmentalism reflects intimate connections with *nastawgan* and N'Daki Menan, for instance through the youth camps.[50] But by long residence or frequent travel, this environmentalism was exposed to the other spaces of Ontario's north, and hence shares some sensibilities with non-Aboriginal resource interests.

That northern space is complex, an intertwining of the holey space of prospecting, mining, and small-scale logging, and of the urban or metropolitan force that generates striated space through polarization of matter flows, a criss-crossing of transportation corridors between nodes of settlement and activity. Southern-style striated development is confined mostly to those corridors. In such a context, it seems reasonable that distinct activities and peoples can coexist on the same land, and so many northerners resist systematic state striation of space and the elaborate politics of allocating people comprehensively to rigorous zones, properties, or timber limits. The state striation of property rights, municipalities, mining stakes, and timber berths is certainly important, but spending months and millions carving up whole districts in this way does not appear to be money well spent. Unless of course the alternative is the galling 1987 proposal from the TWS: that, surely, was "southern" environmentalism.

NorthCARE's language of "multiple use" in the 1980s may therefore have drawn on important northern spatial realities, and we can understand the claim of many resident resource workers that northerners, if left alone, would have solved the problem of mutual accommodation much earlier.[51] But the North Bay environmental organization Northwatch equally alludes to those accommodative realities in its constitutional document: "Northwatch's perspective embodies the principles of a conserver society, with a definition of ecology that encompasses social, environmental and economic justice."[52]

Several prominent northern-based groups were deeply angered by the provincial government's action in revising the results of the Comprehensive Planning Council. An ad-hoc opposition coalition included both Northwatch and the local Friends of Temagami. But most prominent at the blockades at Owain Lake were environmentalists and sympathizers from the south, and the coalition centred on Toronto-based Earthroots. Moreover, the stance towards the old-growth pine of Temagami was manifestly about the "preservation" of a legacy for all Ontarians. Once again, the debate with the provincial government and the public campaign was about apportionment and where the province should draw the boundaries.

- *In Temagami, why did state agencies deploy elaborate land-use planning techniques like the Wendaban Stewardship Authority and the CPP/CPC, and still fail to achieve a settlement?*

For settling the area's land-use dispute, the problem with state-based or striating methods was never properly understood: comprehensive planning is a spatial technique forced to facilitate a debate about spatial effects. Aboriginal people, other northerners, and some environmentalists were coming out of quite different spatial assumptions that a comprehensive shift to *any* zoning solution would have compromised. The community mapping and site-visitation techniques used to promote consensus in the WSA process, by contrast, forced all parties to attend to one another's spaces. Through the mapping and visitation process itself, the WSA hoped to build a new ecumenical space that could coordinate and encompass other space-generating formations without dominating any.[53] But perhaps the WSA succeeded in this precisely because it was cut off from active provincial participation, and therefore from the need to accommodate the logic of striation.

A CONCLUDING NOTE ON GRAND STRATEGY

In Temagami, three forces—environmental, Aboriginal, and resource-municipal—would agree that forest use has been highly destructive within living memory, and that they have not had enough say in its management. Amidst the dispute of the late 1980s and early 1990s, quality jobs in the forest industries, the First Nation's ties with the land, and the ecosystem itself were all undermined at increasing rates. Since at least the Kennedy Commission of the 1940s, the resource industry has assumed two major pillars: centralized state regulation and unlimited raw material exportation to the urban centres further south. At the same time as it creates and reinforces problems in central and northern Ontario, this centralizing power also reflects and reinforces a lack of both community control and of self-limitation in the distant and often-detested south.

What the present situation is, and what the future should hold, remains hotly contested. Environmental groups face especially entrenched local suspicions, and both environmental groups and the First Nation must deal with the actions and suspicions of some of their more militant activists.[54] The hostile relationship of both with local municipal leaders during the worst of the conflict is even more striking. Local business and municipal leaders are essential to the remaking of forest management under genuinely democratic, diversified local control. Their impatience over the CPC and the Aboriginal title experiences taught a difficult lesson: that two essential and understated components of real democratic control are the capacity—and above all permission—to let local conclusions *conclude*. Environmentalists and the First Nation would almost certainly agree. Yet many non-Aboriginal northerners desperately want an industrial revival in familiar patterns, for the sake of their communities' survival and identity, and that is more than just a barrier to a lasting environmental and Aboriginal coalition: the objective availability of sufficient trees is a harsh and advancing limitation.

Resolving this divide with non-Aboriginal resource communities and building local control are no easy tasks for the other two social forces. Since 1995, the provincial Conservatives forwarded a political agenda with little reference to either. MNR reforms were reversed by acts of fiscal decapitation. But a lasting solution almost certainly rests on more than rapidly diminishing the MNR's presence, and offering local appointees the choice between the remaining poor alternatives. From Innis on, we have known that the destructive, pre-emptive pull of the urban social formation is simply too strong in this resource-capitalist society, and staples production too tied up with the worst cyclonic patterns in space.

Perhaps there is the basis for a local alliance to build on the overlapping holey and *nastawgan* spaces. Community forestry, its eye to improving local value-added, environmental sustainability and local control of decision making, has emerged from British Columbia and from a self-reforming environmental movement in Ontario.[55] An inter-community forestry could learn from and transcend the Elk Lake experience in the north of N'Daki Menan. Coordinated in its economic diversification with a "green municipalism" in the south, this might be more than a desirable option: it may be the *only* desirable option for all Ontarians.

If the foregoing reflections bear weight, two key lessons arise from them. First, we have seen that the problems Temagami faces may be explained by the fact that social spaces feed interests and convictions, but do not arise primarily through conscious intentions or goodwill: instead, they arise out of social practice. The same will be true of any solutions. An ecumenical or articulating space in which two nations and many social formations can co-exist will arise only out of a background of ecumenical or articulating practices. Second, spaces will also play a part in future political struggles: a new spatial reality will have to be secured through political processes that operate on an emergent spatial situation. One integral part will be the ability to surprise the opponent in and through the very spaces that are in contestation. And Canada has a number of such spaces within its borders.

The name "Canada" is explained in different ways, much like the country itself. One Aboriginal etymology suggests something like a "row of little huts"; another suggests something like "nothing there" in Portuguese. Chinese transcribes Canada as Jia-ná-dà. Each of the characters in this version has an unrelated meaning, having been chosen above all for its sound. Whether by accident or by design, those meanings are particularly telling: Canada is "Add-Take-Big."

Canada is indeed a *big* country, and some of its ways are not without nobility. But its apparatuses of capture *added* land over a century of internal imperialism and still *take* wealth from it by tax revenues and ground rents. Its history as a single economic unit has centred on the agro-industrial core of southern Ontario, and its colonization of northern Ontario and the prairies left telling spatial marks. As striated space, Canada forged a national symbol out of national policing; its hinterlands are rich—and poor—with the traditions of holey space. Under the market and production pressures of resource capitalism, the institutions of striation gave rise to a "war machine." Normally this has meant a "war with the wilderness"; occasionally, it has become war with those already most policed, especially with the First Nations.

As Basil Johnston has written in *The Manitous*, it is an icy-hearted cannibal-giant that now haunts us. Once built on a human scale with human appetites, it is now consumed by a gigantic and gruesome appetite that merely gnaws and deepens. First Nations, northern Ontarians, environmentalists, and democrats all have before them the task of contesting and transforming that complex force, its checkered land, and its checkered legacy. However they may choose to respond, the road still stands before them.

WORKS CITED

"Bridge Bombing May Be First Shot in New War over Temagami—August 29." <http://kafka.uvic.ca/~vipirg/SISIS/Anishinawbeg/bridge.html> 23 November 1998, 1.

Adkin, Laurie E. "Ecology and Labour: Towards a New Societal Paradigm." In *Culture and Social Change*, edited by Colin Leys and Marguerite Mendell, 75-94. Montreal: Black Rose Books, 1992.

Arnold, Ron. "Loggerheads over Land Use." *Logging and Sawmilling Journal* 18, no. 4 (April 1988): 24-30.

Back, Brian. *The Keewaydin Way*. Temagami: Keewaydin Camp, 1983.

———. "Temagami Wilderness Society's Response to Stewardship Council." *Temagami Times*, June 1990, 6.

Baldwin, Douglas Owen. "Imitation vs. Innovation: Cobalt as an Urban Frontier Town." *Laurentian University Review* 11, no. 2 (February 1979): 23-42.

Baskerville, Gordon, and A.J. Kayll. *An Audit of Management of the Crown Forests of Ontario*. Toronto: Ontario Ministry of Natural Resources, 1986.

Becker, Woody, and Tariq Hassan-Gordon. "Interview With Woody Becker: Family Head with the Makominising Anishnawbeg, November 6, 1996." <http://kafka.uvic.ca/~vipirg/SISIS/Anishi-nawbeg/inter.html> 23 November 1998, 1-3.

Benidickson, Jamie. "Temagami Old Growth: Pine, Politics and Public Policy." *Environments* 23, no. 2 (1996): 41-50.

Braudel, Fernand. *On History*. Chicago: University of Chicago Press, 1980.

Brazeau, David. "Native Families Fight to Reclaim Land." *Sudbury Star*, 2 February 1993.

Brozowski, Roman, and Paul King-Fisher. "Resource Conflict and Land Use Planning in Northern Ontario: The Case of Temagami." In *Geographical Perspectives on the Provincial Norths*, edited by M.E. Johnston, 256-77. Thunder Bay: Lakehead Centre for Northern Studies and Copp Clark Longman, 1994.

Bucknall, Brian. *An Overview of the Legislation*. Paper presented for *Registration Revisited*—a continuing legal education conference. Canadian Bar Association, Toronto, 1987.

Burrows, Robert J. *The Strategy of Nonviolent Defense: A Gandhian Approach*. Albany: State University of New York Press, 1996.

Campbell, Robert M. *Grand Illusions*. Peterborough: Broadview Press, 1991.

Canada. Supreme Court. *Bear Island Foundation et al. v. Attorney-General for Ontario et al.*, [1991] 15 August 1991.

Canada. Supreme Court. *Delgamuukw v. British Columbia*, [1997] 3 S.C.R. 1010ff.

Clark, Bruce. "Bruce Clark Archives—Letter to Verna Friday—Re: *Regina v. Verna Friday*—Section 1." <http://kafka.uvic.ca/~vipirg/SISIS/Clark/verna1.html> 11 December 1995, 1-6.

Clastres, Pierre. *Archeology of Violence*. Translated by Jeanine Herman. Paris: Semiotext(e), 1994.

———. *Society against the State*. Translated by Robert Hurley and Abe Stein. New York: Zone, 1987.

Cronon, William. *Changes in the Land: Indians, Colonists, and the Ecology of New England*. New York: Hill and Wang, 1983.

Davis, Mike. *Ecology of Fear: Los Angeles and the Imagination of Disaster.* New York: Henry Holt, 1998.

Deleuze, Gilles, and Félix Guattari. *Anti-Oedipus: Capitalism and Schizophrenia.* Translated by Robert Hurley, Mark Seem, and Helen R. Lane. Minneapolis: University of Minnesota Press, 1983.

———. *A Thousand Plateaus: Capitalism and Schizophrenia.* Translated by Brian Massumi. Minneapolis: University of Minnesota Press, 1987.

Dunk, Thomas. "Talking about Trees: Environment and Society in Forest Workers' Culture." *Canadian Review of Sociology and Anthropology* 31, no. 1 (1994): 14-34.

di Matteo, Enzo. "Natives Divided by Logging." *NOW*, 19-25 September 1996, 22.

Dunning, R.W. *Social and Economic Change among Northern Ojibwa.* Toronto: University of Toronto Press, 1959.

Fiset, Terry, et al. "Temagami Workshop." In *Sharing the Land: Conference on Emerging Issues in Aboriginal Land Use,* edited by Barrie Solandt, 123-37. Maxwell. Toronto: Canadian Environmental Law Association and Ryerson Polytechnical Institute, 1992.

Friends of the Algonquins. (Pamphlet). Ompah, ON: n.d. (1995?).

Fryer, Roger. "Some Comments on Temagami Issues." In *Temagami: A Debate on Wilderness,* edited by Matt Bray and Ashley Thomson, 61-64. Toronto: Dundurn, 1990.

Gandhi, M.K. *Non-Violent Resistance (Satyagraha).* Edited by Bharatan Kumarappa. New York: Schocken, 1951.

Gordon, Diana. "Prehistoric Occupations at Lake Temagami." In *Temagami: A Debate on Wilderness,* edited by Matt Bray and Ashley Thomson, 153-83. Toronto: Dundurn, 1990.

Gramsci, Antonio. *Selections from the Prison Notebooks.* Translated by Quintin Hoare and Geoffrey Nowell Smith. New York: International, 1971.

Gregg, Richard. *The Power of Nonviolence.* New York: Schocken, 1966.

Harvey, David. *Justice, Nature and the Geography of Difference.* Oxford: Blackwell, 1996.

———. "The Nature of Environment: The Dialectics of Social and Environmental Change." In *Socialist Register: Real Problems, False Solutions* edited by Ralph Miliband and Leo Panitch, 1-51. London: Merlin Press, 1993.

Henton, Darcy. "49 Arrested as Temagami Road Blocked." *Toronto Star*, 13 November 1989, A10.

Hodgins, Bruce W. "Contexts of the Temagami Predicament." In *Temagami: A Debate on Wilderness*, edited by Matt Bray and Ashley Thomson, 123-39. Toronto: Dundurn, 1990.

Hodgins, Bruce W. *Wanapitei on Temagami: A Story of Adventures*. Peterborough: Wanapitei, 1996.

Hodgins, Bruce W., and Jamie Benidickson. *The Temagami Experience: Recreation, Resources, and Aboriginal Rights in the Northern Ontario Wilderness*. Toronto: University of Toronto Press, 1989.

Hodgins, Bruce W., and Jonathan Bordo. "Wilderness, Aboriginal Presence and the Land Claim." In *Co-Existence? Studies in Ontario-First Nations Relations*, edited by Bruce W. Hodgins, Shawn Heard, and John S. Milloy, 67-80. Peterborough: Trent University, Frost Centre, 1992.

Jessop, Bob. *State Theory: Putting the Capitalist State in Its Place*. University Park: Pennsylvania State University Press, 1990.

Johnston, Basil. *The Manitous: The Spiritual World of the Ojibway*. New York: HarperCollins, 1995.

Johnston, Diane. "River Valley Bridge Explosion Still under Investigation." *Temiskaming Speaker*, 4 September 1996, 90 of 109 <www.net.nt.net/~tpc/tlcautio.htm>.

———. "Spiked Trees Found in Owain Lake Forest." *Temiskaming Speaker*, 11 September 1996, 81 of 109 <www.net.nt.net/~tpc/tlcautio.htm>.

Katt, Raymond, Steve Massabi, and Verna Friday. "Temagami Natives Renounce Treaty Negotiations and Assert Their Sovereignty." News Release, 25 February 1993.

Keil, Roger. "Green Work Alliances: The Political Economy of Social Ecology." *Studies in Political Economy* 44 (Summer 1994): 7-38.

Kleinfelder, J.A., and A. Yesno. "The People North of 50: In Quest of Understanding." Paper produced for the Royal Commission on the Northern Environment, 1984.

LaDuke, Winona. "A Society Based on Conquest Cannot be Sustained." In *The New Resource Wars*, edited by Al Gedicks, x-xi. Montréal: Black Rose, 1994.

Laronde, Mary. "Co-Management of Lands and Resources in N'Daki Menan." In *Rebirth: Political, Economic, and Social Development in First Nations*, edited by Anne-Marie Mawhiney, 93-106. Toronto: Dundurn, 1990.

Lawson, James. "*Nastawgan* or Not? First Nations Land Management in Temagami and Algonquin Park." In *Sustainability—The Challenge: People, Power, and the Environment*, edited by L. Anders Sandberg and Sverker Sörlin, 189-201. Montréal: Black Rose, 1998.

Liddell Hart, B.H. *Strategy: The Indirect Approach.* London: Faber and Faber, 1967.

Macdonald, Craig. *Historical Map of Temagami (Te-mee-ay-gaming).* Toronto: Ontario Geographic Names Board, 1985.

———. "The Nastawgan: Traditional Routes of Travel in the Temagami District." In *Nastawgan: The Canadian North by Canoe and Snowshoe*, edited by Bruce W. Hodgins and Margaret Hobbs, 183-87. Toronto: Betelgeuse Books, 1985.

Mackay, Donald. *Heritage Lost: The Crisis in Canada's Forests.* Toronto: Macmillan, 1985.

Ma-Kominising Anishnabaeg. "Update, August 4, 1997: Restoration of Sharpe Rock Inlet and Diamond Lake Creek." Anti-Colonial Action Alliance <http://kafka.uvic.ca/~vipirg/SISIS/Anishnabeg/aug1997. html> 23 November 1998, 1-2.

Matakala, Patrick W. "Decision-Making and Conflict Resolution in Co-Management: Two Cases from Temagami, Northeastern Ontario." Ph.D. diss., University of British Columbia, 1995.

McNab, David T. "We Hardly Have Any Idea of Such Bargains: Teme-Augama Anishnabai Title and Land Rights." In *Circles of Time: Aboriginal Land Rights and Resistance in Ontario*, 45-74. Waterloo: Wilfrid Laurier University Press, 1999.

McNeil, Kent. *Common Law Aboriginal Title.* Oxford: Clarendon Press, 1989.

———. "The Temagami Indian Land Claim: Loosening the Judicial Strait-Jacket." In *Temagami: A Debate on Wilderness*, edited by Matt Bray and Ashley Thomson, 185-221. Toronto: Dundurn, 1990.

M'Gonigle, Michael, and Ben Parfitt. *Forestopia: A Practical Guide to the New Forest Economy.* Madeira Park: Harbour, 1994.

Miller, Christopher L. "The Postidentitarian Predicament in the Footnotes of *A Thousand Plateaus*: Nomadology, Anthropology, and Authority." *Diacritics* 23, no. 3 (Fall 1993): 6-35.

Morantz, Toby. "The Judiciary as Anthropologists: New Insights into Social Organization: The Teme-Augama Anishnabay Case." In *Papers of the 23rd Algonquian Conference*, edited by William Cowan, 285-97. Ottawa: Carleton University, 1992.

Murdoch, Jonathan, and Terry Marsden. "The Spatialization of Politics: Local and National Actor-Spaces in Environmental Conflict." *Transactions of the Institute of British Geographers* New Series no. 20 (1995): 368-80.

"Native Leader Wants Temagami Deal Salvaged." 16 November 1993, *Globe and Mail*, A3.

"Natives Reject Deal Again." 3 March 1994, *Globe and Mail*.

Northwatch. *Northwatch Structure Paper*. Photocopy. 12 August 1995.

O'Connor, James. "The Second Contradiction of Capitalism." In *The Greening of Marxism*, edited by Ted Benton, 197-221. New York: Guilford, 1996.

Ontario (A.G.) v. Bear Island Foundation, [1991] 2 S.C.R. 570.

Ontario Community Forestry Group. *Lessons Learned, 1991-1994: Taking Stock of Ontario's Community Forestry Experience*. Toronto: Queen's Printer, 1995.

Ontario Forest Policy Panel. *Diversity: Forests, People, Communities— A Comprehensive Forest Policy Framework for Ontario 28*. Toronto: Queen's Printer, 1993.

Ontario. Ministry of Natural Resources. *Direction '90s*. Toronto: Queen's Printer, 1991.

———. "Description of Land-Use Zones in the Temagami Comprehensive Planning Area." *Fact Sheet* (1996): 7.

———. "Highlights of the Temagami Land-Use Strategy." Toronto: Queen's Printer, 1996, 1.

———. *Lake Temagami Plan for Land Use and Recreational Development*. Toronto: Queen's Printer, 1973.

———. "A Report on the Status of Forest Regeneration." Toronto: Queen's Printer, 1993.

———. *Response of the Government of Ontario to the Temagami Comprehensive Planning Council Recommendations*. Toronto: Queen's Printer, 1996.

———. *Sustainable Forestry: Managing Ontario's Forests for the Future*. Toronto: Queen's Printer, 1993.

Ontario Native Affairs Secretariat [ONAS]. Office of the Chief Negotiator. "Ontario's Offer to the Teme-Augama Anishnabai." 1993, 5.

Ontario Old Growth Policy Advisory Committee. *Conserving Ontario's Old Growth Forest Ecosystems: Highlights and Recommendations*. Toronto: Queen's Printer, 1994.

Polanyi, Karl. *The Great Transformation* 1944. Reprint, Boston: Beacon Press, 1967.

Prefasi, Ron. "Temagami." In *At the End of the Shift: Mines and Single-Industry Towns in Northern Ontario*, edited by Matt Bray and Ashley Thomson, 156-60. Toronto: Dundurn, 1992.

Rea, K.J. *The Prosperous Years: The Economic History of Ontario, 1939-1975*. Toronto: University of Toronto Press, 1985.

Rogers, Edward S. "Leadership among the Indians of Eastern Subarctic Canada." In *Perspectives on the North American Indians*, edited by Mark Nagler, 57-71. Toronto: McClelland and Stewart, 1972.

Ross, Rupert. *Dancing with a Ghost*. Markham: Octopus, 1992.

Sharp, Gene. *The Politics of Nonviolent Action*. Boston: Porter Sargent, 1973.

Sherlock, Faith Ann. "Jailed, But Innocent at Heart." *Anglican Journal*, December 1992, 18.

Shute, Jeremy J., and David B. Knight. "Obtaining an Understanding of Environmental Knowledge: Wendaban Stewardship Authority." *Canadian Geographer* 39, no. 2 (1995): 101-11.

Skidmore, Judith. "Canadian Values and Priorities: A Multiple-Use Perspective." In *Temagami: A Debate on Wilderness*, edited by Matt Bray and Ashley Thomson, 65-68. Toronto: Dundurn, 1990.

Speck, Frank. "The Family Hunting Band as the Basis of Algonkian Social Organization (1915)." In *Cultural Ecology*, edited by Bruce Cox, 58-75. Toronto: McClelland and Stewart, 1973.

Steedman, Ian. "Trade Interest versus Class Interest." *Economia Politica* 3, no. 2 (August 1986): 187-206.

Storper, Michael, and Richard Walker. *The Capitalist Imperative: Territory, Technology and Industrial Growth*. Oxford: Basil Blackwell, 1989.

Sun Tzu. *The Art of War*. Translated by Samuel B. Griffin. Oxford: Oxford University Press, 1963.

"Temagami Land Battle Climaxing, Natives Say." *Toronto Star*, 23 March 1993, A10.

Temiskaming Municipal Association. Presentation to Premier Peterson, 26 October 1987.

Temiskaming Speaker Editors. "Land Claim Madness." *Temiskaming Speaker*, 16 August 1995.

Thoreau, Henry David. *Walden; or, Life in the Woods/On the Duty of Civil Disobedience*. Ed. Norman Holmes Pearson. New York: Rinehart, 1960.

Township of Temagami. *Old Growth, New Growth*. Pamphlet. Temagami: 1995.

Temiskaming Municipal Association. Municipal Advisory Group. "An Overview of the Bear Island Land Claim and Caution from the Municipal Perspective: Its History, Its Impacts, Its Issues, Our Losses, Our Costs." Mimeo. January 1995.

———. Municipal Advisory Group. *Position: Bear Island Land Caution*. Mimeo. 12 April 1994.

Temagami Wilderness Society. "Position-in-Principle." 17 July 1987.

Uhler, Russell S. *Canada-United States Trade in Forest Products*. Vancouver: UBC Press, 1991.

Unland, Karen. "Temagami Remains a Tinderbox." *Globe and Mail*, 2 September 1996, A6.

Walkom, Thomas. "Temagami Battle Is about Who Uses Bush Best." *Toronto Star*, 26 October 1989.

Watson, Denis McLean. "Frontier Movement and Economic Development in Northeastern Ontario, 1850-1914." Master's thesis, University of British Columbia, 1971.

Wildlands League. "Fact Sheet no. 1: Ontario's Forest Industry—Where Have All the Loggers Gone?" *The Forest Diversity/Community Survival Project* no. 1 (Spring 1995).

Wilson, Hap. *Temagami Canoe Routes*. Hyde Park, ON: Canadian Recreational Canoeing Association, 1992.

Winfield, Mark S., and Greg Jenish. "Ontario's Environment and the 'Common Sense Revolution.' *Studies in Political Economy* no. 57 (Autumn 1998): 129-47.

Wolin, Sheldon S. "[The Economy of Violence]." In *The Prince: Niccolò Machiavelli*, edited by Robert M. Adams, 185-94. New York: W.W. Norton, 1977.

Wroe, Darlene. "After 96 Years: Temagami MNR Building Closes—Services Now Provided Out of North Bay." *Temiskaming Speaker* 2 October 1996, 44 of 109 <www.net.nt.net/~tpc/tlcautio.htm>.

Echoes of Resistance

Coercion and Injustices in Canadian Prisons

Chapter 13

PEGGY O'REILLY-SHAUGHNESSY

Historically, there have been profound injustices in many aspects of government policy towards Aboriginal peoples. The ingrained views, based on ignorance or prejudice that lay behind such policies, are a distinct indicator of the intentions of the policy-makers of the times. The criminal justice system's framework was already well-grounded in Western traditions when its first penitentiary was built in Kingston, Ontario, in 1835 (Portsmouth). During the first 150 years of (un)justice in Canada, Aboriginal prisoners were condemned, marginalized, reduced to silence, and virtually kept "invisible" within the penitentiary walls. The penitentiary system was devised with rules and consequences depriving Aboriginal prisoners of their culture, identity, and self-respect. Even as early as 1890, Japanese, Chinese, and Jewish immigrants were allowed visits by their pastors and rabbis, and pains were taken to provide whatever was necessary for the celebration of Hebrew and "heathen" sacraments.[1] However, Aboriginal prisoners were left out of this process because of the Indian Act, which outlawed many of

Notes on pages 272-73.

their spiritual practices; they were then co-opted within the Christian denominations behind the wall. With "civilization" came prisons in which the church prevailed. Christianity's main function was to take the "savages" and "civilize" them, or in the case of the prison system, take the "deviants of society," those who fall outside "societal norms," and create "law-abiding citizens."

The history of the incarceration of Aboriginal peoples is a complicated one to trace within the penitentiary system of Canada. The presence of Aboriginal prisoners during the early years seems to be well hidden within this machine. However, it is evident that Native prisoners lived within the walls of the penitentiary. And the attitude toward the "invisible Indian" can be found in documented annual reports. For example, in a report from Kingston Penitentiary in 1856, Rev. Mulkins notes, "the mortality has been very great among the Indians....It is remarkable, and very suggestive that the ravages of death should be so fearful among this decaying race."[2] Comments such as "decaying race" reflect and acknowledge the continuing attempts of the church and the state to assimilate Aboriginal peoples, especially those hidden behind the wall.

The inherent coercion of the state and church towards Aboriginal prisoners continued throughout the history of the penitentiaries in Canada and is still practised today. However, Aboriginal prisoners continued to resist and defend their Indigenous rights. Although these struggles to survive as "Indians" were never documented within Correctional Services of Canada (CSC). As one prisoner stated,

> During the early years, if you were caught talking to a group of Brothers they [administration] would get nervous....As if we were trying to organize something eh...it was nothing to have a bunch of "Indians" in the "hole" [solitary confinement] at one time. They didn't want us talking in a group on the yard or nothing. Many of the Brothers really resisted the "man" [warden], they just wanted to practise their spirituality...they didn't care if they spent a year in the "hole" [laughs].[3]

Native prisoners' struggles would not only see them spend time in the "hole"—death would occasionally be the outcome of resistance. Elders such as Art Solomon, who became known for his time spent working with Native prisoners in Ontario, reported:

Don St. Germaine was murdered in cold blood at Kingston penitentiary. Why is murder not a murder when it is committed by a prison
guard against a defenseless man?…All of this was done by people
who profess to be Christians, two of the commandments say, "Thou
shalt not kill" and "Thou shalt love they neighbour as thyself."[4]

These very Christians would continue to be responsible for the Native
prisoners behind the walls. Even to this day, the chaplain has the final
say on when a sweatlodge ceremony will be allowed and when the
reception hall can be used for Native ceremonies. It is like a slap in the
face to have to walk down towards the Native grounds because the
church is always in clear view and always in control.

The Native Brotherhood movement eventually began inside the
prison. It originated in the late 1950s in Manitoba's Stony Mountain
Penitentiary. This group was initiated by Native prisoners who were
disturbed by the increasing numbers of Native peoples coming into
contact with the law and eventually being incarcerated.

The Native Brotherhood would become the sole responsibility of the
Social Development Department. This department was responsible for
any social group and recreational event pertaining to the general
prison population. Many staff members within the institution viewed
the Native Brotherhood as just that—a recreation. As one Native prisoner stated, "some look upon our group as just a place where we go
and hang out…have a coffee…and read a book. Most of them think us
Natives get too much!"[5] Such comments are commonly heard among
the Brotherhood membership, especially where staff are unaware or do
not understand what happens at a Native Brotherhood meeting. Most
non-Aboriginal staff and inmates tend to assume that because they cannot see something highly structured (that is, no visible immediate
measurable results) then nothing of importance has taken place.

After several years, the Native Brotherhood was eventually given
permission to have elders visit their group. As Solomon explains: "For
the past eight years, the Native spiritual ways have gone into the prisons in Ontario as a social thing, in other words as a privilege not as a
right."[6] Many elders who attempted to visit the Native brothers and to
pray with the sacred pipe encountered problems at the main gate of
the prisons. Some were viewed as activists by the penitentiary staff and
therefore looked upon as criminals. Elders who were allowed visits

with Native prisoners were confronted by guards handling their medicines and other sacred items. These items were exposed to x-ray machines and some were denied entry into the prison because they were supposedly a "security risk" in the eyes of the prison authorities. But because Solomon and other elders argued: "Native spiritual ways must go into the prisons under the established principle of *freedom of religion* and with the same respect and rights that are accorded to any other faith tradition."[7]

Unlike the religious freedom rights accorded to other faiths, Native spiritualities are not viewed respectfully at certain times by some of the prison officials. For example, during a mid-winter ceremony at Warkworth Institution, I witnessed an elder being refused entrance to the prison. Later a guard approached me and asked "how do I know who an elder is? Anyone could come to this front gate and say they are an Elder!" However, this particular elder was holding an eagle staff, which was approximately six feet in height with many "sacred" items attached. If someone presented themselves at the front gate with a black shirt with a white collar around their neck and stated they were a priest, would their ministry be questioned?[8]

The struggle for the practising of Native spirituality continues behind the wall. The case of the Butler brothers is a good example. In 1981 Darrelle (Dino) Butler and Gary Butler crossed into Canada from the United States to help organize a rally in support of Leonard Peltier. (This rally was organized because many people believed Peltier was unjustly convicted of the murders of two FBI agents in the United States.) On entering Canada, they were met by Vancouver police who attempted to detain them for questioning about an attempted bank robbery. This resulted in a high-speed chase in which the Butlers allegedly fired at the police. They were arrested and charged with attempted murder of the two police officers as well as with weapon charges. Before judge and jury, they were convicted of the lesser-included offence of discharging a firearm with the intent to endanger the life of a person.[9]

The Butlers were eventually moved to Kent Institution, a maximum security federal penitentiary in British Columbia. In 1983, after the introduction of the Charter of Rights and Freedoms Act, the two cousins began a spiritual fast to protest the denigration of the practice of Native spirituality behind the wall. This protest would echo across Canada and draw support from the national media along with a public outcry. This in turn forced Svend Robinson, NDP Member of Parliament, to raise this issue in front of the House of Commons. When Solicitor General Gerald Kaplan, who was in charge of the Correctional Service of Canada, was questioned regarding the situation at Kent Institution, his response was "I have no sympathy for the Indians on a hunger strike at Kent Penitentiary, especially since they spent several weeks fattening up before beginning the fast."[10] Such comments suggest that the attitudes of CSC towards Aboriginal prisoners have barely changed since the opening of its first penitentiary.

On 2 May 1983, Darrelle Butler ended his spiritual fast after thirty-four days. Subsequently, CSC adopted guidelines specifically geared towards the cultural needs of Aboriginal peoples.[11] Butler's struggle for the recognition of Native spirituality can be seen as a mechanism of resistance to the coercion and injustice found in Canadian penitentiaries. Effectively, his actions have helped pave the way for the practising of Native spirituality within the walls of the federal prison system of Canada.

Did change occur through Dino Butler's echo that was finally heard outside the prison walls? When we resist something so strongly, it creates an echo so loud that it goes beyond its source; but, once the response from that echo has returned, it has been dramatically altered. But is our everyday resistance so "silent" that we can hardly hear it or recognize it ourselves? Does it become so silent, that it does not even justify a response?

Aboriginal peoples hold "distinct legal rights" as stated within the constitution of Canada which "recognizes and affirms" existing Aboriginal and treaty rights. This legal fact is reflected in the "distinct" legal rights of Aboriginal prisoners in the Correctional and Conditional Release Act (CCRA) which was passed in Parliament in 1992. The overall intent of the CCRA was to legislatively recognize both the unique circumstances and special needs of Aboriginal prisoners. However, although the principles within this act specify that "all correctional policies, programs and practices respect gender, ethnic, cultural and language differences," it is not uncommon to hear comments from Native prisoners like this one: "being an Indian is a way of life, my way of life, and a part of me as a North American Indian...why must I ask permission to be an Indian for three hours per week."[12]

Why is it that so much money is directed within Correctional Service of Canada to reports, commissions, and investigations when recommendations are seldom heard and implementations of new policies seldom seen? What was Correctional Service of Canada's intent to entrench in law the guidelines for practising Native spirituality—were laws established in order to "hush" the echo? One can only become suspicious because for over a century the state outlawed through the Indian Act many Native spiritual practices.

Why is it that CSC would allow Aboriginal prisoners access to land within the prison walls, put up a teepee, allow an elder to construct a sweat lodge, and practise four Native ceremonies per year? Is it so they can practise their traditional beliefs? Or is it to create images and symbols for the "other" to see—the very symbols that society identifies as "traditional," "authentic," or "Indianness." Do all these things silence the "echo" of protest? Are all these images available within the prison walls so non-Aboriginal people can look out onto the yard, see the tepee, and think "yes" the government does care about those "Indians?" Were Native prisoners finally allowed to practise their traditional beliefs because the government sees the importance of such traditions? Or were those traditions put in place for white people to view such images? Are policies created for Aboriginal religion in order to hide the over-representation of Aboriginal peoples in federal prisons and pretend the state wants to solve such problems?

As Foucault describes in *Discipline and Punish*,

> Discipline "makes" individuals; it is the specific technique of a power that regards individuals both as objects and as instruments of its exercise....The success of disciplinary power derives no doubt from the use of simple instruments: hierarchical observation, normalizing judgment, and their combination in a procedure that is specific to it—the examination. The exercise of discipline presupposes a mechanism that coerces by means of observation; an apparatus in which the techniques that make it possible to see induce effects of power and in which, conversely, the means of coercion make those on whom they are applied clearly visible.[13]

Aboriginal peoples of Canada have long been objectified through representation, symbols, and objects; they have always remained outside the norms of Canadian society, which has largely been determined by white, middle-class men. They have been defined first by the Indian Act and again by the Canadian Constitution of 1982. They have been quantified and reduced in statistical analysis to their over-representation in the federal prison system in Canada. This estimation of such over-representation within the federal prison system however, is probably significantly under-estimated. Such statistics regarding the over-representation of Aboriginal peoples is determined by who is a Status "Indian" and who is not. It is solely defined and calculated by the Canadian government's definition within the Canadian constitution.

Many problems within CSC's policies towards the practising of Native spirituality remain. Spirituality has been allowed to be a practice to a certain extent since the early 1980s because of Native prisoners' struggle and resistance throughout the history of the penitentiary system in Canada. The problems that remain today are not only with the policies themselves but also with the limitations and constraints on how such policies will be implemented within the prison walls.

It is interesting to observe how Native prisoners have learned to take the very tools used to objectify them to create strategies of resistance toward the coercion and injustices of the Western traditional prison system. By going into the teepee or the sweatlodge, they are hidden from the "seeing eye," away from the "calculated gaze" of the "keeper."[14] This escape allows the Native prisoner to pray as a Native without being harassed by the guards. It temporarily removes prisoners from the very architecture of the prison. Time no longer is measured by seconds, minutes, hours, days, or years. It becomes a space, a private space where only Native prisoners are allowed; a chance to pray on Mother Earth herself, not on the cement that has been created within the architecture of the machine; a sacred place, an illusion of freedom. The Native prisoner is no longer individualized or classified within this space—he is able to form a community, a Native community. This community all wants similar things, the chance to be able to practise a way of living as North American Indians. As Solomon explains, "I have come to the conclusion that...after going into the prison of Canada for twelve years, there is nothing so much in need of correction as the Corrections System of Canada."[15] Since the founding of the first penitentiary, much has changed towards of Aboriginal prisoners practising their traditional beliefs. But inherent coercion of Aboriginal prisoners by the state and the church remains to this day within the walls of the penitentiary of Canada. From the definition of who is Native to when and where Native prisoners can practise their spirituality, Native inmates remain at the hands of these two groups: the state and the church.

Echoes of resistance will continue to be a large part of the Native prisoners' way of life until respect has been given towards their cultural beliefs. Unfortunately, Native men have died behind prison walls for such rights, but their spirit will remain as the fight continues. Don St. Germaine, Art Solomon, and others not mentioned who have died fighting for the rights to practise Native spirituality will be thanked in prayer as the fight against coercion and injustices continue behind the prison walls.

REFERENCES

Couture, Joseph. *Aboriginal Behavioural Trauma: Towards a Taxonomy.* Saskatoon: Corrections Canada, 1994.

Constitution Act 1982. Ottawa: Ministry of Public Works and Government Services of Canada.

Foucault, Michel. *Discipline and Punish: The Birth of the Prison.* New York: Vintage Books, 1977.

James, J.T.L. *A Living Tradition: Penitentiary Chaplaincy.* Ottawa: Ministry of Supply and Service of Canada, 1990.

Matthiessen, Peter. *In the Spirit of Crazy Horse.* New York: Viking, 1983.

O'Reilly-Shaughnessy, Peggy. Interviews at Warkworth Institution. Warkworth, ON, June 1997, May 1999.

————. Journal entries, 1994-99.

R. v. Butler (Darrelle Dean); R. v. (Gary Leroy) Butler. [1985] 2 C.N.L.R.

Solomon, Arthur. *Eating Bitterness: A Vision Beyond the Prison Walls.* Toronto: NC Press, 1994.

Waldram, James. *The Way of The Pipe: Aboriginal Spirituality and Symbolic Healing in Canadian Prisons.* Peterborough: Broadview Press, 1997.

Woods, Gerald. "The Quality of Mercy: The Reform Tradition in Canadian Federal Corrections." Manuscript, Ottawa Solicitor General's Library, 1992.

Female Narratives of Resistance

The Significance of Gender and Food
in the Writings of Louise Erdrich

UTE LISCHKE

On a recent visit to Birchbark Books in Minneapolis, Minnesota (the bookstore owned by Louise Erdrich), it was very evident that food is a significant aspect of native spirituality. Food, most particularly wild rice (Manomin), corn (Mandamin), and licorice were prominently displayed alongside the books on the shelves.[1] During our conversation, Erdrich also commented on the importance of gender in her writings. She emphasized her roots and their relationship to her work. Her mother is from the Turtle Mountain Reservation in North Dakota. Her father, Ralph Erdrich, was born soon after his family immigrated to the United States. Her German grandfather had been a master butcher in southern Germany and their ancestral home, Erdrichshof, still stands near Pforzheim. She considers her German roots to be an extremely important influence on all of her writings. Upon arrival in North America, the Erdrich family had to adapt to new ways. Yet they were also still connected to Europe. For example, Erdrich recalled that her German grandfather fought for Germany in the

Notes on pages 273-75.

201

First World War. However, during the Second World War, her father was fighting for the American side, while her German relatives living near Pforzheim were fire-bombed by the Americans. Yet the family held together. Erdrich said, "We just had to get through it."[2] Aboriginal and European peoples are irrevocably conjoined and we are all here to stay.

Before the Erdrich family ever arrived on North American soil, there existed the romanticized (and male) European notion of wilderness, that is "land which is wild, uncultivated, and inhabited only by wild animals; a wild, uncultivated, or uninhabited region." The word wilderness itself comes from the old English word for wild deer.[3] In this view, all things are categorized and disconnected. North American Aboriginals have no such notion of, or word for, "wilderness" in their cultures or languages. Part of non-Aboriginal conceptions about wilderness have to do with Europeans' views of the North as an abstract space. The concept of "North" is geographically defined according to the compass, for example, a "northerly wind" or a person from the "North." In North America, the "North" still refers to that which is sparsely populated, pure, untouched by "civilization." But the North for Aboriginal people is real and practical since it is one of the four sacred directions—a place where the spirits of the Bear dwell.[4]

If Europeans once had a different relationship with what became known as the wilderness, sometimes known as the North, it has been essentially forgotten in the recent past of Europe and by the European newcomers to Turtle Island.[5] A product of our collective imagination, these ideas of wilderness and of the North must be explored and also included in gender studies. This chapter explores these notions of wilderness as they intersect with food and gender in the writings of Louise Erdrich.

In female narratives of resistance, food represents, as a product of Mother Earth, one of the most significant attributes of women's writings.[6] Mother Earth is female and women are, for Aboriginal people, the source of the creation and re/creation within the circle of life. Mother Earth is animate and an all-encompassing (instead of interconnected and linear) female being—everything is interconnected—the animals, the plants, the birds, the four natural elements of earth, water, air, and fire, as well as the four sacred directions. This is the source of the food that nourishes us and gives us life; it is also "wondrous" and spiritual.[7] When Europeans arrived in North America, they had to adapt to the new sources of food, and they also had to rely on Aboriginal peoples for their teachings about food. And it is the presence of Aboriginal voices themselves that tells their stories, thereby resisting European myths about North America.

In her memoir *Becoming Myself*, a bildungsroman in which she describes the "actualization of the 'true' self," Maria Tippett, the biographer of Emily Carr,[8] has remarked on the importance of the land on her own intellectual and spiritual growth.[9] Her perceptions reveal that women's experiences are often fundamentally different from those of European men. Much like Erdrich, Tippett experiences nature as a challenge to her for potential growth, transformation, and self-understanding. It is a different experience from men's relationship to the wilderness since women generally have a resistance to "conquer" the wilderness. Instead, through a more pragmatic approach, women tend to adapt, learning about and working with the elements. There is a sense of being "still," experiencing loneliness and solitude through the human body:

> I was often lonely that autumn and winter—and sometimes even terrified. Nocturnal sounds such as the night prowlings of a raccoon, the scratching of a bat, the chafing of one tree against another, and the scuttering of a mouse—sometimes over my blankets—sent me, flashlight in hand, to investigate. During the day the sounds from the forest and shore seemed to be in their proper place. I was well-compensated for my night-time fears: "There is something marvellous in the routine of solo life here. Rising when I please, puttering about, getting the fire going while preparing breakfast, then setting into work. The first few blissful hours when my mind is clear, when old worries dare not impose on my writing."... Roughing it in a cabin in the woods not only enabled me to come "to terms with ideas by myself without interruption from outside," but living in the midst of Mayne Island's richly forested landscape also helped me "to experience E's [Emily Carr] solitude, E's forest, [and] E's loneliness."[10]

Tippett confronts the European ideas of wilderness. The result is a narrative of resistance, which celebrates the becoming of herself. This had also been true for Emily Carr. During her sojourn alone in the woods, the natural world became fused with her own images:

> connecting her life to present ecological concerns and the moral precepts they have generated. Psychoanalytic elements embed-

ded in the visual and verbal vocabularies of modernism and piv-
otal to the development of biographical form in the twentieth century, reinforce the significance of nature with their own codes. In
addition, this combination of factors—nature, ecology, moral pre-
cepts, psychoanalytical perceptions and life narrative—merge to
support and explain Carr's affinity to aboriginal Canadians,
dwellers on the threshold between the Victorian outpost of
Empire and the wilderness.[11]

Women such as Tippett and Carr have a highly spiritual view of their
environment; they "enter" the forests and embrace the loneliness
therein, often overcoming their "fear" of the wilderness by adapting it
to their more immediate life experiences and needs. They have used
their apparent loneliness in the forest as a conduit to productivity.
Whereas Tippett explores her relationship as a woman to the woods,
Erdrich, in her writings, resists "normal" gendered roles by crossing the
boundaries between male and female roles. Males are able to suckle,
women become priests, and men aim to bake the perfect cake. Such
reversals, especially when connected to the concept of food, relate to
the nourishment of the soul, to the survival of the human spirit, and to
women's bodies.

EUROPEAN NOTIONS OF THE LAND

Alberto Manguel has written in his *Reading Pictures: A History of Love
and Hate* that

> Sometime in the sixteenth century, the illustrious essayist Francis
> Bacon observed that for the ancients, all the images that the world
> lays before us are already ensconced in our memory at birth. "So
> that as Plato had an imagination," he wrote "knowledge was but
> remembrance; so Solomon giveth his sentence, that all novelty is
> but oblivion." If this is true, then we are all somehow reflected in
> the many and different images that surround us, since they are
> already part of who we are: images that we create and images that
> we frame; images that we assemble physically, by hand, and
> images that come together, unbidden, in the mind's eye; images of
> faces, trees, buildings, clouds, landscapes, instruments, water, fire,
> [and it may be added earth and air] and images of those images—
> painted, sculpted, acted out, photographed, printed, filmed.
> Whether we discover in those surroundings images faded memo-
> ries of a beauty that was once ours (as Plato suggested) or whether

they demand from us a fresh and new interpretation through whatever possibilities our language might offer us (as Solomon intuited), we are essentially creatures of images, of pictures.[12]

From this suggestion, Manguel argues that it is important to be able to "read pictures." Pictures are images—which also tell stories, if we care to listen to them. This is significant. The images come from dreams of the land, which in their turn tell stories about us as well. In this sense, we also read the images as part of the land and as part of ourselves— where we are from and where we now are. European women who set-tled in the North American "wilderness" often chose to adapt to and work with the land rather than to recreate and reconstruct an imagined European notion of wilderness. Their voices are significant.

In their introduction to the volume of the *Journal of Canadian Studies* that is dedicated to the study of "Refiguring Wilderness," the authors equate "North" and "Wilderness" with "concepts of the mind and of experience…coalesced over the last century to constitute an imagined cultural version of Canada.…It is a wasteland, a nest of wild beasts.…It is a container of a myriad of complex relationships. It is a landscape of the mind." Furthermore, the authors suggest that for Europeans, "wilderness was possession, a source of wealth and power, sovereignty and empire."[13] In one sense, European attitudes to wilderness repre-sent, at least in part, the creation of Europe and Europe's own ancient past. It only recently came to be applied to the North American context. The loss of the European wilderness around the late sixteenth, early seventeenth century, required a mourning, which needed to find a public expression, especially when it was related to a loss of a culture. Simon Schama points out in his *Landscape and Memory*, "neither the frontiers between the wild and the cultivated, nor those that lie between the past and the present, are so easily fixed. Whether we scramble the slopes or ramble the woods, our Western sensibilities carry a bulging backpack of myth and recollection."[14] Yet underneath that soil which generation upon generation has depleted, lies a "rich loam of memory." It is impossible to deny that our collective pasts, "like the slow mold of the seasons, forms the compost of our future."[15]

This intellectual endeavour happened in Europe throughout the Middle Ages and indeed the Renaissance.[16] Those who were dissatis-fied with the political and cultural developments had two choices. They could participate in escapism and fantasy by reading exploration and travel literature, or they could leave Europe behind and sojourn to distant lands to seek out their own adventures. German landscapes in general and forests in particular, have held a particular fascination not only for Germans, but also for Europeans and North Americans. This landscape has become closely connected to the concept of Heimat, defined by Schama, for example, as *der Holzweg*, the track through the woods.[17] In part, it is also a longing for the memory of the forest and the land and a return to what was perceived to be primeval wilderness. In truth, it is about a past and a spirit of place that may be more Eurocentric myth than reality. European colonizers went to North America in an attempt to "liberate the past from the grand narrative schemes of classical historiography and to resurrect the inner *life* of the past, in all of its concrete fullness."[18] Leaving Europe and its cultural traditions behind for the "wilderness" of the "Americas," the colonizers established a new "cultural memory" through which they established the "other" by eliminating Aboriginal people and the landscape that already existed there. Instead of finding something new and embracing it, Europeans exploited and debased the land and the people who were the keepers of Mother Earth.

The idea of journeying into foreign lands in order to discover the "self" is part of western European male culture. For example, in Ludwig Tieck's early romantic novel *Franz Sternbald's Wanderings* (1798), a young artist goes out into the world, not quite knowing his course. During his journeys, he passes through a large forest, in which all the trees cry out to him, attempting to detain him. Memories overcome him until he is totally bewildered by these unaccustomed feelings. Coming to a clearing, he has the strange feeling that, in his youth, he had been there before and that something very eventful had occurred that he is now unable to remember. Intoxicated, he hears the sound of the forest horn and, unable to restrain himself from overwhelming sadness, the pain of memory and undefined hopes, he cries out:

> Am I mad, or what is happening to this foolish heart? What invisible hand plucks all the strings of my being, at once so tenderly and so terribly, and scares out from their hiding places all the dreams and magic appearances, all the sights and tears and forgotten songs? Oh, I feel it in myself that my spirit strives after something that is more than earthly and is granted to no man. With magnetic force, the invisible heaven draws my heart to itself, and mixes up together all my premonitions, all the joys that have

been wept over and forgotten, all the impossible ecstasies, all the unfulfilled hopes.[19]

Clearly a piece of German Romantic prose, this writing is filled with all the components of its style: it invites and warns; it mentions distant music that awakes memory and desire; it features a young person in limbo between past and future, a mind full of tumult, inexplicable regret, and undefined longing; premonitions of unfulfilled individuality and lost identity; a peculiar sense of German inwardness, remoteness from reality, intimate community between self, and the mysterious forces of nature and God.[20]

Beneath these exotic and interesting elements are forces of terror and violence and death, the "tangled mysteries of the German forest."[21] Like the young artist, those who endeavoured to become the colonizers were also bent upon discovering, like Goethe's hero Wilhelm, of the novel *Wilhelm Meister's Apprenticeship,* a sense of their being. Goethe's emphasis is on the main character's *Bildung,* his growth as an individual, rather than on the realities of human existence. The colonizers sought, within the wilderness of the newly discovered land, to complete their identity. More often than not, their road led, as it did with Franz Sternbald, to the wood, the German wood, the home of the fairy stories, the place of longing and of memories, of terror and of transformation, in short, a spiritual habitat. Bogumil Goltz wrote in the 1860s that:

> it is the wood in which all of her secrets and all of her favours are found together....What the evil, over-clever, insipid, bright, cold world encumbers and complicates, the wood-green, mysterious, enchanted, dark, culture—renouncing but true to the law of nature—must free and make good again. Whoever has a heart in his body must regret that he cannot stay in the wood and live on berries.[22]

Yet it is a sinister wood. Hansel and Gretel find themselves at the witch's house, the young bride in the fairy tale of the Robber Bridegroom finds herself among cannibals in her fiancé's woods, and Red Riding Hood, the protagonist of the ultimate European imperial fairy tale, which teaches children to fear the wilderness, confronts the big, bad wolf.

The literary historian Robert Pogue Harrison has noted that the objective of the Grimm brothers in their philological undertaking was to restore the lost "unity of German culture" by "recovering whatever remained of the original traditions." Their stories, as allegories, were

chiefly about the "theme of restoration,"—restoration of life and then
unity, which "relies upon the dialectic of separation and reunion."[23]
The forest was essential as a place that provided meaning. As a setting
for most of the fairy tales, the forests recaptured a past and a space that
provided cultural identity.

Separation from the forest, the loss of space and thus a loss of identity, occurred in the seventeenth and eighteenth century in Europe,
which coincided with the height of European expansion overseas during a period of social upheaval in Europe itself. Europeans felt a sense
of loss of their own land. For some, wilderness was lost to abuse and
rapid degradation, despite the fact that conservationist measures had
been initiated.[24] For example, already in 1592, John Manwood, a monar-
chist, had composed a treatise of the laws of the forest in England in
which he recalled the old laws pertaining to reforestation and preservation of wilderness. He hoped that these old initiatives could once
again be applied so that the wilderness could be saved from "the ravages of human exploitation."[25]

By the nineteenth century, similar efforts were made in Germany to
"preserve" the forests. Once the forests were depleted of wildlife by an
ever-infringing humanity, only tame "beasts of pleasure" remained to
be hunted by the well-to-do. Thus depleted, new hunting grounds had
to be found. Metaphorically, this "lack," or empty space was equated
with a loss of identity. The male colonizers' search for new wilderness
was intended to fill the empty space, the loss of identity in their lives.
Fantasy and adventure-seeking activities became a frequent substitute
and the American West became a popular destination to escape European crises. New *Lebenswelt* and *Lebensraum* were secured in an exotic
foreign land, which represented strength and purity—hence the concept of a "wild" west and a strong, true north. This, in part, explains
why Germans are still attracted to Canada (and North America) as a
unique place. A Eurocentric myth of the wilderness was created.[26]
European white males colonized America.

In the early twenty-first century, the concept of the wilderness is in
the process of becoming almost wholly imaginary. This can be both
strength and a weakness. The idea of wilderness, as the context for
rediscovery, is important in re-establishing what Walter Benjamin
refers to as the "'aura' that contains vague reminders of a lost kinship
between subject and object. The deadly Cartesian separation between
the *res cogitans* and *res extensa* gives way, in the forests of symbols, to an

ecstatic psychological state—a 'transport of the mind and senses'—
which recovers the realm of correspondences in their predifferentiated
unity."[27] The difficulty is that few of us can survive in a purely imaginative place. When the American philosopher David Thoreau declared
in his journal in 1856 that he had:

> finally "reached a new world." He meant, of course, that he had
> stayed in the same place. But in that place he had discovered a
> spot so wild that the "huckleberries grew hairy and were inedi-
> ble." The discovery made him shudder with pleasure....Holding
> the things in the palm of his hand he began, suddenly, to be car-
> ried through time and space: "Here grows the hairy huckleberry
> as it did in the [female] Sachem's day and a thousand years before,
> and concerns me perchance more than it did her....I experience
> exactly the same sensations as if I were alone in a bog in Rupert's
> Land, and it saves me the trouble of going there....It is in vain to
> dream of a wildness distant from ourselves. There is none such. It
> is the bog in our brain and bowels, the primitive vigor of Nature
> in us, that inspires that dream.[28]

This interaction has also happened, albeit on a small scale, in many
female narratives such as in the writings of Louise Erdrich whose work
embodies both the German and the Aboriginal concepts of the land.

RESISTANCE: A FEMALE CAPTIVITY NARRATIVE
—*THE ANTELOPE WIFE*

The female literary tradition of the captivity narrative is particularly
apparent in the writings of Louise Erdrich, an Anishinabe/Cree writer of
German/Jewish descent who currently resides in Minneapolis. Her
works encompass both the European and the Aboriginal traditions.
Erdrich was born in 1954. She is a Chippewa/Cree person of the
Bird/Bear Clans (also known among them as Anishinabe and by anthro-
pologists/linguists as Ojibwa) on her mother's side, and German/Aus-
trian/Jewish/Catholic heritage, on her father's side respectively.[29]
Indigenous knowledge always comes from specific places. The indigenous knowledge that informs Erdrich's writings comes from these places
and the families who reside there.[30] But during the period of colonization, it was important to learn and adapt various kinds of knowledge.

For example, in Louise Erdrich's *The Birchbark House*, Angeline, the
sister of Omakayas (Little Frog), the female protagonist of the story,

goes to the mission school in the spring to learn the white man's language. She comes home and shows her Nokomis (grandmother) the language "which looked like odd tracks." Angeline explains to her that the drawings are "letters….One follows the next. You look at them, just like tracks. You read them. They have a meaning and a sound." Her Nokomis responds "Howah! That's a good idea! Like our picture writing." Omakayas remembers "last winter, before the sickness began, she had seen Fishtail walking from the mission school. Had he learned to make the white man's tracks? Had he learned to write his name? Had he learned to read the words of the treaties so that his people could not be cheated of land?"[31] Reading tracks is important because it helps in the hunt. Reading the white man's "tracks" is important so that one does not get cheated out of land and become a captive to the white man's power.

Louise Erdrich provides stories that are related to the captivity narrative to reveal the interrelationship of the human race and the fact that through fear, we are able to learn and find new meanings and self-understanding. Colin Calloway in his *New Worlds for All: Indians, Europeans, and the Remaking of Early America*, has defined captives and captivity *narratives as* follows:

> Many of these cultural converts entered Indian country as captives, against their will, but they were subjected to powerful acculturative pressures by their captors, and some came to prefer their new life to their old. Still others chose to live with Indians, whether in preference for the Natives' way of life or to escape from their own society. Some of these "white Indians" even fought alongside their Indian friends and relatives in their wars against the whites.[32]

There were others, however, who feared being taken captive. They had the view of Indians as savages who butchered and killed innocent women and children. This notion has been challenged and, more recently, scholars have studied captivity narratives as sources for "valuable information on Indian societies, on intercultural interaction, and on gender relations in early America. Captives in Indian societies sometimes provided ethnographic data and a view of events from Indian country." This ethnographic data challenges Euro-American preconceptions about Aboriginal people.[33] Captivity narratives are powerful tools of Aboriginal resistance to Europeans since they also contain pictures. And they abound, not only in North American writings, but also in the imagination of the Europeans. For example, Franz Kafka once wrote about his romanticized notion of being Indian:

> If one could be an Indian, up and ready, askew, high in the air, atop a speedy horse, quivering excitedly above the shaking earth, shedding one's spurs, for there really were no spurs, throwing off the reins, since one needed no reins, barely seeing the land ahead, a barren heath, as horse and rider disappeared.[34]

Aboriginal societies have always held a charm for Europeans, and Germans have a romantic wildness of the soul, which is often found in their *unziemliches Verlangen*, or unseemly longing, to be an "Indian" or for things "Indian." Many Germans have attempted to live in their own "Aboriginal" communities and tried to remake themselves in the process.[35]

In her poetry, fiction, and prose, Erdrich evokes a longing and desire for the other that reflects the split in herself—the European and the Indian. In *The Blue Jay's Dance*, her autobiography of a birth year, she refers to this as her "Horizon Sickness" when she says "I'm homesick." Countered by her husband's response "This is home," Erdrich concludes, "each of us is absolutely right."[36] Her horizon sickness is the desire to return to her family and roots in Minnesota, where one can see earth and sky merge in the distance and where sunsets linger. For her, place—the place of the Grand Sky—is everything.

In 1997 Erdrich published a major novel entitled *The Antelope Wife*. This narrative conjoins the European and the Anishinabe cultures. The novel documents in a female narrative the resistance and the interconnections between white and red; between Europe and Turtle Island. In the beginning of *The Antelope Wife*, twin sisters are weaving with a single sinew thread, furiously competing with each other to set one more bead in the pattern and "trying to upset the balance of the world."[37] The twins are juxtaposed, two women and yet one, one sewing with light, one with dark, one's beads white and pale, the other's deep red and blue-black indigo, one using an awl made of an otter's sharpened penis bone, the other that of a bear. The pattern they are creating is woven onto a single sinew thread. They are at once different, yet the same, united by the ambitions of their lives' work. Both are absolutely necessary for the maintenance of the methaphoric balance of their world.

This balancing and juxtaposing is continued throughout the novel. The story continues with Scranton Roy, a soldier, and the son of a Quaker family from Pennsylvania, who has just killed an old Ojibway woman. He gives chase to a dog carrying a tikinagun on its back, enclosing a child in moss and trailing blue beads. Horrified by the spectacle of his killing of an old woman, whose face reminds him of his mother's, Roy becomes a deserter and gives chase to the dog. When he finally entices the dog to stop and eat, he is able to remove the child. When he places the baby girl to his breast, she begins to suckle and eventually is nurtured by his milk. This suckling pattern will repeat itself when Roy later nurses his own child after the mother's death. The novel ends with the story of Scranton Roy's return to the Anishinabe village. Responding to the visions he has of the woman he had killed, he arrives at the village with his grandson Augustus, the son of the girl nursed on his milk, who trades his red beads to Ten Stripe Woman, relative of the woman his grandfather killed, for a silent young girl. In this way, the Roy family becomes connected to the family of Richard Whiteheart Beads, the Shawanos. White and Red, like the beads, are separate and then conjoined.

Between the beginning and end of *The Antelope Wife*, like beads in a necklace, are intricately patterned stories—voices from Erdrich's family histories—that are part of the broader circle of life and time. Each story also has a parallel story, circumscribing the circles of contact and interaction into ever-smaller degrees of separation. Each story may have a beginning and an end, but as the reader is taken to the edge of the earth where the horizon meets the sky, one becomes acutely aware of the distance that needs to be travelled before we are able to begin to understand the complex questions raised by the author at the end of the stories:

> Did these occurrences have a paradigm in the settlement of the old scores and pains and betrayals that went back in time? Or are we working out the minor details of a strictly random pattern? Who is beading us? Who is setting flower upon flower and cutglass vine? Who are you and who am I, the beader or the bit of colored glass sewn onto the fabric of this earth? All these questions, they tug at the brain. We stand on tiptoe, trying to see over the edge, and only catch a glimpse of the next bead on the string, and the woman's hand moving, one day, the next, and the needle flashing over the horizon.[38]

Thus, the past, present, and future are fused as one. By posing these questions, Erdrich also challenges the notion of what is fact and what is fiction and questions the "Euro-American assumptions about 'civilized' and 'savage' life."[39] To illustrate this point, she uses the tradition of the "captivity narrative." For example, in *The Antelope Wife*, by contrasting the European longing to become "red" with the compassionate adoption of the "white man" by Aboriginal society, as well as by adapting the reversal of gender roles (the soldier Roy suckles two babies and the captive German male takes over a woman's kitchen and bakes a Blitzkuchen—the cake of all cakes), Erdrich articulates the universality and connectedness of the human race. Erdrich's richly woven tapestry, which cuts across family generations during the span of a century, is an autobiographical account of the blending of her own family, white and red, German/Jewish/Catholic, and Aboriginal.

The various stories are poignantly told and unified by means of the captivity narrative, which appears just past the middle section of the book as chapter 13, "The Blitzkuchen." The focus of this narrative is on food and its preparation, which is the domain of the woman to create and re/create life, and sustain and transform the family. In this narrative, the baking of a cake is a ceremony, as a holy occupation as hunting is for men.[40] It also becomes a narrative of the joining of white and red in a marriage—a joining of names and families. As much as Klaus Shawano, the narrator and namesake of this captivity narrative, had kidnapped the mysterious and elusive antelope wife, an act which precipitates his future suffering, his father had kidnapped a German soldier at the end of the Second World War to take revenge on the Germans for killing his cousin. The naming of Klaus, after the captured German, and his brother Frank's obsession to recreate the *Blitzkuchen* baked by the German, is one of the primary ideas in this novel. Louise Erdrich uses it as a metaphor to illustrate the consequences of this Aboriginal initiative on German culture.

As much as *The Antelope Wife* may have been "written out of dread…written by a writer who was afraid of what was about to happen and didn't know how to stop it" (that is, Richard Whiteheart Bead's suicide in the novel may have presaged Michael Dorris's suicide a short while later—the novel was written before Dorris's suicide in April of 1997), Erdrich emphasized that the book was written as a response to her ancestral origins, which shaped her life as a Native American.[41] In an interview with Mickey Pearlman in 1989 Erdrich gives this account of her mixed-blood past:

> I think…that if you believe in any sort of race memory, I am getting a triple whammy from my background—in regard to place and home and space.…The connection that is Chippewa is a connection to a place and to a background, and to the comfort of knowing, somehow, that you are connected here before *and before* the first settler.…Add to that the German part of my family is most probably converted Jews and the Jewish search for place, and you have this awful mix. A person can only end up writing—in order to resolve it. You can even throw in the French part of the background—the wanderers, the voyagers, which my people also come from. There is just no way to get away from all this, and the only way to resolve it, without going totally crazy looking for a home, is to write about it. The Germans have a word for it—*unziemliches Verlangen,* unseemly longing.…I feel that I am very fortunate to have some place to put these longings because otherwise they would become very destructive.[42]

Cultural encounters in North America between the "Indian" and the German have been complex and have taken many unusual forms. One of these forms has been cultural adoption. This form was usually initiated by the "Indian" to "capture" and adapt the European to live as an "Indian." But these cultural encounters are not only frozen in the past through the writings of Euro-Americans. They also continue to exist in the early twenty-first century as living diplomatic and cultural strategies of Aboriginal people, which enable them to resist total assimilation and to survive.[43]

BLITZKUCHEN—STORIES AND VOICES OF RESISTANCE

Erdrich understands and has used the strategy of cultural adoption in *The Antelope Wife.* In the chapter entitled "The Blitzkuchen," Erdrich tells the story by using the framework of a captivity narrative. However, it is also a story of how the Chippewa "Klaus Shawano" got his name. The story is set just after the Second World War and the word Blitz here has several connotations, being connected to the German use of lightning air strikes during the war as well as to the Anishinabe concept of lightning as a transforming agent. The Chippewa capture a German soldier who is being held near the reservation in a prisoner-of-war camp. The Chippewa men force the German to test his survival skills by baking a *Blitzkuchen,* lightning cake—or a cake made in a hurry, a cultural construct, or a chance (or otherwise) sexual encounter, much to the consternation of the Chippewa woman. This apparently comic story of a "German" captivity narrative, blended with a naming ceremony, as told by Erdrich, highlights the complexities of cultural encounters. It also is a commentary on the cross-cultural gender relations and conflicts, which have complicated the relationship between Euro-Americans and "Indians."

Klaus Shawano recounts the following story of his naming. After returning from the Second World War, his father continued to be haunted by the death of his cousin at the hands of German soldiers. His valiant attempts to save him had failed. The old tribal warrior, overcome with anger, and aware of the proximity of Germans in the nearby camp, encouraged Shawano to fetch him a soldier. On a moonless night, then, Shawano clipped a hole in the wire fence, snuck into the work camp and did what he was told:

> The men were summoned the next morning to his house. "Of course, I stole the German at night," said Shawano....Asinigwesance...was excited by this ancient working out of the old-way vengeance,..."I dropped the gunnysack over the Kraut's head when he came outside to take a leak,...Bound his arms behind him. Goose-stepped him."...And the man, his head covered by the gunnysack, was quiet with a peculiar stillness that was not exactly fear. Nor was it sleep. He was awake in there....Maybe some expected to see a crazy eagle....but they did not see an eagle. Instead, blinking out at us from spike tufts of hair, a chubby boy face, round-cheeked, and sparkling brown eyes. The men all reared back at the unexpected sense of warmth and goodwill from the German's pleasant smile. *"Owah!"*...His hands were chubby, his skin almost as brown as ours. Around his circle eyes his stubby hair poked out like a quill headdress. His smell—that came off him too now—was raw and fearful odor like the ripe armpit stink of porcupine. He moved quite slow, like that creature, his deep eyes shining with tears, and he took us all in one by one and then cast his eyes down, bashful, as though he would rather be under the porch or inside his own burrow.[44]

Erdrich plays around with the word porcupine which, in this clan, is both a storyteller and a trickster. The prisoner of war, a chef, offers to bake a cake in order to save his life. After much anticipation, the effect is startling:

> We are all people of simple food straight from the earth and from
> the lakes…suddenly this: a powerful sweetness that opened the
> ear to sound….They breathed together. They thought like one per-
> son. They had for a long unbending moment the same heartbeat,
> same blood in their veins, the same taste in their mouth. How,
> when they were all one being, kill the German?…So that is how
> the German was adopted into the Shawano clan, how Frank got
> fixed on duplicating that sweet hour, and how I got my name.[45]

The Roy and Shawano families are of mixed blood and race but maintain their Anishinabe traditions. They are also sensitive to how various
cultural backgrounds are more or less suited for compatibility: "Some
bloods they go together like water—the French Ojibwas; You mix those
up and it is all one person. Like me [Cally]. Others are a little less pre-
dictable. You make a person from a German and an Indian, for instance,
and you're creating a two-souled warrior always fighting with them-
self."[46] Erdrich uses the example of her German heritage to show how
this transforms some into two-souled warriors confronted with an
inner struggle for survival.

This mixed heritage is also reflected in the character of Frank
Shawano, the baker, who reincarnates the spirit of the German prisoner of war. Klaus, the original prisoner, redeemed himself by baking a
Blitzkuchen that lived on in legends as the cake of all cakes. In Frank's
obsessive mission to recreate the recipe, he has lost his seventh sense,
his sense of humour:

> "What are you making?"…Blitzkuchen!…He's trying to recon-
> struct the recipe….The cake is a fabulous thing, he says. The cake is
> holy. Extraordinary with immense powers of what sort nobody
> knows. He calls it the cake of peace. The cake of loving sincerity.
> For years, he tells, me, he has searched and tested for the exact
> recipe. In fact, the hunt for this recipe could be called his life
> quest….He lost his sense of humor. Now he is the only Indian alive
> without one….Frank is working again on his life project. This cake
> is from an old German recipe given by an actual prisoner of war to
> Frank's father. The cake of all cakes. The blitzkuchen. Early in his
> life he tasted it—light as air with a taste of peach…."It explodes on
> your palate,"…"That is my calling. But I will never stop attempting
> the blitzkuchen."[47]

Baking, for Erdrich, is clearly a holy occupation. Even though sometimes the baker is a male, he performs a female action using Mother

Earth to make the cake. The male baker is transformed by the trickster into a woman, crossing genders, becoming female. Much like the gender crossing of the soldier Scranton Roy, who suckled and raised two children as an act of resistance to established gender roles, the act of baking is also one of resisting, of survival, and ultimately one of spiritual transformation in which something new, the *Blitzkuchen,* is created and re/created. It is ceremony—feasting—at which stories are told and voices are heard.

Cally's grandmother visits the bakery where she becomes acquainted with Frank's quest to master the perfect cake: "She takes an immediate bite. "Needs something." "What?" I say, thinking I can clue in Frank… she gives a secret little smile. A familiar expression from up north. I'm the one suspicions of her now. She's toying with me, this old bulldog lady. She knows, but she won't tell."[48] It was not until his wedding to Rozina that Frank was able to reproduce the cake and discover the missing ingredient: "The crowd began to taste the cake exclaiming as they did, nervously, in trepidation, but unable to resist the next bite after the first, the next and next delicate yet dense bite of *Blitzkuchen.* And so it was, so the secret was discovered. The final and the missing ingredient—fear. And they all ate together, and they all were their loved ones moving in the present."[49] In this way, the family is transformed by Frank's cooking. He, like the prisoner of war, used the cake as a transforming agent.

But things are not at all what they appear to be in Louise Erdrich's writings. The metanarrative is one of resistance. The wedding is one in which diverse cultures are joined together for the generations yet unborn. New beads are to be added to the ancient ones and the family history continues with the adoption of the Europeans into it. The families are transformed, become interconnected, and survive together. Within the "beading" of her narrative of resistance, Erdrich meshes her German/Jewish roots based on the German romantic tradition with the Aboriginal oral tradition to explore this "triple whammy" of her origins. The numerous German quotations and the citing of Goethe, among other German writers, attests to what she learned from her father. It is important that the German/Jewish aspects of Erdrich's heritage be more fully analyzed in order to begin to understand the questions Erdrich poses at the end of her novel. Clearly, the telling and recording of stories became, for Erdrich, part of the healing process in resolving her own crisis of identity and belonging, including a resolution of the concept of unseemly longing. Indeed, it is her richly configured and interwoven heritage that provides her with the basis for weaving such delicately intricate patterns into the stories of her life experiences. It is one of the most significant examples of a female narrative of resistance, which focuses on gender and its relationship to food and with it, ceremony. In so doing, it also transforms, in the process, both European and Aboriginal people into a new people.

THE LAST REPORT ON THE MIRACLES AT LITTLE NO HORSE

Female narratives of resistance are about identities and their transformations. Erdrich's latest set of stories begins in 1996 in *The Last Report On the Miracles at Little No Horse*, when Father Damien Modeste, a crossdressing woman priest (who is not a priest at all), writes to the Pope reporting on the miracles at the Reservation, Little No Horse.[50] In fact, there are no miracles at all in any sense of the word, Catholic or otherwise. The stories take us back to the early twentieth century (1912) where Erdrich's third novel *Tracks* begins. The story opens with a creation story of a flood on the Red River which catapults Agnes DeWitt, a southern German, into the role of Father Damien Modeste who is drowned by the flood. Agnes assumes his identity and takes his money and proceeds to Little No Horse in his stead. It is here that she meets up with Nanapush who transforms her life from an apparent Catholic priest (who Nanapush knows is not a priest) into an understanding of Anishinabe spirituality through the use of the sweat lodge and a vision quest after Agnes attempts suicide.

In *Last Report* Nanapush not only uses his power of storytelling and healing but also transforms Agnes from the inside out, making her a better person. In this process, Nanapush and the Chippewa of Little No Horse adopt and capture Agnes. Nanapush also exposes the absurd Catholic "miracles" of Pauline Puyat who has become Sister Leopolda and who, after her death, is being considered as the first mixed-blood saint. Instead of "miracles," Agnes tells the truth of the matter to the Pope's emissary—the truth that the so-called saint is a murderer twice over. Agnes puts to rest the notion of the miracles and holds up to scrutiny, with poignant Anishinabe spirituality and all of its inherent powers, the Catholic Church and the overwhelming damage that was done to Aboriginal people in the twentieth century (and, by implication, well before the last century). In telling the stories in *Last Report*, Agnes truly becomes her own new self, German and an adopted Chippewa, and develops a better relationship with the people of Little No Horse.

At the beginning of this century, Europeans must learn to deal with their sense of loss and anxiety, which is closely connected to history and identity, and with it their associations with the concept of wilderness. The various voices that appear in women's writings must be heard. These Aboriginal voices also reveal that women, as writers and storytellers, continue in their role as teachers to propagate this knowledge, as is shown in the capacity of Scranton Roy, the soldier, to leave the warring ways to become a nurturing father; and Agnes to assume the role of Father Modeste. As far as these elements exist in the world of imagination and myth, it is an internal search for one's identity, a quest for spirituality. The "wild nest" of the imagination must include the understandings of women and their gendered relationship to the land and to Mother Earth/Mother Nature. Only then will we be able to understand Aboriginal people and nature, not as wilderness in the European sense, but of nature and the natural world as a living memory site, a spiritual process that is not dead. And it is the projection of this potential of the imagination and the images within it that is still worthy of investigation and ultimately of the transformation of our identities on Turtle Island.

The Resistance of Little Charlie Wenjack and His Legacy at Trent University

Chapter 15

BRUCE W. HODGINS
JOHN S. MILLOY

It was in October 1966 that twelve-year-old Charlie Wenjack died trying to walk home after escaping from his hated residential school in Northwestern Ontario. One of us (Bruce W. Hodgins) was then already in his second year of teaching history at Trent University which was in its third year of operation. Charlie had been born in 1954, one year after Hodgins graduated with an Honours B.A. in history from what became Wilfrid Laurier University. If Charlie had survived and made it to Trent Native Studies and beyond, he might have attended a recent Trent or Laurier Aboriginal Colloquium at Wanapitei. He would have been younger than many of us attending. Native Studies was inaugurated at Trent in 1968.[1] Walter Currie, a Status Indian who already had a distinguished career in the Ministry of Education, was the first chair, although Ken Kidd, the great Canadian anthropologist, was the primary moving force. Bruce Hodgins was for several years an outside member of its departmental committee. Harvey McCue, an Anishinabe from Lake

Notes on pages 275.

221

Simcoe, had graduated from Trent and immediately, in 1968, joined the department.

In late 1972, as construction began on what was temporarily called College no. 5, a low-grade controversy developed over what it should be called. For a time, it looked as if Peter Robinson, a town college, would be shut down and its name moved to this new college on the Nassau campus. But the provincial funding regulations happily blocked that plan. Instead, the students in the Native Studies Department, led by Terry McCue and Ed Metatawabin, suggested and strongly promoted the name "Charlie Wenjack College." Many of these students, like Charlie Wenjack, had gone through the culturally genocidal residential school system but, unlike Charlie, they had somehow survived. They were angry, radical, and determined. They lost. The college was named Otonabee. As a typical Trent solution, the students received a sop: the largest lecture hall or stage theatre on campus and adjacent to Otonabee was, almost two years later, named the Wenjack Theatre. How did this happen and what does it signify?

It was Ian Adams, a great rising star among a group of young radical left-leaning journalists, who made the name of Charlie Wenjack famous. Born in Africa and raised in Britain, Pakistan, and then Canada, Adams was a world traveller before entering journalism. He was an angry young man. For much of his youth and young adulthood he was very literate, yet very poor. He took as his beat the large-scale poverty existing in rich Canada. More than one-quarter of Canadians lived in poverty when Pierre Trudeau's federal Liberal government was still cautious and concerned with fiscal responsibility and the Ontario Conservative government appeared socially reactionary, committed to retrenchment, and quick to blame the poor themselves. Native people were one of Ian Adams's categories of the poor.

On 31 July 1965, before Charlie died, Adams's major article appeared in the *Weekend Magazine* which was syndicated to dozens of Canadian dailies. It was entitled "The Indians: An Abandoned and Dispossessed People." It involved an in-depth study of Native people in the large Kenora District of Northwestern Ontario. Not mentioning Charlie, it described and decried the extent of the region's socio-economic poverty. It was the story of a people "rejected and discriminated against" by "white society with hate and bitter hostility." After Charlie's body was found in October 1966, Adams was soon on the site. He was also present at the brief inquest. He researched, he interviewed, he wrote. His articles on Charlie Wenjack and residential schools for Native children appeared in various newspapers, and in magazines. Especially important was the article in *Maclean's,* of 2 February 1967.[2] The articles all merged with the new left radicalism of the late 1960s, with the socio-economic scandals of society, and with verbal battles before and after the appearance in 1969 of the Pierre Trudeau/Jean Chretien integrationist White Paper on Indian Affairs.

Twelve-year-old Charlie Wenjack had run away from the residence of Cecilia Jeffrey School in Kenora, Ontario, an Indian residential school like many others which had "problems" with attempted runaways. The usually unsuccessful and recaptured runaways frequently sustained extreme corporal punishment, deprivation, and psychological abuse. Little children were taken to Cecilia Jeffrey and other such schools from remote northern Cree villages. They were often undernourished and nearly always forbidden to speak Cree. They were generally kept there for years without vacation trips home to their parents. A great number died at these schools. Hundreds of kids ran away from such schools; most were recaptured. A few were successful, but probably more died in the attempt. These deaths were the ultimate resistance.

Charlie's home was far to the north at Ogoki Post (HBC) on the Martin Falls Reserve in the Albany valley of Northwestern Ontario. As Ian Adams wrote, Charlie "collapsed and died of hunger" close to the railway track which he desperately thought might take him to his family hundreds of kilometres away. He had no food. After his body was found, it was sent home in the company of his sisters who were also students at the school. Despite commitments, there was no real investigation into the death of Charlie Wenjack. Instead, federal authorities continued their verbal pillory of the messenger Ian Adams, calling him an irresponsible junior lefty linked to Aboriginal political activists.[3]

In late 1969 and 1970, Ian Adams wrote a best-seller non-fiction book entitled *The Poverty Wall!*[4] The second chapter was called "Why Did Charlie Wenjack Die?" Indians were among the poorest of Adam's categories of the poor. Other categories included the inner city unemployed, families with single mothers, the unorganized working poor, and the elderly. The situation was getting worse, he argued, as the rich became richer and at the same time more unconcerned.

In the Wenjack chapter, Adams mentioned the cultural component of the "Indian question," but he underplayed its centrality. He identified, condemned, and noted Indian opposition to the Chrétien-Trudeau

White Paper which proposed the phasing out of Indian reserves and Indian status, and the transferring of financial support for Indians to the provinces (which in most cases were even more socially irresponsible than the federal authorities).

There followed a modest response by the Trudeau government on the general poverty issue. It involved the so-called David Croll Senate Committee on Poverty and its *Poverty Report*. Adams and others on the left responded with *The Real Poverty Report*. Trudeau, between 1972 and 1974 was in his minority government and most responsive phase, and he moved to increase social spending on various income and welfare measures. Ironically, in 1972 all three political parties (led by Trudeau, Robert Stanfield, and T.C. Douglas) were moving to explore the concept, pushed by Ian Adams and others, for a guaranteed annual income and a negative income tax—that is, a payment to the poor regardless of their status and lifestyle. Alas, it did not materialize.

On the Native issues, the core of the 1969 White Paper was rejected as policy between 1972 and 1974. Canada was now full-steam ahead into land claims, increased Indian Affairs spending, support for cultural and linguistic activities, a speed-up on closing the remaining residential schools, and the official rejection of assimilation and cultural genocide. But Ian Adams, like T.C. Douglas and J.S. Woodsworth of the old social democratic left, had unfortunately missed or downplayed the cultural issues. Adams recognized cultural genocide in the residential schools question, but analytically he considered overall Indian issues as primarily ones of abject poverty and bureaucratic condescension and apathy. This is truly ironic when one realizes that, before Charlie died, Indian Affairs and its officials and many church officials who actually ran most of the schools were clear about the matter. They saw it as an Indian question, not a poverty question. Charlie Wenjack was reacting to a clear policy of intended destruction of Indian culture and to the enforced but clearly impossible elimination of the so-called Indian problem by mean of total assimilaion.

Meanwhile at Trent University, for almost two years beginning in 1973, the memorializing of Charlie Wenjack became the major political issue of the students in the Native Studies Department. The student leadership was determined to memorialize Charlie Wenjack by insisting that College no. 5 be named Charlie Wenjack College. They submitted the proposal formally to the university's names committee whose membership was moving decisively toward the name Otonabee, which members now suddenly emphasized as the Indian name for the upper Trent River, meaning in Anishinabe "sparkling" or "fast flowing water." The other Aboriginal alternatives had been *Kino-magauin* (place of thinking) and *Wendake* (Huronia). All other colleges were named after specific persons. The committee resolved unanimously on Otonabee; so on a motion by Jim Jury and John Burbridge, it asked senate for approval, with the added provision that some part of the college, perhaps the theatre, should later be set aside to honour Charlie Wenjack. Senate accepted "Otonabee" unanimously, with two abstentions. The second motion concerning Wenjack seemed to occasion considerable debate and was carried on division, twelve yeas, five nays, and eight abstentions. So the matter of naming College no. 5 seemed settled. It would and did become Otonabee College. But what about Charlie Wenjack?

There had been a proposal, promoted presumably by Tom Symons and Ken Kidd, to name the theatre "Monture Hall," after the elder Mohawk physician who had recently died. Dr. Monture had been an advisor in the establishment of the Native Studies Department. With the downtown Rubidge Hall areas (including old Monture House owned by Trent) about to be sold, this name had seemed quite appropriate. Clearly, some Trent faculty wanted no recognition of Charlie Wenjack, a kid who had rejected "Western" or "colonist" education. A few, however, who had wanted "Wenjack" as the College's name might settle for the theatre. To us, it seems bizarre and a mystery that the student paper *Arthur* ignored the controversy completely. Were the Trent University Native Students Association (TUNA) students still that alienated from other students? The University's official *Fortnightly* merely reported the tabling of reports, noting the votes: certainly no controversy.

In 1974 the thrust of the Wenjack proposal finally went to the new Otonabee College names committee for a final consideration. Harvey McCue (Native Studies) was the spokesperson for it. He reported to the college council that the committee had long debated and studied the issue and believed that Dr. Monture had given much more to Trent and Native Studies than had Charlie Wenjack, who had simply died objecting to residential schools. But the TUNA students, led by Terry McCue of Rama, and Ed Metatawabin (of far northern Fort Severn), had been very forceful in their presentation. Harvey McCue now argued that

BLOCKADES AND RESISTANCE

Dr. Monture deserved more than just a theatre named in his honour. So, obviously with some hesitation, the committee was finally recommending "Wenjack Theatre." The report was accepted.

Vice-President Richard Sadlier wrote Charlie's parents for permission. He invited them, as well as Charlie's sister and Andrew Rickard, Grand Chief of Treaty 9, to attend the dedication. The parents briefly replied in the affirmative, but only Chief Rickard actually came to the dedication, held on 24 November 1974, where there was a full house in the theatre itself. Terry McCue, his wife, and Ed Metatawabin were furious. Terry's letter to Chair Walter Currie (and copied to V.P. Richard Sadlier) was eloquent. It shows the depth of the feeling and the outrage:

26 November 1974.

Professor Walter Currie,
The Chairman,
Department of Native Studies,
Trent University.

Dear Professor Currie:

I am writing this letter officially to declare my displeasure and disgust with that ridiculous sham the University called the dedication of the Wenjack Theatre.

Over two years ago the University asked for submissions of names, to the naming committee, for an "Indian" name for the then "College Five." Many names were submitted, but the Native students on campus at the time felt that Charles Wenjack College was the most appropriate. Subsequently, Ed Metatawabin and myself were asked to represent T.U.N.A. at a meeting with the Names Committee to present the name and our reasons for choosing it.

We told them that while Charley [sic] Wenjack was indeed a symbol of all the brutality and ugliness represented by Indian education in Canada here was a chance to end that. By naming the college "Wenjack" we felt that Trent could begin building a new hope among Indians of this country for a better deal in education: that instead of Charley Wenjack being a negative symbol his death could be the symbolic cornerstone, not of defeat and pain, but of a positive force spearheaded by Trent with its Native Studies Program.

For reasons of their own, I suppose, they chose another name for the college, and the theatre was named after Charley Wenjack. We probably should have fought against this action but I am sure we all felt that something was better than nothing.

However, what truly disgusts me was that nowhere in that whole farce of Sunday, the 24th, was there a mention of the students' suggestion of the name. Nowhere was there a mention of the spirit we felt was integral in the use of Charley's name. Not one member of the T.U.N.A. Executive that fought for that was present. My wife and I were there only by chance—we happened to re-enrol this year.

If one were to judge by the ceremony, one would be led to believe that the University, through its Names Committee, came up with the name out of the blue. What a damn lie. I felt sick when I saw the dignitaries seated in the front row being introduced by the President.

What the hell did Elizabeth McLuhan or the Mayor of Peterborough have to do with Wenjack and what that name stands for? Where was Ed Metatawabin or Marie MacGregor or any of the other students who fought for and believed in that name?

I feel disgusted and sold out and I'm sure my brothers and sisters would feel the same if they had been there to witness that bit of treachery by the University which so prides itself in its "Indian Program." The old spectre of Indian Affairs with its "token" Indian involvement rushing forward crying, "See what we have done for these people," haunted that theatre on Sunday last.

As a "sold out" Indian, I would like to suggest that the Native Studies Department, unless it approves of this type of action, demand:

(i)   THAT the University send letters of apology to all Native students enrolled here when the name was suggested. That is the least they deserve.

(ii)   THAT the University, through the *Fortnightly* or *Arthur*, publicly acknowledge this omission and, along with it, print an article explaining the meaning behind the name.

(iii) THAT some form of censure be taken against the staff member who participated in this rip-off.

Yours sincerely,
Terry McCue.

P.S. I would ask that this letter be read into the official minutes of the next departmental meeting and that a copy be forwarded to Mr. R.H. Sadleir.

The dedication ceremony was reported substantially in the *Examiner* of 25 November and briefly in the *Fortnightly*.

Bitterness among the students continued for awhile, but then it faded away. Within a few years, most non-Native students and many faculty had no knowledge whatsoever of whom the Wenjack Theatre commemorated. It was just a name. But faculty members of the Native Studies Department and incoming Native students did not forget. The residential schools issues returned to the newspapers and to a central place in the Aboriginal agenda in the 1990s. Academically it became particularly important to two historians, James Miller and one of the authors of this paper (John Milloy). It was very important to the Royal Commission on Aboriginal Peoples and its *Report*, for which John Milloy did the major research on the schools question. In 1999, this research appeared as Milloy's *"A National Crime."*

Neither Indian Affairs, nor Prime Minister Chrétien have yet adequately addressed the thrust of the *Report* on most matters. Native people suffered and the family of Charlie Wenjack still await a specific apology and some financial compensation, though the general apology and offers of considerable general financial support have been made. A plaque honouring the name of Charlie Wenjack now exists at the entrance to his theatre. The residential schools are gone, Charlie Wenjack has been memorialized, but overall Aboriginal resistance continues.

The Struggle Continues

BRUCE W. HODGINS

Epilogue

This volume, *Blockades and Resistance,* has described in fifteen chapters the diverse ways in which Aboriginal peoples in Canada, especially in Ontario (and with two examples from the United States and Europe), have resisted and blockaded attempts to deny them their right to portions of their traditional and dynamic cultures. While there have been many successes, the struggle continues as part of a broad international struggle for the recognition, implementation, and entrenchment of diverse Aboriginal rights.

The occasion for this book was the tenth anniversary of the great Temagami blockade of 1989. Although one pickup truck did drive the Red Squirrel Road extension in late December of that year, it was the only vehicle ever to do so except ATVs and snowmobiles. Then the snows came. The spring breakup washed out the hastily constructed culverts and ditches. The extension was never used for access to logging the old-growth pine, nor for anything else. The millions of dollars spent to construct the road and to arrest the blockaders was all wasted. All three Ontario political

Notes on page 276.

parties, including the Liberals who had issued the contract, admitted that it had been a serious mistake. In this sense, the blockades were a success. But the ultimate goal of the blockades, the recognition of Aboriginal title to N'Daki Menan, to the public but not private lands of the Temagami country, was not achieved. Indeed, the Supreme Court of Canada "found" that the Native community of the Temagami area, even though they had probably not signed the Robinson Treaty of 1850, had passively "adhered" to it over several generations. They had thus substituted treaty rights for Aboriginal land title. The Crown (primarily, it seems, in the right of Ontario) however, had failed in its fiduciary responsibility to the Aboriginal people of Temagami. The Temagami people had not received what they should have received under the Robinson Huron Treaty. Based on the number and size of the traditional families, the treaty should have included at least 112 square miles and compensation for not receiving it, at least since the time when they had "adhered." In the 1880s, Ontario had refused to transfer to Canada such land for a proper Indian reserve, claiming that the local Indians were not a proper band as then loosely defined. The Bear Island Reserve, which they finally received only in 1972, long after it had become the site of their village, covered less than one square mile.

Long and painful negotiations finally resulted in a signed agreement in principle. The agreement, among many things, involved the transfer of 112 square miles of land bordering along most of the eastern and northern shores of Lake Temagami and stretching fairly deeply inland. Chief Gary Potts and some others were disinclined toward Indian reserves. He found the concept demeaning, too restrictive, and too tied to the old Indian Act with its distant federal control. So the 112 square miles would have been unalienable, private, freehold land under the laws of Ontario. But in late 1993, this agreement failed to secure full Aboriginal ratification. For some years, there had been two Aboriginal bodies or governments, the Temagami First Nation (TFN) (formerly the Temagami Band of Ojibwa) and the Teme-Augama Anishnabai. The First Nation involved only the Status Indians, while the much broader later body involved all those people, Status, non-Status and Métis, who could trace ancestry back to the traditional extended families. Gary Potts had been chief of both bodies and continued as chief of the TAA. The two bodies had worked closely together during the blockades and the negotiations. The agreement carried overwhelmingly with the TAA.

It was defeated twice, and overwhelmingly so, by the TFN whose constitution then basically allowed only adult Status Indians living on Bear Island to vote. Most of the shoreline would have been subject to the provincially endorsed Skyline Reserve, with no development, no cottage construction for leasing purposes, etc.

There was an impasse. Ontario took the agreement off the table. Gary Potts did not stand for re-election to the TAA and was replaced by Doug McKenzie as chief. The leadership of the Temagami First Nation changed several times. In 2000, Raymond Katt replaced Jim Twain as chief. It is now Alex Paul.

With the two bodies, the TAA and the TFN, working together, in late 1999 Ontario agreed to a slow restarting of new negotiations with the 112 square miles of set-aside lands, now styled the "Proposed Settlement Lands," back on the table. After preliminary talks and the establishment of negotiating teams, a side table, and consultative committees, negotiations in the summer of 2001 became intense. This time there would be no co-management, but up to three square miles of special lands for heritage sites for each of the traditional families. In the spring of 2001, on provincial urging, two federal representatives finally appeared at meetings for the first time. On questioning, the two women announced almost casually, that if Ontario acquiesced, all 112 square miles could become Indian reserve land. Actually, this harkened back to the federal proposals of the mid-1880s, though largely in different locations on the lake. The Aboriginal leadership seemed likely to endorse this fully.

Meanwhile, the municipality of Temagami had, under Ontario policy, expanded to encircle the lake and stretch far to the west and the south. Privately held provincial land under the 1993 agreement would now have been inside the "Town of Temagami" and subject to municipal taxation and planning regulation. Indian reserve lands would not be so constrained. While there was sudden surprise at this federal initiative, and considerable alarm among many cottagers over the future of the Skyline Reserve, this concern was soon tempered by Ontario and TAA/TFN assurances that the transfer could be accompanied by legally binding commitments to respect most of the Skyline Reserve. The town and Bear Island also opened serious discussions with Ontario toward the establishment of a jointly administered community forest covering part of the area. A new agreement is supposed to be signed in 2003. I feel guardedly optimistic about it.[1]

Meanwhile, as noted in the various chapters of this book, there have been other blockades and lots of resistance throughout Canada. The blockade and armed resistance at Kahnesetake-Oka in southwestern Quebec in July 1990 was particularly serious. This time the army faced Mohawk protestors including the warriors. Then, in 1995, there were standoffs both at Gustafsen Lake in interior British Columbia and at the former Ipperwash Provincial Park. The Ipperwash stand off led to the death of Anishinabe Dudley George at the hands of the provincial police, with suspicions concerning aggressive police behaviour stretching back and up to the highest Ontario officials. In 1996, the Cree and Inuit of Northern Quebec made it absolutely clear that if Quebec seceded from Canada, it could not take Cree and Inuit lands and people with it.[2] Meanwhile, the Cree demanded control of their own forests; both groups would like more self-government and their own territory, even if technically still part of Quebec. Finally, since 1999, the people of Burnt Church, New Brunswick, and other Mi'kmaq have resisted federal attempts to restrict their own Supreme Court decision to give the Mi'kmaq a priority right (within conservation supremacy) to the lobster and other fisheries of the area.[3]

There has been progress. On 1 April 1999, Nunavut was created in the eastern and central Arctic, with an Inuit-dominated territory with public government and a generous land settlement.[4] Also, the Nisga'a agreement in British Columbia has been signed, ratified, and constitutionally entrenched—despite a large and ominous British Columbian backlash.

Yet so many comprehensive agreements need still to be negotiated, especially in British Columbia, Labrador, and New Brunswick. The matter of recompense for physical and psychological abuse from the former federally owned and religiously run residential school system remains on the table. Despite a federal apology, this leaves the four largest churches with vast numbers of class action suits which allegedly could bankrupt some of them or parts of them. Across the country, Aboriginal people resist a cheap solution.

Canada has not been unique in facing blockades and resistance from Aboriginal peoples. Since 1989, many such peoples have done so. In Australia, the decades of resistance to land confiscation by Eddie Mabo and his friends worked its way through the courts until, in 1994, the High Court of Australia not only recognized the Torres Strait Islanders' right to their traditional (agricultural) lands, but extended Aboriginal rights to claim long-time occupied lands throughout Australia. The court explicitly rejected the *Terra Nullius* doctrine which had sanctioned unilateral Aboriginal displacement. This was followed by the Wik decision in 1996 that opened the way for claims to some of the vast extent of land held under long-term pastoral leases throughout the country wherever some long-term occupancy could effectively be asserted. Yet in Australia, the federal government refuses to apologize, is not very co-operative, and seems to be riding a backlash. More resistance is inevitable.[5]

In New Zealand, long-time resistance and protest has led to Pakeha (i.e., European)-New Zealand recognition and constitutional entrenchment of the Maori version and translation of the 1840 Treaty of Waitangi. The parchment document is now enshrined in a large new building under armed and mainly Maori guard. Imagine Canada doing that for the Royal Proclamation of 1763 and the great Treaty of Niagara of the following year! In New Zealand, the 1992 Sealords Fishery Agreement and the South Island Ngai Tahu Settlement of 1998-99 followed years of resistance and tedious negotiation.[6]

The Sami (Laplanders) of northern Norway, Sweden, and Finland continue to resist assimilation, push for constitutional entrenchments of rights to lands and culture, and often push for solutions not all that different from those of Nunavut and even of Greenland, both Inuit controlled. In Mexico, the Zapatistas of Chiapas have fought for land settlements, genuine federalism, and the constitutional entrenchment of Aboriginal rights throughout the country.[7] President Fox, who does not control congress, seems somewhat sympathetic to these demands. There is, of course, huge Aboriginal resistance in Thailand (from the karens and other "hill tribes") and Indonesia (especially in West Irian or Western New Guinea). Resistance by many Native Americans in the United States also still continues.

Back in Canada, 45 percent of First Nations people now live in cities; even the "reserve" population continues to grow. Their resistance to serious but undercover attempts at assimilation and continued marginalization are growing. There seems little means for initiating meaningful discussions. Even negotiations for recognized specific and comprehensive claims move slowly and at great cost. This is true even when the range of likely solutions is clear to the three parties, federal, provincial, and Aboriginal. Why, for instance, could not all the smallish specific claims for the large and relatively well-off Walpole Island First Nation north of Windsor be settled within a year? Is fear of backlash or of cost holding back the federal and/or provincial politicians? Then there is the Caldwell First Nation of southwestern Ontario, people who finally reached an agreement that involved securing their first and scattered reserve by using public funds to buy their land on the open market, only to find resistance to the deal from local farmers and other non-Aboriginal local people.

Let us close with some words by Gary Potts, written just before the Temagami blockade of 1989:

> We intend to maintain our honour and integrity as our forefathers have done in dealing with the Crown since 1763. We began our struggle for justice in 1877, and after 112 years, have no intention of giving up....Our principle of sharing with all people will continue, a commitment based on the principles of sustained life, sustained development, and stewardship.[8]

PREFACE

1 Christian F. Feest, ed., *The Cultures of Native North Americans* (Cologne: Könemann Verlagsgesellschaft mbH, 2000), 18.

INTRODUCTION

1 David T. McNab, private communication with Gary G. Potts, 30 April 1999.

2 David McNab, *Circles of Time: Aboriginal Land Rights and Resistance in Ontario* (Waterloo: Wilfrid Laurier University Press, 1999), 94-95.

3 See Geoffrey York and Loreen Pindora, *Peoples of the Pines: The Warriors and Legacy of Oka*, 2nd ed. (Toronto: McArthur, 1999) for an extended journalistic treatment of the Oka blockade.

4 For recent work in the field of Aboriginal Studies in Canada, see Keith Thomas Carlson, Melinda Marie Jette, and Ken Coates, "An Annotated Bibliography of Major Writings in Aboriginal History, 1990-1999," *Canadian Historical Review* 82, no. 1 (March 2001): 122-71. This list runs to forty-nine pages of work in the past decade. See also Ken Coates, "Writing First Nations into Canadian History: A Review of Recent Scholarly Work," *Canadian Historical Review* 81, no. 1 (March 2000): 99-114.

5 The meeting ground is also part of circles of time. See McNab, *Circles of Time*, 27-49.

6 For another example of Toronto being known as the "meeting place" or the "gathering place," see McNab, "'In the Middle of the Fly-way': Visitors to the Gathering Place: A Story of Where the Water Meets the Sky," paper presented at Faculty/Graduate Seminar, First Nations House, University of Toronto, 16 January 1998.

7 Robert A. Williams Jr., *Linking Arms Together: American Indian Treaty Visions of Law and Peace, 1600-1800* (New York: Oxford University Press, 1997).

8 Bob Rae, "The Road to Self-Determination," in *Aboriginal Self-Determination, Proceedings of a Conference Held September 30-October 3, 1990*, ed. Frank Cassidy (Halifax and Lantzville, BC: Oolichan Books and The Institute for Research on Public Policy, 1991), 151.

9 Bob Rae, "The Road to Self-Determination," 154.

10 Paul Williams, "The Senecas Did It!" Paper presented at the American Society for Ethnohistory Conference, London, Ontario, 20 October 2000.

CHAPTER 1

1 It will be recalled that the Supreme Court of Canada decision in the Bear Island case was handed down on 6 August 1991 more than seven years before Delgamuukw. Delgamuukw and the Marshall decisions of 1999 could not change the "legal fact" of the Bear Island case of 1991. Only a new trial for the Bear Island citizens will change things legally. See McNab, *Circles of Time*, 45-74.

CHAPTER 4

1 Central portions of this chapter appeared in a somewhat different form in my "Refiguring Wilderness: A Personal Odyssey," *Journal of Canadian Studies* 33, no. 2 (Summer 1998): 12-26.

2 Bruce W. Hodgins and Jamie Benidickson, *The Temagami Experience: Recreation, Resources, and Aboriginal Rights in the Northern Ontario Wilderness* (Toronto: University of Toronto Press, 1989).

3 Bruce W. Hodgins, "Context of the Temagami Predicament," in *In Temagami: A Debate on Wilderness*, ed. Matt Bray and Ashley Thomson (Toronto: Dundurn, 1990), 123-39.

4 "Context," 110-11, and the article by Kay Chernook, "Be What You've Come Here For," in *Circles of Strength: Community Alternatives to Alienation*, ed. Helen Forsey (Gabriola Island: New Society, 1993), 117-26.

5 Copies of almost all of the papers of the Wendaban Stewardship Authority are in the possession of the second chair of the WSA, James Morrison, in Haileybury. I have an imperfect set. The plan, of course, exists in the files of MNR (North Bay and Peterborough), and of ONAS (Toronto). For his part, Jamie Benidickson published an early, upbeat article on the WSA in 1992.

6 Bruce W. Hodgins, John S. Milloy, and Shawn Heard, eds., *Co-existence? Studies in Ontario-First Nations Relations* (Peterborough: Trent Frost Centre, 1992); see especially David McNab, "Making a Circle of Time: The Treaty-

Making Process and Aboriginal Land Rights in Ontario," 27-49. This later became McNab's analysis of Aboriginal Land Rights and Resistance in Ontario, entitled *Circles of Time*.

7 Supreme Court of Canada, *Bear Island Foundation v. The Attorney General of Ontario*, [1991] S.C.R. 570.

8 See also Bruce W. Hodgins and Kerry A. Cannon, "The Aboriginal Presence in Ontario Parks and Other Protested Places," in *Changing Parks: The History, Future and Cultural Context of Parks and Heritage Landscapes*, ed. John S. Marsh and Bruce W. Hodgins (Peterborough: Trent Frost Centre, 1995), 50-76; and Bruce W. Hodgins, "The Crown Domain and the Aboriginal Self-Governing Presence in Northern Ontario," in *Earth, Water, Air and Fire: Studies in Canadian Ethnohistory*, ed. David T. McNab (Waterloo: Wilfrid Laurier University Press, 1998), 245-62.

CHAPTER 5

1 Colin G. Calloway, *New Worlds for All: Indians, Europeans, and the Remaking of Early America* (Baltimore: Johns Hopkins University Press, 1997), 155.

2 The Teme-Augama Anishnabai include the citizens of the Temagami First Nation as well as those Aboriginal people who are regarded by the federal government as "non-Status Indians" but who are also associated with the Temagami First Nation.

3 David T. McNab, *Circles of Time: Aboriginal Land Rights and Resistance in Ontario* (Waterloo: Wilfrid Laurier University Press, 1999), 45-74.

4 Hodgins and Benidickson, "Aboriginal Rights, Resource Management, and the Northern Ontario Wilderness," in *The Temagami Experience: Recreation, Resources, and Aboriginal Rights in the Northern Ontario Wilderness* (Toronto: University of Toronto Press, 1989), 267-89.

5 Hodgins and Benidickson, *The Temagami Experience*, 270-71.

6 I am basing this information on my recollections of events as well as on my private diary and my date book for 1988.

7 The environmental part of these proceedings and their background is discussed accurately from an outsider's perspective in Gerald Killan, "The Development of a Wilderness Park System in Ontario," in *Temagami, A Debate on Wilderness*, ed. Matt Bray and Ashley Thomson (Toronto: Dundurn Press, 1990), 85-120.

8 I am basing this information on my recollections of events as well as on my private diary for 1988, and my date book for March-May 1988 for which there are no entries for Temagami or for any meetings about it.

9 Thomas R. Berger, *Northern Frontier, Northern Homeland: The Report of the Mackenzie Valley Pipeline Inquiry*, vol. 1 and 2 (Ottawa: Queen's Printer, 1977).

10 I am basing this information on my recollections of events as well as on my private diary for 1988 and my date book for the same time period. For example, in 1986-87 Kerrio, perhaps unaware of what his senior officials were doing, allowed the OMNR senior bureaucracy to ditch the proposed Ontario-wide fishing negotiations by artificially creating a racist backlash led by Ontario's negotiator, and other senior officials. The same results can be seen, in terms of the racist reaction to the Algonquins of Golden Lake land claim in 1990-91, as well as to fishing. The aftermath of the failed fishing negotiations with the Chippewas of Saugeen and Nawash, the litigation, and the court judgment in favour of the Chippewas, also fuelled the reaction of white racists. The fishing negotiations failed and the local ones with the Chippewas of Saugeen and Nawash resulted in a negative court decision for Ontario. The OMNR bureaucracy and its authoritarian methods have not changed regardless of which government has been in power at Queen's Park.

11 Bruce W. Hodgins, "Contexts of the Temagami Predicament," in *Temagami, A Debate*, 123-40; Bruce W. Hodgins and Jonathan Bordo, "Wilderness, Aboriginal Presence and the Land Claim," 67-80. In *Co-Existence? Studies in Ontario-First Nations Relations*, edited by Bruce W. Hodgins, Shawn Heard, and John S. Milloy. Peterborough: Trent University, Frost Centre, 1992.

12 Even in 1988, road blockades were not a "new" strategy of resistance in Ontario. As early as 14 April 1987, there was local talk of blockading the bridge across Highway 621 within the Big Grassy Reserve on Lake of the Woods as a result of a dispute regarding the ownership of the Big Grassy River as part of the reserve. Private diary, 14 April 1987 and my "Action Memo" to Mr. Ted Wilson, Director, Office of Indian Resource Policy, dated 14 April 1987.

13 Hodgins and Benidickson, *The Temagami Experience*, 267-89; Hodgins and Bordo, "Wilderness," 67-80; I am basing this information on my recollections of events as well as on my private diary for 1988 and my date book for 1988, especially entries in the date book for 31 May; 2, 3, 7, 8, 13, 16, 21, 23, 24 June; 11 July; and 5, 9, 11, 18, 22 August for the immediate reaction to the blockade.

14 I am basing this information on my recollections of events as well as on my private diary for 1988 and my date book for 1988, entries on 13, 22 September; 5, 6 October; 9, 14, 18, 29 November; 6, 13, 15 December. The daily cost of arresting the TAA was then estimated by the OPP to be about $2 million a day. This, of course, compares unfavourably with the cost of building the road which was estimated to be about $4 million in total.

15 This advice by the OPP is similar to their actions taken during the summer of 1990 during the Oka crisis. But it is in sharp contrast to the actions taken by the OPP at Ipperwash in September 1995. The change in the OPP actions in September 1995 which led to the events at Ipperwash could have come only directly from the Premier's Office.

16 I am basing this information on my recollections of events as well as on my private diary for 1988-89 and my date book for 1988-89. For 1989 I rely on date book entries for 30 January; 2, 7, 9, 10, 21, 28 February; 3, 22, 27, 28 March; 10, 17, 20, 26 April; 1, 11, 29 May; 20, 21 June; 26 July; 22 August; 18 September; and 1, 2, 19 October.

17 Date book, 1988.

18 This description of the TAA blockade of 1988 has been taken from McNab, *Circles of Time*, 45-74.

19 Journal entries on 1-8, and 11-16 January 1989.

20 It was not until the following year that monies from this fund were accessed from the management board of Cabinet. The monies were not used to fund First Nations' "economic participation" but rather were given to First Nations directly through contribution agreements with the directorate to assist them in negotiating agreements with the province. Indirectly, they may have assisted in Aboriginal economic development.

21 McNab, "Drawings, Volume 2, 1989," entries for February 1989.

22 McNab, "Drawings, Volume 2, 1989," entries for March 1989.

23 The reader should note the irony here since Peter Robinson was a brother of William Benjamin Robinson who had negotiated the so-called Robinson Treaties which the TAA did not participate in or sign or adhere to this day. Subsequently, Gary Potts in the late 1990s became a member of Peter Robinson College. He is currently doing graduate work at the Frost Centre for Canadian Studies and Native Studies.

24 McNab, "Drawings, Volume 2, 1989," entries for April-August 1989.

25 The ruling can be found in the *Canadian Native Law Reporter*, 1990, 4 C.N.L.R., 3-6.

26 McNab, "Drawings, Volume 2, 1989," entries for January-December 1989.

27 Bob Rae, *From Protest to Power, Personal Reflections on a Life in Politics* (Toronto: Viking Penguin Books, 1996), especially 109-10. In his "personal reflections," Rae attributes his intervention in the issue as a result of a meeting with Chief Gary Potts.

28 Someone, perhaps even the senior bureaucrat himself, leaked the policy to the NDP before it was announced in the legislature and it was ripped to shreds by the NDP when Scott introduced it. Scott was furious at this turn of events. The senior bureaucrat was the primary author of this policy. See his "Ontario's Approach to Aboriginal Self-Government," in *Co-existence? Studies in Ontario-First Nation Relations*, ed. Shawn Heard, Bruce W. Hodgins, and John S. Milloy (Peterborough: Frost Centre for Canadian Heritage and Development Studies, 1992), 50-57. He was, at the time, a life-long NDP supporter. He was one of the people purged from a position of power from the Ontario Native Affairs Secretariat by Michael Harris's political minions in 1996.

29 McNab, "Drawings, Volume 3," entries for April 1990.

30 "Province and Teme-Augama-Anishnabai Sign Historic Stewardship Agreement," 23 April 1990 and also "Statement by the Honourable Ian Scott Minister Responsible for Native Affairs on the Signing of a Land Stewardship Agreement between the Province of Ontario and the Teme-Augama Anishnabai Monday, April 23, 1990, 11:00 A.M." news release, Ontario Ministry of Natural Resources.

31 These events up to 1992 are described in Hodgins and Bordo, "Wilderness, Aboriginal Presence and the Land Claim," 67-80.

CHAPTER 6

1 N. Scott Momaday, *The Way to Rainy Mountain* (Albuquerque: University of New Mexico Press, 1969), 4.

2 Paul A.W. Wallace, *The White Roots of Peace* (1946; reprint, Saranac Lake, NY: Chauncy, 1986), 7.

3 Ibid., 8.

4 *The Oxford English Dictionary* (Oxford: Clarendon Press, 1971), 581-82.

5 Ibid., 523-24.

6 Ibid.

7 This view differs somewhat from a wide-spread, traditional Native belief that all things, even stones, are living things, i.e., animism.

8 Paula Gunn Allen, ed., *Spider Woman's Granddaughters* (New York: Ballantine, 1989), 9.

9 N. Scott Momaday, foreword to *Keepers of the Earth: Native American Stories and Environmental Activities for Children*, by Michael J. Caduto and Joseph Bruchac (Golden, CO: Fulcrum, 1988), xvii.

10 Wallace, *White Roots*, 8.

11 John C. Mohawk, prologue to Wallace, *White Roots*, xxi.

12 Ibid., xxi.

13 Wallace, *White Roots*, 9-10.

14 Ibid., 9.

15 Mohawk, prologue, xxii.

16 Steve Wall and Harvey Arden, *Wisdomkeepers: Meetings with Native American Spiritual Elders* (Hillsboro, OR: Beyond Words, 1990), 109.

17 Meredith Raine and Jennifer Dittman, "Native American Fest Kicks Off," *The Daily Athenaeum*, 14 September 1992, 1, 2.

18 Barbara Burke Ankrom, "Native Tribute," *West Virginia University Alumni Magazine* 16, no. 1 (1993): 21.

19 Ibid.

20 Tim Noisette, "Community Gathers for Tree Planting," *The Daily Athenaeum*, 21 October 1996, 10.

21 Ibid.

22 Annie Dillard, *Pilgrim at Tinker Creek* (1974; reprint, New York: Harper Perennial, 1988), 33-34.

23 Personal fax, 15 December 1999.

24 Bruce W. Hodgins and Jamie Benidickson, *The Temagami Experience: Recreation, Resources, and Aboriginal Rights in the Northern Ontario Wilderness* (Toronto: University of Toronto Press, 1989), 6.

25 Ibid., 269.

26 Wall and Arden, *Wisdomkeepers*, 107.

27 Wallace, *The White Roots*, 47.

CHAPTER 7

1 J.V. Wright, *Ontario Prehistory* (Ottawa: National Museum of Man, 1972), 48-49. Cole Harris maintains that about 2000 B.P. "native silver deposits at Cobalt Ontario were exploited to produce beads, ear spools and other ornaments," (*Historical Atlas of Canada*, vol. 1 [Toronto: University of Toronto Press, 1987], 4).

2 For detailed discussion on the reasons why some Aboriginal people aided the newcomers in locating mineral deposits, see Rhonda Telford, "Aboriginal Knowledge and Use of Minerals in Ontario" in "'The Sound of the Rustling of the Gold Is Under My Feet Where I Stand; We Have a Rich Country': A History of Aboriginal Mineral Resources in Ontario" (Ph.D. diss., University of Toronto, 1996), 21-113.

3 Union of Ontario Indians (UOI) "Robinson Huron Treaty 1850, Historical/Contemporary Documents, P. Williams" letter, 20 August 1840, Shinguacouse et al. to "Father." The spelling "Shinguacouse" is maintained throughout the text, but other spellings appear in citations as they were in the original documents. Elizabeth Arthur, ed., *Thunder Bay District, 1831-1892* (Toronto: Champlain Society, 1973), xl. References to "Macdonell" refer to Allan Macdonell. Angus Macdonell will be referred to in full. Public Archives of Ontario (PAO), RG1, vol. 3, ser. A VII, "The Report of the Select Committee on the Copper Mines, on the North Side of Lake Superior," selected segment by Francis James, 1866. Ontario, *Report of the Royal Commission on the Mineral Resources of Ontario and Measures for their Development* (Toronto: Warwick and Sons, 1890), 256.

4 National Archives of Canada (NAC), RG10, vol. 123, pp. 6192-6198, petition no. 225, 5 July 1847, "Memorial: Indians at the Sault Ste Marie praying that they may receive compensation for their lands now occupied by the whites." The first mining location appears to have been issued to John Prince, who applied for Spar Island on 1 July 1845. (*Report of the Royal Commission*, 255). *British Colonist*, 18 December 1849, "The Indian Troubles—Let-

ter from Mr Allan Macdonell," 2. Shinguacouse's speech discussed above might have been referring to Allan Macdonell as one of those who came "stealing" along the shores in 1845, but it was more likely to be John Prince who obtained the first location. By at least 1846, Shinguacouse decided to trust Macdonell, sharing with him the location of some mines.

5   Ontario, *Report of the Royal Commission*, 255; Robert Surtees, "Indian Land Cessions in Ontario, 1763-1862" (Ph.D. diss., Carleton University, 1982), 238-39; also H.V. Nelles, *Politics of Development* (Toronto: Macmillan, 1974), 20. James Morrison, "The Robinson Treaties of 1850: A Case Study," 31 March 1994 (for Royal Commission on Aboriginal Peoples [RCAP]) 38-41. "British Justice" *Lake Superior Journal*, 8 November 1849, 2. Also "List of Mining Locations Granted on Lake Superior, 1846" (see Logan's Report to Commissioner of Crown Lands [CCL], 1847) in Arthur, *Thunder Bay District*, 49-50. Many more mining applications were received than locations granted. According to the *Royal Commission*, thirty applications were received for Lake Superior in 1845, increasing to one hundred the following year; one application was received for Lake Huron in 1845 and thirty-three the following year (255).

6   PAO, RG1, A-1-6, vol. 25, no. 4, file 2120, pp. 21675-21677, letter 27 April 1846, Alexander Vidal to D.B. Papineau, CCL "Respecting Claim of Indians to the Lands at Sault Saint Marie which he was ordered to survey," pp. 21675-21677. Ontario Native Affairs Secretariat (ONAS), ILF no. 130400 "Garden River Indian Reserve, #14" "Report of the CCL relative to Indian Settlements at Garden River, Lake Huron, etc." 26 April 1848, J.H. Price (includes Vidal's 21 February 1848 Report). Also MNR, Survey Branch, "Mining Locations on the River St Mary and Echo Lake," Vidal, 1848, Plan no. 8904 D17.

7   NAC, RG10, vol. 612, letter, 10 June 1846, Chinquak to Ironside, pp. 116-117. Vol. 123, pp. 6071-6749, petition no. 225, 5 July 1847 "Memorial: Indians at the Sault St Marie praying that they may receive compensation for their lands now occupied by the whites" pp. 6192-6198; response, Major Campbell, 14 July 1847, pp. 6189-6191.

8   NAC, RG10, vol. 123, petition no. 225, pp. 6192-6198.

9   Chute, "A Century of Native Leadership" (Ph.D. diss., McMaster University, 1986), 227. Elgin arrived in Canada in 1847 to usher in responsible government. See W.L. Morton, "James Bryce," *Dictionary of Canadian Biography*, vol. 9, 1861-70 (Toronto: University of Toronto Press, 1976), 89-93. "Bruce-Lord Elgin," 9. NAC, RG10, vol. 123, 5 July 1847, Petition of William McMurray Chinguakose, Joseph Nabenagojing, Charles Pahyabetahsung, and John Kabaoose, pp. 6190-6198.

10   Reference to this report in Elgin's correspondence to Grey, 23 November 1849, Doughty *Elgin-Grey Papers*, vol. 4, p. 1485. Excerpts published in the *Lake Superior Journal*: "Indian Commissioner Arrived—Treaty with the British Indians," 24 August 1850, 2; the *Globe*: "The Indian Difficulties," 21

December 1849, 98 (this is the lengthiest reproduction); and in the *Montreal Pilot*: "The Indian Difficulty," 27 December 1849, 2. Spragge's letter went out under the name of J.H. Price, Papineau's successor. Morrison, "The Robinson Treaties," 53-54.

11 "The Indian Troubles," *British Colonist*, 18 December 1849. This is the only reference to a prior deputation having gone to Montreal, unless Macdonell meant the earlier deputation to Toronto to see McMurray. "British Justice," *Lake Superior Journal*, 8 November 1849, 2. Also NAC, RG10, vol. 513, pp. 76-77; letter, 31 July 1848, Campbell to T.G. Anderson, pp. 76-77.

12 UOI, "Robinson Huron Treaty 1850, Historical/Contemporary Documents, P. Williams," transcripts, Shinguacouse's speech, August 1848, pp. 1-2; Peau-de-Chat's reply to questions by government representatives, 19 August 1848, pp. 2-3. NAC, RG10, vol. 534, letter, 20 August 1848, Anderson to Major Campbell, pp. 255-58. Anderson identified the proposed treaty area as a block extending northward from the edge of Lake Huron to the height of land and west to the mouth of the Pigeon River. Thus, only the area containing the mining locations was to be included.

13 Chute, "A Century of Native Leadership," 229-30. NAC, RG10, vol. 173, letter, 9 October 1849, Anderson to Major Campbell, pp. 100434-100436 (in Chute, "A Century of Native Leadership," 240).

14 "The Indian Troubles," *British Colonist*, 18 December 1849. Reference to Macdonell's queries on the validity of the location tickets from Morrison, "The Robinson Treaties," 64. Macdonell raised the issue in a letter to Campbell on 21 April 1849. A deputation did go to Montreal in July 1849.

15 PAO, RG1, A-1-7, vol. 7 (12), letter, 19 June 1849, Cameron to Price, pp. 1 and 2; also MU 275, Henry Blanchard Papers; Chute, "A Century of Native Leadership," 244. PAO, RG1, A-1-7, vol. 7 (12), letter, 19 June 1849, James Cameron to James Price, CCL, pp. 2-3.

16 "The Chippewa Indians and the Mining Companies," *The Illustrated London News*, 15 September 1849, vol. 15, 180. Chute notes that part of Shinguacouse's speech to Elgin was reprinted in the *Montreal Gazette* ("A Century of Native Leadership," 244).

17 Macdonell to editor, *Toronto Patriot*, 19 December 1849.

18 *Toronto Patriot*, 19 December 1849. This incident refutes the arguments of the Wightmans that Macdonell was in control and caused the Mica Bay incident for his own reasons. Nancy and Robert Wightman, "The Mica Bay Affair: Conflict on the Upper-Lakes Mining Frontier, 1840-1850," *Ontario History* 83 (1991).

19 "The Indian Difficulties," *British Colonist*, 3 December 1849.

20 PAO, RG1-360-0-52 "Michipicoten Island," 1852-1853, letters, 12 January 1852, illegible to Allan Macdonell; and 29 January 1853, Macdonell to John Rolph, CCL.

21 Vidal/Anderson, Report, pp. 163136-67; Appendix A, pp. 163142-44 and 163128-89.

22 "The Indians on Lakes Huron and Superior," *British Colonist*, 16 November 1849, 3. Vidal/Anderson, Report, pp. 163143 and 163145.

23 "The Indian Troubles—Letter from Mr Allan Macdonell," *British Colonist*, 18 December 1849.

24 Vidal/Anderson, Report, Appendix C, pp. 163147-48.

25 Vidal/Anderson, Report, pp. 163129-31. At the time of the Mica Bay incident, Angus Macdonell was no longer a shareholder in the company, having divested himself of all shares in September. ("Quebec Mining Company's Office," *Toronto Patriot*, 9 March 1850). The *Patriot* does not state the status of Allan Macdonell or Wharton Metcalfe. But Nancy and Robert Wightman claim that both had also sold their shares in September ("The Mica Bay Affair," 200). NAC, RG10, vol. 612, letters, 12 November 1849, Rev Frederick O'Meara to Major Campbell, Civil Sec, pp. 393-97; 14 November 1849, Charles Thompson to Robert Baldwin, pp. 398-400; and "Disturbances at the Lake Superior Mines," *The Globe*, 23 November 1849.

26 Bonner likely did not relish the thought of having to deal with another large group of Ojibwa as he had to do when Peau-de-Chat and party came calling in July of 1849 (for Bonner's account see *Toronto Patriot*, 2 February 1850; Macdonell's account, *Toronto Patriot*, 19 December 1849).

27 NAC, RG10, vol. 612, letter, 16 November 1849, Anderson to Robert Baldwin, pp. 402-403. The Wightmans refer to this particular account by Anderson as "balanced." See also MR-BR, Anderson's Journal, 16 November, 24.

28 NAC, RG10, vol. 612, letter, 30 November 1849, Mr. Meredith Assisting Civil Secretary to Ironside, pp. 404-406; and vol. 572, 11 January 1850, Ironside to Meredith. The troops arrived late due to bad weather; see "The Troops to the Indian Country," *British Colonist*, 25 January 1850.

29 NAC, RG10, vol. 612, arrest warrant based on John Bonner's sworn statement to George Ironside, 3 December 1849, pp. 420-21. NAC, RG10, vol. 572, letter, 11 January 1850, Ironside to A.E. Meredith, Assistant Secretary, Knight, "Mica Bay Affair," 49. See also Robert Saunders, "John Beverley Robinson," 9 *DCB* pp. 668-78 for additional information. "The Proceedings Against the Indians," *British Colonist*, 14 December 1849; see also "The Indian Difficulty," *Montreal Pilot*, 27 December 1849.

30 NAC, RG1-360-0-61.1 "Montreal Mining Company," 1846-1851; letter, 31 December 1849, W.D. Cockburn, Secretary, MMC to CCL.

31 Such an outcome to the arrest and supposed upcoming trials was predicted by the *Toronto Patriot*, which believed the whole proceedings against the Ojibwa chiefs, the Métis, and the whites was a farce and a waste of "public money...resulting in a loss of public character wholly unjustifiable." See

"Indian Affairs," 31 May 1850, NAC, RG10, vol. 514, letters, 22 May 1851, Colonel Bruce to the AG; also vol. 572, 22 May 1851, Colonel Bruce "To Chiefs Shingwokoose and Neb-ena-goo-ling and to Pierre La Sage and to Charles Boyer." This pardon might explain why no trial records seem to exist. In 1846 he became chief commissioner of public works, a position he held until the entrenchment of Baldwin's Reform Party (Julia Jarvis "William Benjamin Robinson," *Dictionary of Canadian Biography*, vol. 10 [Toronto: University of Toronto Press, 1976], 622-24). Jarvis presents incorrect information regarding Mica Bay: on page 623 she states that the incident occurred in 1848 and that this led to the despatch of Vidal and Anderson. It was, however, the other way around: Mica Bay occurred in November 1849, only a few days *after* Vidal and Anderson had departed. Furthermore, their report was not presented to the government until 5 December 1849, almost a month *after* the Mica Bay affair. PAO, Jarvis-Powell Papers; letters 2 February 1843, Jarvis to father. Also J.B. Robinson Papers; 24 and two on the 25th of March 1847. Robinson relinquished this position so that he could sit in the legislature. His resignation was accepted on 27 July 1848. PAO, MSS Misc Coll 1848, no. 9, MU 2110, Archibald Campbell (Montreal Mining Company) to W.B. Robinson.

32 NAC, RG10, vol. 180, no. 4113, pp. 104186-104189, no. 31, OIC 8 January 1850, "Claim of Indians to the Lands on Lake Superior"; vol. 513, pp. 219-20, letter, 11 January 1850, Bruce to Robinson.

33 PAO, RG1-360-0-61.3 "Montreal Mining Company," 1856-1864, letter, 25 March 1850, Cockburn to Price. "Indian Difficulties to be Settled—Treaty to be Held—Mining Operations to be Renewed," *Lake Superior Journal*, 15 May 1850, 2.

34 Alexander Morris, *The Treaties of Canada with the Indians v. Belfords* (1880; reprint, Toronto: Clarke and Company, 1971), 17-18.

35 Morris, *The Treaties of Canada*, 18.

36 "British Justice," *Lake Superior Journal*, 8 November 1849, 2. Also "List of Mining Locations Granted on Lake Superior, 1846" (see Logan's Report to the Commissioner of Crown Lands, 1847) in Arthur, *Thunder Bay District*, 49-50. To date it has not been possible to obtain specific figures denoting either profit or production from the Lake Superior mines held by the Montreal Company to 1850. By 1850, that company alone paid the government at least £3750 or $15,000 in various fees. PAO, RG1-360-0-61.1 "Montreal Mining Company," 1846-1851. See "Statement shewing the payments made to the Crown Land Department by the Montreal Mining Company—On Lands on Lakes Huron and Superior," 16 September 1856. By 1870, the company lost about $400,000 and sold eighteen locations on Lake Superior to a group of Americans for $225,000. See Thomas Gibson, *Mining in Ontario* (Toronto: T.E. Bowman, 1937), 46. According to the 1895 report of the

Ontario Bureau of Mines, the Bruce Mines on Lake Huron produced three million dollars worth of copper between 1846 and 1876 (Gibson 122). Morris, *The Treaties of Canada*, 18-19.

37 Morrison, "The Robinson Treaties," 145.

38 Morris, *The Treaties of Canada*, 16.

39 Ibid.

40 PAO, RG1-360-0-61.2 "Montreal Mining Company," 1852-1857. See "Memo on a letter from the Secretary of the Montreal Mining Company dated 23 November 1847" (n.d.).

41 PAO, RG1-360-0-49 "Memorandum per Mining Locations Falling Within Indian Reserves"; see "Report relative to certain Mining Locations."

42 Robinson Treaties, 4.

43 Robinson Superior Treaty, 3; Robinson Huron Treaty, 4.

44 Morris, *The Treaties of Canada*, 17.

45 NAC, RG10, vol. 572, letters, 10 January 1850, Ironside to Bruce; and vol. 185, no. 4767, 27 December 1850, "W.B. Robinson on the alleged dissatisfaction of Chinguakonce with the late Treaty" to Bruce, pp. 107760-107763. Lise Hansen, "Research Report: The Anishinabek Land Claim and the Participation of the Indian People Living on the North Shore of Lake Superior in the Robinson Superior Treaty, 1850," Ontario Native Affairs Secretariat, 1985; regarding the independence of the presents from the Treaty, see p. 41, about the distance, see pp. 57-58 and 61.

46 Four 6,400, and one 340-acre mining locations were encompassed in the reserve. Vidal had surveyed these locations in 1847 and 1848. Shinguacouse was not alone. Many other mining locations were situated on land which the Ojibwa wished for themselves. Two fell within the Thessalon reserve; one in Mississaugi; two at Serpent River; two at Spanish River; and one at White Fish River. PAO, RG1-360-0-49, n.d. but at or after 1853. File: "Memorandum for Mining Locations Falling Within Indian Reserves." See, "Report relative to certain Mining Locations upon Lake Huron and its vicinity assigned to the Locatees previously to the Treaty of 9 September 1850 with the Lake Huron and other Indians..." (n.p.), author unknown.

47 Rhonda Telford, "The Nefarious and Far-Ranging Interests of Indian Agent and Surveyor John William Keating, 1837 to 1869," in *Papers of the 28th Algonkian Conference*, ed. David H. Pentland (Winnipeg: University of Manitoba, 1997).

48 Chute, "A Century of Native Leadership," 283-85. PAO, RG1-360-0-52 "Michipicoten Island" 1852-1853, letter, 29 January 1853, Macdonell to John Rolph, CCL. Macdonell's petition was denied. RG1-360-0-71 "Reports to Executive Council" 1845-1864. See "Extract from a Report of a Committee of the Hon the Executive Council on Land Applications, dated 7 April 1853

approved by His Excellency the Governor General in Council on the 19th of the same month."

49 PAO, RG1-360-0-41, "List of Mining Locations on the North Shores of Lakes Huron and Superior for which patents have been issued," n.d. The Bonner family continued to hold this location as late as 1898-99 and possibly longer. RG1-273-3-9.1 "Island of Michipicoten."

50 Knight, "Mica Bay Affair," 58. Knight credits this information to Chaput who in turn obtained it from the *Lake Superior Mining Journal*. I was not able to obtain a copy of this. I attempted to find parallel accounts in Canadian newspapers: *British Colonist, Globe, Toronto Patriot*, and the *Montreal Pilot*. The incident was not reported there, nor in the correspondence of the Manitowaning Superintendency.

51 Even in this context, "ownership" may have meant something more like "stewardship" or "guardianship."

CHAPTER 8

1 This chapter is part of a continuing project in which Michael Ripmeester and I are engaged concerning the cultural history of the Alderville First Nation. For previous explorations of some of the ideas here, see Brian S. Osborne and Michael Ripmeester, "Kingston, Bedford, Grape Island, Alnwick: The Odyssey of the Kingston Mississauga," *Historic Kingston* 43, (1995): 83-111; "The Mississaugas between Two Worlds: Strategic Adjustments to Changing Landscapes of Power," *The Canadian Journal of Native Studies* 17, no. 2 (1997): 259-91; Brian S. Osborne and D. Swainson, *Kingston: Building on the Past* (Westport: Butternut, 1988); Michael Ripmeester, "'It is Scarcely to be Believed...': the Mississauga Indians and the Grape Island Mission, 1826-1836," *The Canadian Geographer* 39, no. 2 (1995): 157-68.

2 For "landmarks" see Maurice Halbwachs, *The Collective Memory* (New York: Harper and Row, 1980). For "lieux de mémoire," see Pierre Nora, ed., *Realms of Memory: The Construction of the French Past*, Vol. 1, *Conflicts and Divisions* (New York: Columbia University Press, 1996); *Realms of Memory*, Vol. 2, *Traditions* (New York: Columbia University Press, 1997): and *Realms of Memory*, Vol. 3, *Symbols* (New York: Columbia University Press, 1998). In the context of this Colloquium, the 1988 and 1989 barricades on Red Squirrel Road erected by the Teme-Augama Anishnabai focused attention on N'Daki Menan as a "landmark" of protest and a "lieux de mémoire" for those involved.

3 For more on art as historical document, see Brian S. Osborne, "The Artist as Historical Commentator," *Archivaria* 17 (1983-84): 41-59.

4 *Mississagua Indians in Canada*, by Captn. B. Hall, R.N. in Jim Burant, *Friendly Spies on the Northern Tour: The Sketches of Henry Byam Martin* (Ottawa: Sup-

plies and Services, 1982), 53. See also Daniel Francis, *The Imaginary Indian: The Image of the Indian in Canadian Culture* (Vancouver: Pulp, 1992).

5 "The Town of Kingston and its Fortifications, 1796," (NAC). For more on the role of power in the production of maps, see J.B. Harley, "Maps, Knowledge and Power," in *The Iconography of Landscape*, ed. D. Cosgrove and S. Daniels (Cambridge: Cambridge University Press, 1988), 227-312; "Deconstructing the Map," in *Writing Worlds: Discourse, Text and Metaphor in the Representation of Landscape*, ed. T. Barnes and J. Duncan (London: Routledge, 1992), 231-47; "Rereading Maps of the Columbian Encounter," *Annals of the Association of American Geographers* 82, no. 4 (1992): 522-42.

6 James C. Scott, *Weapons of the Weak: Everyday Forms of Peasant Resistance* (New Haven: Yale University Press, 1985); James C. Scott, *Domination and the Arts of Resistance: Hidden Transcripts* (New Haven: Yale University Press, 1990).

7 Scott, *Weapons*, xiii.

8 Steve Pile and Michael Keith, eds., *Geographies of Resistance* (New York: Routledge, 1997), xi.

9 Cresswell, Tim, *In Place/Out of Place: Geography, Ideology, and Transgression* (Minneapolis: University of Minnesota Press, 1996), 23.

10 Steve Pile, "Introduction: Opposition, Political Identities and Spaces of Resistance," in *Geographies of Resistance*, ed. Pile and Keith, 3.

11 The leading scholar on Mississauga cultural history is Donald B. Smith. See Donald B. Smith, "Who are the Mississauga?" *Ontario History* no. 67 (1975): 211-22; "The Dispossession of the Mississauga Indians," *Ontario History* no. 73 (1981): 40-53; and *Sacred Feathers: The Reverend Peter Jones (Kakkewaquonaby) and the Mississauga Indians* (Toronto: University of Toronto Press, 1987), 17. See also Peter Schmalz, *The Ojibwa of Southern Ontario* (Toronto: University of Toronto Press, 1991). See also Michael Ripmeester, "Vision Quests into Sight Lines: Negotiating the Place of the Mississaugas in South-Eastern Ontario, 1700-1876" (Ph.D. diss., Queen's University, 1995).

12 Chief Robert Paudash, "The Coming of the Mississaga," *Ontario Historical Society, Papers and Records* 6 (1905): 7-11.

13 R. White, *The Middle Ground: Indians, Empires, and Republics in the Great Lakes Region, 1650-1815* (Cambridge: Cambridge University Press, 1991); J.S. Sosin, *Whitehall and the Wilderness: The Middle West in British Colonial Policy, 1760-1775* (Lincoln: University of Nebraska Press, 1961).

14 Not only did the 1819/1822 cessions of lands allow Euro-Canadian settlement and the construction of the Rideau waterway, the waterway also effected a major hydrological change in the heart of the Mississauga homeland. Rivers were diverted, lakes formed, lands drowned, and fauna and flora habitats modified. The degree to which this also influenced the Aboriginal peoples of the day has not received much attention.

15 Much of what follows is derived from several sources: George Copway, *The Traditional History and Characteristic Sketches of the Ojibway Nation* (1851; reprint, Toronto: Coles, 1972); Peter Jones, *The Life and Journals of Kah-ke-wa-quo-na-by (Reverend Peter Jones) Wesleyan Methodist Missionary* (Toronto: A. Green, 1860); A.D. McMillan, *Native Peoples and Cultures of Canada: An Anthropological Overview* (Vancouver: Douglas and McIntyre, 1988); R. Orr, "The Mississaugas," *Annual Archaeological Report. Appendix to the Report of the Minister of Education* (Toronto: A.T. Wilgress, 1915); C. Vecsey, *Traditional Ojibwa Religion and Its Historical Changes* (Philadelphia: American Philosophical Society, 1983); William W. Warren, *History of the Ojibway People* (St. Paul, MN: Minnesota Historical Society, 1984). See also, Smith, *Sacred Feathers*.

16 Jones, *Life and Journals*, 108.

17 Smith, *Sacred Feathers*, 6-8; Vecsey, *Traditional Ojibwa*, 78-79. Totems included Eagle, Reindeer, Otter, Bear, Buffalo, Beaver, Catfish, Pike, Birchbark, White Oak, Bear's Liver.

18 These treaties and purchases have proven to be problematic in recent years with claims that these lands were also traditional hunting grounds—"homelands"—for the Lake of Two Mountains (Oka) Algonquian peoples.

19 F.A.F. La Rochefoucault-Liancourt, *Travels through the United States, the Country of the Iroquois and Upper Canada in the Years 1795, 1796, & 1797* (London: R. Phillips, 1799), 292; Isaac Weld, *Travels through the States and the Provinces of Upper and Lower Canada during the Years 1794, 1796, & 1797* (London: Stockdale, 1807), 2: 85-86.

20 La Rouchfoucault-Liancourt, *Travels*.

21 Mary Quayle Innis, ed., *Mrs. Simcoe's Diary* (Toronto: Macmillan, 1965), 72.

22 Queen's University Archives, Barnabus Bidwell Papers, Marshall S. Bidwell of Stockbridge to Barnabus Bidwell, 24 April 1816.

23 *Christian Advocate and Journal* 10, no. 43 (17 June 1836): 179.

24 Ripmeester, "Vision Quests," 185.

25 For Aboriginal attitudes to the missionary project that relate to what follows, see James P. Ronda, "'We are well as we are': An Indian Critique of Seventeenth-Century Christian Missions," *William and Mary Quarterly* 34 (1977): 66-82; Jean-Guy Goulet, "Religious Dualism among Athapaskan Catholics," *Canadian Journal of Anthropology* 3, no. 1 (1982): 1-18. More particularly, see Jean-Guy Goulet, *Ways of Knowing: Experience, Knowledge, and Power among the Dene Tha* (Lincoln: University of Nebraska Press, 1998).

26 G.G. Findlay and W.W. Holdsworth, *The History of the Wesleyan Methodist Missionary Society* (London: Epworth Press, 1921); J. Comaroff and J. Comaroff, *Of Revelation and Revolution: Christianity, Colonization, and Consciousness in South Africa*, Vol. 1 (Chicago: University of Chicago Press, 1991), 43-48; J. Comaroff and J. Comaroff, *Ethnography and the Historical Imagination* (Boul-

der: Westview Press, 1992); Robert Coleman, "Nothing to do but to save souls": John Wesley's Charge to His Preachers (Grand Rapids: Francis Asbury, 1990), 31-32.

27 Coleman, *Nothing to do,* chap. 1.

28 John Webster Grant, *A Profusion of Spires: Religion in Nineteenth Century Ontario* (Toronto: University of Toronto Press, 1989), 109; F.A. Norwood, "The Invisible American—Methodism and the Indian," *Methodist History* 8, no. 2 (1970); Bruce D. Forbes, "And Obey God, etc.: Methodism and American Indians," *Methodist History* 23, no. 1 (1984): 17; Comaroff and Comaroff, *Of Revelation,* 60-80. It is important to remember, however, that the efforts of the Methodists were not sanctioned by the Crown or colonial administration. The memory of the American Revolution and the War of 1812, together with the American origins of many Methodists in the 1820s, rendered them a threat to the established church and society of Upper Canada. They were seen as purveyors of dangerous republican ideas and—in the words of one somewhat intemperate commentator—as "canting American scoundrels"!

29 For more on the Grape Island experience, see Osborne and Ripmeester, "Kingston, Bedford," "The Mississaugas," and Ripmeester, "It is scarcely," and "Vision Quests."

30 *Christian Advocate and Journal* 3, no. 14 (5 December 1828): 54.

31 *Christian Guardian* 1, no. 13 (13 February 1830): 98-99.

32 Ibid.

33 Jones, *Life and Journals,* 102-103, 280-86. See 284-86 for references to the inspection of homes and the bestowing of praise or criticism.

34 This out-reach missionary role of Grape Island is an important element of my ongoing research with Michael Ripmeester.

35 *Christian Advocate and Journal* 5, no. 27 (4 March 1831): 105.

36 *Christian Advocate and Journal* 1, no. 51 (24 August 1827): 201; *Christian Guardian* 2, no. 2 (27 November 1830): 6.

37 *Christian Advocate and Journal* 3, no. 14 (5 December 1828): 54.

38 *Methodist Magazine,* October 1826, 395.

39 Jones, *Life and Journals,* 71-82.

40 Ibid., 139.

41 See Comaroff and Comaroff, *Of Revelation,* 219.

42 Vecsey, *Traditional Ojibwa,* 154-59, 164-68.

43 Ibid., 54.

44 See Comaroff and Comaroff, *Of Revelation,* 244.

45 Jones, *Life and Journals,* 184.

46 *Christian Advocate and Journal* 10, no. 43 (17 June, 1826): 170.

47 Jones, *Life and Journals,* 54.

48 Smith, *Sacred Feathers,* 74-76.

49 National Archives of Canada (NAC), RG10, Minutes of a Council held at the Post at York, 30 January 1828, vol. 791, pp. 7195-7197, C-13499.

50 Jones, *Life and Journals*, 84, 106-108; NAC, RG10, Paudash Papers, "Petition of the Mississauga Nations of Indians residing at the River Credit, Lake Simcoe, Rice Lake, Grape Island, Mud Lake, Colborne, River Credit," 11 February 1832.

51 *Christian Guardian* 4, no. 46 (25 September 1833): 182-83.

52 NAC, RG10, Comm. G. Clarke to Col. Givins, Kingston, 9 May 1832, vol. 51, pp. 56295-6, C-11016.

53 Queen's University Archives, Miscellaneous, "Petition to Sir John Colborne, Lieutenant Governor, from Gananoque Mississaugas."

54 NAC, RG10, "Major General Darling to Earl Dalhousie," vol. 792, pp. 7425-7426A, C-13499.

55 NAC, RG10, J.B. Clench to Gen. Clarke, Kingston, 8 September 1832, vol. 51, pp. 56752-3, C-11017.

56 NAC, RG10, J.B. Clench to Col. Givins, Kingston, 10 September 1832, vol. 51, pp. 56755-6, C-11017.

57 *Methodist Magazine* 10, no. 2 (February 1827): 83; *Methodist Magazine* 11, no. 3 (March 1828): 114; *Methodist Magazine* 11, no. 6 (June 1828): 229.

58 "Canada—the Rideau Canal," from a correspondent to the *London Sun*, a supplement to the *Montreal Gazette*, 27 June 1833.

59 *Christian Guardian*, September 1833.

60 NAC, RG10, W. Macaulay to Col. J. Givins, Kingston, 11 July 1831, vol. 48, pp. 54381-3.

61 NAC, RG10, W. Chewitt to J. Givins, York, 28 July 1831, vol. 48, pp. 55023-24, C-11015; M. Macaulay to J. Givins, Kingston, 22 July 1831, vol. 48, pp. 55025-27, C-11015.

62 NAC, RG10, S'ltrn. Givens to Col. J. Givins, Richmond and Napanee, 25 May 1831, vol. 48, pp. 55025-27, C-11015.

63 How this trauma and these strategies were represented over the next 160 years of reservation life at Alnwick becomes a natural progression of this analysis. This question is central to our ongoing research with the Alderville First Nation.

CHAPTER 9

1 See, for example, Bruce Trigger, "Ethnohistory: The Unfinished Edifice," *Ethnohistory* 33, no. 3 (1986): 253-67; Calvin Martin, "Ethnohistory: A Better Way to Write Indian History," *Western Historical Quarterly* 9, no. 1 (1978): 41-56; Raymond Fogelson, "The Ethnohistory of Events and Nonevents," *Ethnohistory* 36, no. 2 (1989): 131-47.

2 See Michel Foucault, *Power/Knowledge: Selected Interviews and Writings 1972-1977*, ed. C. Gordon, (New York: Pantheon 1989); H. Harootunian, "Foucault, Genealogy, History: The Pursuit of Otherness," in *After Foucault: Humanistic Knowledge, Post-Modern Challenges*, ed. J. Arac (London: Rutgers University Press, 1988), 110-37.

3 Fogelson, "The Ethnohistory of Events and Nonevents."

4 Marshall Sahlins, "Goodbye to *Tristes Tropes*: Ethnography in the Context of Modern World History," *Journal of Modern World History* 65 (1993): 1-25.

5 Gavin Smith, "Pandora's History: Central Peruvian Peasants and the Recovering of the Past," in *Between History and Histories: The Making of Silences and Commemorations*, ed. Gerald Sider and Gavin Smith (Toronto: University of Toronto Press, 1997).

6 James Scott, *Domination and the Arts of Resistance: Hidden Transcripts* (New Haven: Yale University Press, 1990).

7 See James Scott, *Weapons of the Weak: Everyday Forms of Peasant Resistance* (New Haven: Yale University Press, 1985). For a treatment of everyday forms of resistance as inconsequential, see Gerald Sider, "Against Experience: The Struggles for History, Tradition, and Hope among a Native American People," in *Between History and Histories*, ed. Sider and Smith.

8 Anja Nygren, "Struggle over Meanings: Reconstruction of Indigenous Mythology, Cultural Identity, and Social Representation," *Ethnohistory* 45, no. 1 (1998): 31-63; Lynette Turner, "Consuming Colonialism," *Critique of Anthropology* 15, no. 2 (1995): 203-12.

9 Foucault, *Power/Knowledge*, 49-50.

10 James Scott, *Domination and the Arts of Resistance*. See also Ronald Wendt, "Answers to the Gaze: A Genealogical Poaching of Resistances," *Quarterly Journal of Speech* 82 (1996): 251-73.

11 See Jon Simons, *Foucault and the Political* (London and New York: Routledge, 1995); Leslie Paul Thiele, "The Agony of Politics: the Nietzschean Roots of Foucault's Thought," *American Political Science Review* 84, no. 3 (1990): 907-25; Wendt, "Answers to the Gaze."

12 See Smith, "Pandora's Histories"; Scott, *Domination and the Arts of Resistance*.

13 Gayatri Chakravorty Spivak, "Can the Subaltern Speak?" in *Marxism and the Interpretation of Culture*, ed. C. Nelson and L. Grossberg (Urbana: University of Illinois Press, 1988).

14 Clifford Geertz, *Works and Lives: The Anthropologist as Author* (Stanford: Stanford University Press, 1988), 135

15 See James Scott, "Everyday Forms of Peasant Resistance," in *Everyday Forms of Peasant Resistance*, ed. J. Scott and B.J. Tria Kerkvliet (Totowa: Frank Cass, 1986), 22-31.

16 See A. Appadurai, "Putting Hierarchy in Its Place," in *Rereading Cultural Anthropology*, ed. G. Marcus (Durham: Duke University Press, 1992) 34-47.

17 Geertz, *Works and Lives*.

18 Inga Clendinnen, *Ambivalent Conquests: Maya and Spaniard in Yucatan, 1517–1570* (Cambridge: Cambridge University Press, 1987), xi.

19 See Yi-Fu Tuan, *Morality and Imagination: Paradoxes of Progress* (Madison: University of Madison Press, 1989), x.

20 Michael Ripmeester, "Vision Quests into Sight Lines: Negotiating the Place of the Mississaugas in South-eastern Ontario, 1700-1876" (Ph.D. diss., Queen's University, 1995); Michael Ripmeester, "'It is scarcely to be believed...': The Mississauga Indians and the Grape Island Mission, 1826-1836," *The Canadian Geographer* 39 (1995): 157-68; B. Osborne and M. Ripmeester, "The Mississaugas between Two Worlds: Strategic Adjustments to Landscapes of Power," *Canadian Journal of Native Studies* 17, no. 2 (1997): 259-91.

21 For more on the agricultural village and its functioning, see Ripmeester, "Vision Quests into Sight Lines"; "It is scarcely to be believed..."; and Osborne and Ripmeester, "The Mississaugas between Two Worlds."

22 For more on the use of spatial organization in reform projects, see Michel Foucault, *Discipline and Punish: The Birth of the Prison* (New York: Vintage, 1979); Chris Philo, "'Enough to Drive One Mad:' The Organization of the Space in Nineteenth Century Lunatic Asylums," in *The Power of Geography: How Territory Shapes Social Life*, ed. Jennifer Wolch and Michael Dear (London: Unwin Hyman, 1989); Timothy Mitchell, *Colonising Egypt* (Berkeley: University of California Press, 1991).

23 For a general discussion of these principles, see John Ransom, *Foucault's Politics* (Durham and London: Duke University Press, 1997) and John and Jean Comaroff, *Of Revelation and Revolution: Christianity, Colonization, and Consciousness in South Africa*, Vol. 1 (Chicago: University of Chicago Press, 1991).

24 John Sunday to Col. S.P. Jarvis, Alderville, 2 April 1844, Records Relating to Indian Affairs (RG10) Government Archives Division National Archvies of Canada, vol. 138, p. 79187, C-1148 (hereafter cited as NAC).

25 John Sunday, John Simpson, et al. to T.G. Anderson, Alnwick, 26 April 1858, NAC, RG10, vol. 411, p. 6, C-9616.

26 Gordon Taylor, *The Mississauga Indians of Eastern Ontario* (M.A. thesis, Queen's University, 1981), 101-108.

27 The personal census for Alnwick in 1871 is lost.

28 Canada, *Report of the Special Commissioners to Investigate Indian Affairs in Canada* (Toronto: Stewart Derbishire and George Desbarats, 1858), Appendix 29, 278-79.

29 John Sunday Jr. to W. Bartlett, Alnwick, 31 August 1866, NAC, RG10, vol. 414, p. 701, C-9618; W. Bartlett to William Spragge, Toronto, 7 September 1865, NAC, RG10, vol. 549, p. 69, C-13359; Alnwick Indians to W. Bartlett, Alnwick,

30 November 1870; NAC, RG10, vol. 414, p. 1049-1050, C-9619; Alnwick Indians to W. Bartlett, Alnwick, 3 March 1873, NAC, RG10, vol. 414, p. 1101, C-9619.

30 W.R. Bartlett to Jacob Storm, Toronto, 17 February 1868, NAC, RG10, vol. 551, p. 290, C-13360.

31 Petition of the Alnwick Indians to His Excellency Lord Monck, Governor-General of Canada, Alnwick, 20 September 1866, NAC, RG10, vol. 414, pp. 770-772, C-9618.

32 Ibid.

33 The following discussion relies heavily upon Scott, *Domination and the Arts of Resistance*, particularly chapter 4.

34 The census for 1871 reports that the fur trade brought in about $2,300. Recorded timber sales were valued at $1,284. The only other product for which dollar values are recorded are the products of the orchard for 1861. The value of these products was $85 (Census of Canada, Agriculture, 1861, 1871; *Sessional Papers*, no. 8, 8[7], 1875), 21-22.

35 K. Kelly, "Wheat Farming in Mid-Nineteenth-Century Ontario," *The Canadian Geographer* 15, no. 2 (1971): 107-108.

36 Kenneth George, "Dark Trembling: Ethnographic Notes on Secrecy and Concealment in Highland Sulawesi," *Anthropological Quarterly* 66, no. 4 (1993): 230-39.

37 Gilbert Herdt, "Secret Societies and Secret Collectives," *Oceania* 60 (1990): 360-81.

38 For more on Bedford Township, see Ripmeester, "Vision Quests into Sight Lines"; Ripmeester, "It is scarcely to be believed..."; Ripmeester and Osborne, "The Mississaugas between Two Worlds."

39 See, for example, Keith Basso, "'Speaking with Names': Language and Landscape among the Western Apache," in *Rereading Cultural Anthropology*, ed. George Marcus (Durham: Duke University Press, 1992), H. Kuper, "The Language of Sites in the Politics of Space," *American Anthropologist* 74, no. 3 (1972): 411-25; Ted Swedenburg, *Memories of Revolt: The 1936-1939 Rebellion and the Palestinian National Past* (Minneapolis and London: University of Minnesota Press, 1995); James Fentress and Chris Wickham, *Social Memory: New Perspectives on the Past* (Oxford and Cambridge: Blackwell, 1992).

40 Herdt, "Secret Societies and Secret Collectives."

41 George, "Dark Tremblings," 235.

42 See, for example: Anastasia Shkilnyk, *Poison Stronger than Love: The Destruction of an Ojibwa Community* (New Haven: Yale University Press, 1985); Geoffrey York, *The Dispossessed* (London: Vintage U.K., 1990); H. Robertson, *Reservations Are for Indians* (Toronto: James Lewis and Samuel, 1970); K. Erikson and C. Vecsey, "A Report to the People of Grassy Narrows," *American Indian Environments: Ecological Issues in Native American History* (Syra-

cuse: Syracuse University Press, 1980); J. Timpson, S. McKay, S. Kakegamic, et al. "Depression in a Native Canadian in Northwestern Ontario: Sadness or Spiritual Illness," *Canada's Mental Health* 36, nos. 2/3 (1988): 5-8.

43 For a discussion of substance abuse as an attempt to escape the rigours of everyday life, see Stanley Cohen and Laurie Taylor, *Escape Attempts: The Theory and Practice of Resistance to Everyday Life* (New York: Routledge, 1992), especially chapter 5.

44 See, for example, Heidi Nast and Steve Pile, eds., *Places through the Body* (London and New York: Routledge, 1998).

45 See Peter Stallybrass and Allan White, *The Politics and Poetics of Transgression* (Ithaca: Cornell University Press, 1986); B. Babcock, *The Reversible World: Symbolic Inversion in Art and Society* (Ithaca: Cornell University Press, 1978), 263-64.

46 John Sunday to T.G. Anderson, Alnwick, 25 November 1846, NAC, RG10, vol. 410, p. 135-36, C-9616; Chiefs of Alnwick to W.R. Bartlett, Alnwick, 19 October 1858, NAC, RG10, vol. 414, p. 193-94, C-9618.

47 For more on these policies, see J.R. Miller, *Skyscrapers Hide the Heavens: A History of Indian-White Relations in Canada* (Toronto: University of Toronto Press, 1991) and J. Tobias, "Protection, Civilization, Assimiliation: An Outline History of Canada's Indian Policy," in *Sweet Promises: a Reader on Indian—White Relations in Canada*, ed. J.R. Miller (Toronto: University of Toronto Press, 1991).

48 Patricia Mann, *Micro-Politics: Agency in a Postfeminist Era* (Minneapolis and London: University of Minnesota Press, 1994); Michel de Certeau, *The Practice of Everyday Life* (Berkeley: University of California Press, 1984).

49 See also, Deborah Reed-Danahay, "Talking about Resistance: Ethnography and Theory in Rural France," *Anthropological Quarterly* 66, no. 4 (1993): 221-29; Wendt, "Answers to the Gaze."

50 De Certeau, *The Practice of Everyday Life*, 18.

51 See David Butz and Michael Ripmeester, "Finding Space for Resistant Subcultures," *Invisible Cultures: An Electronic Journal for Visual Studies* no. 2 (1999): 1-16 <http://www.rochester.edu./in_visible_culture>; Stallybrass and White, *The Politics and Poetics of Transgression*, 58. Several authors point out, however, that extrication from a particular exercise of power can lead to unanticipated entanglement in others. See Lila Abu-Lughod, "The Romance of Resistance: Tracing Transformations of Power through Bedouin Women," *American Ethnologist* 17, no. 1 (1990): 41-55; Simons, *Foucault and the Political*.

52 See Foucault, *Discipline and Punish*.

53 See David Butz and Michael Ripmeester, "Making Space for Resistant Subcultures"; Steve Pile and Michael Keith, eds., *Geographies of Resistance* (London and New York: Routledge, 1997); Reed-Danahay, "Talking about

Resistance"; de Certeau, *The Practice of Everyday Life*; Mona Domosh, "Those Gorgeous Incongruities: Polite Politics and Public Space on the Streets of Nineteenth-Century New York City," *Annals of the Association of American Geographers* 88, no. 2 (1998): 209-26.

54 De Certeau, *The Practice of Everyday Life*, 18.

55 W.R. Bartlett to C. Walcot, Toronto, 18 February 1862, NAC, RG10, vol. 546, p. 223, C-13358.

56 John Snake, Robert Wilkins, James Smoke, and John Paul to W. Bartlett, Alnwick, January, 1860, NAC, RG10, vol. 414, p. 323, C-9618.

57 See Scott, *Domination and the Arts of Resistance*, 203; John D. Rogers, "Cultural and Social Resistance: Gambling in Colonial Sri Lanka," in *Contesting Power: Resistance and Everyday Social Relations in South Asia*, ed. D. Haynes and G. Prakash (Berkeley: University of California Press, 1991).

58 Wesleyan Methodist Missionary Society (London) Archive, North America, Synod Minutes, Box 90, Fiche 77, "Report for 1841." School of Oriental and African Studies, University of London. Hereafter cited as WMMS.

59 WMMS, Box 90, no. 81, "Report for 1846."

60 Methodist Episcopal Church Society, *Annual Reports*, 1859-1860 and 1876-1877.

61 Methodist Episcopal Church Society, *Annual Reports*, 1865-1866.

62 See for example, John S. Milloy, *"A National Crime": The Canadian Government and the Residential School System* (Winnipeg: University of Manitoba Press, 1999); Celia Haig-Brown, *Resistance and Renewal: Surviving the Indian Residential School* (Vancouver: Tillicum Library, 1988).

63 *Missionary Notices*, December 1852, 188.

64 T.G. Anderson, Appendix 29, *Canada, Report of the Special Commissioners to Investigate Indian Affairs in Canada* (Toronto: Steward Derbishier and George Desbarats) 1858, p. 251.

65 Col. R. Bruce to T.G. Anderson, Quebec, 27 May 1853, NAC, RG10, vol. 411, p. 272-73, C-9616.

66 Col. R. Bruce to Rev. E. Wood, Quebec, 19 June 1852, NAC, RG10, vol. 411, p. 464-67, C-1916.

67 W.R. Bartlett to William Spragge, Toronto, 10 February 1864, NAC, RG10, vol. 547, p. 585-88, C-13359.

68 W.R. Bartlett to P. Pennefather, Toronto, 4 December 1860, NAC, RG10, vol. 545, p. 230, C-13358.

69 W.R. Bartlett to R. Pennefather, Toronto, 15 December 1858, NAC, RG10, vol. 544, p. 105-106, C-13357.

70 Rev. T. Hurlburt to T.G. Anderson, Alnwick, 19 November 1856, NAC, RG10, vol. 412, p. 32-33, C-9617.

71 Rev. T. Hurlburt to T.G. Anderson, Alnwick, 31 March and 1 April 1858, NAC, RG10, vol. 412, p. 5-10, C-9617.

72 The following discussion is based upon Haig-Brown, *Resistance and Renewal*, 70-71. Haig-Brown suggests that the skills learned in the schools were intended to prompt dissatisfaction with the parents' way of life.

73 Rev. T. Hurlburt to T.G. Anderson, Alnwick, 31 March and 1 April 1858, NAC, RG10, vol. 412, p. 5-10, C-9617.

74 On the continued preservation and protection of Native cultures, see David McNab, *Circles of Time: Aboriginal Land Rights and Resistance in Ontario* (Waterloo: Wilfrid Laurier University Press, 1999).

CHAPTER 10

1 Situated where the Canadian National rail line running through Horne-payne then north of Lake Nipissing intersects with the local stretch of the Trans-Canada Highway (built during World War II), the predominately Franco-Ontarian town of Longlac (population approximately 1,800) began as a North West Company trading post before being incorporated into the Hudson's Bay Company system; A.J. Ray, "The Hudson's Bay Company and Native People," *Handbook of North American Indians*, vol. 4, *History of Indian-White Relations*, ed. Wilcomb Washburn (Washington DC: Smithsonian Institution, 1988), 338.

2 Anthony Hall, "Treaties, Trains, and Troubled National Dreams: Reflections on the Indian Summer in Northern Ontario, 1990," *Law, Society, and the State: Essays in Modern Legal History*, ed. L.A. Knafla and S. Binnie (Toronto: University of Toronto Press, 1995).

3 As of 1991, of all 21,356 Treaty 9 "Indians," 13,952 lived on their reserves; Government of Canada, Royal Commission on Aboriginal Peoples, *Report* (Ottawa: Minister of Supply and Services, 1996), 1:161, table 6.1. As of 1998, of the 702 people on the Ginoogaming band list, only 263 (plus 25 non-members) lived there; *Ginoogaming First Nation: Community Information Book, 1998* (Longlac, ON: Ginoogaming First Nation, 1998), 5. Some people historically associated with Ginoogaming have never lived there, but rather north around Aroland and east around Hornepayne; see Paul Driben, *Aroland is Our Home: An Incomplete Victory in Applied Anthropology* (New York: AMS Press, 1986), 28.

4 As of the early 1990s, nearly 36 percent of Ginoogaming enrollees were "C-31s"; S. Clatworthy and A.H. Smith, "Population Implications of the 1985 Amendments to the Indian Act: Final Report" (Winnipeg and Perth: Four Directions Consulting and Living Dimensions, 1992), 84.

5 D.C. Scott, "The Last of the Indian Treaties," *Scribners* 40 (November 1906): 578.

6 James Morrison, *Treaty Research Report: Treaty 9 (1905-06), The James Bay Treaty* (Ottawa: INAC Treaties and Historical Research Centre, 1986), 17.

7 Peter Kulchyski, ed. "St. Catherine's Milling," in *Unjust Relations: Aboriginal Rights in Canadian Courts* (Toronto: Oxford University Press, 1994), 21.

8 E.B. Titley, *A Narrow Vision: Duncan Campbell Scott and the Administration of Indian Affairs in Canada* (Vancouver: UBC Press, 1986), 66. For example, although a doctor accompanied the commissioners in their travels, unlike several of its precursors, Treaty 9 contained no mention of a "medicine chest."

9 According to the James Bay Treaty (para. 12) this was "with a view to show the satisfaction of His Majesty with the behavior and good conduct of His Indians, and in extinguishment of all their past claims."

10 Titley, *A Narrow Vision*, 66.

11 Government of Canada, *The James Bay Treaty* (Ottawa: Queen's Printer, 1964), 11.

12 Robert White-Harvey, "Reservation Geography and the Restoration of Native Self-Government," *Dalhousie Law Journal* 17, no. 2 (1994): 587.

13 By contrast, the size of neighbouring Long Lake no. 58 First Nation is only one pitiful square mile; Hall, "Treaties, Trains, and Troubled National Dreams," 290.

14 J.S. Long, "'No Basis for Argument': The Signing of Treaty 9 in Northern Ontario, 1905-06," *Native Studies Review* 5, no. 2 (1989): 33.

15 Survey by J. Dobie, Department of Indian Affairs Land Registry Office, Reserve General Register.

16 "The Ogoki Saga," *Inland Seas* 4, no. 1 (1948): 15.

17 Karl Froschauer, *White Gold: Hydroelectric Power in Canada* (Vancouver: UBC Press, 1999).

18 W.T. Easterbrook and Hugh G.J. Aitken, *Canadian Economic History* (Toronto: University of Toronto Press, 1958), 524.

19 Ontario Hydro, *The Gifts of Nature: The Story of Electricity at Work in the Province of Ontario* (Toronto: Ontario Hydro, 1961), 28.

20 A.W.G. Wilson, *Geology of the Nipigon Basin, Ontario* (Ottawa: Dept. of Mines, Geological Survey Branch Memoir no. 1, 1910), 145.

21 G.W. Kyte, *Organization and Work of the International Joint Commission* (Ottawa: J.O. Patenaude, 1937), 3.

22 "The Ogoki Saga," 15.

23 See International Joint Commission, *Correspondence and Documents relating to the St. Lawrence Deep Waterway Treaty 1932, Niagara Convention 1929, and Ogoki River and Kenogami River (Long Lake) Projects and Export of Electrical Power* (Ottawa: J.O. Patenaude, 1938).

24 In 1932, it amounted to only about 425,300 tons. By 1939 exports to the US recovered to just over 637,950 tons (Easterbrook and Aitken, *Canadian Economic History*, 540).

25 Rolf Knight, *Indians At Work* (Vancouver: New Star, 1978), 160; Morris Zaslow, *The Northward Expansion of Canada, 1914-67* (Toronto: McClelland and Stewart, 1988), 153, 171.

26 Government of Ontario, Order-in-Council of 8 May 1937.

27 Government of Canada, Order-in-Council of 2 March 1943.

28 American Society of Civil Engineers (ASCE), "Diversion of Water from the Albany River Watershed to the Great Lakes Basin: Ogoki Diversion/Long Lake Diversion" (N.p.: ESCE, mimeo., 1946), 10-12. The paper industry had grown rapidly when, during the second half of the nineteenth century, methods using wood pulp rather than textile fibres were developed. Thereafter what the industry required was cheap pulp and plenty of low-cost energy to operate its mixing vats and pressing mills. Water was the answer because it both delivered logs to the mills and generated the electricity to run them.

29 D.M. Rosenberg, "The Environmental Assessment of Hydroelectric Impoundments and Diversions in Canada," *Canadian Aquatic Resources*, ed. M.C. Healey and R.R. Wallace (Ottawa: Fisheries and Oceans Canada, 1987), 86-88.

30 ASCE, "Diversion," 12.

31 Government of Ontario, *Report of Department of Lands and Forests for 1938* (Toronto: Government Printer, 1939), appendix 14.

32 Hydro Electric Power Commission, memo of 22 October1940.

33 Ginoogaming First Nation Claim 2 (1996), para. 17, and ASCE, "Diversions," 11.

34 Text with MNR map of Long Lake.

35 Rosenberg, "The Environmental Assessment," 71.

36 Fikret Berkes, "The Intrinsic Difficulty of Predicting Impacts: Lessons from the James Bay Hydro Project," *Environmental Impact Assessment Reports* 8, no. 3 (1988), 207-208.

37 International Joint Commission, *Correspondence Relating to Kenogami River (Long Lake) Project and Export of Electrical Power* (Ottawa: J.O. Patenaude, 1938), 11-13.

38 Easterbrook and Aitken, *Canadian Economic History*, 553-54.

39 International Joint Commission, *Correspondence and Documents Relating to the Great Lakes-St. Lawrence Basin Development, Supplement no. 1* (Ottawa: Edmond Cloutier, 1941).

40 ASCE, "Diversion," 7-10. On its consequences, see Paul Driben and D. Auger, *The Generation of Power and Fear: The Little Jackfish River Hydroelectric Project and the Whitesand Indian Band* (Thunder Bay: Lakehead University, Centre for Northern Studies Research Report no. 3, 1989).

41 ASCE, "Diversion," 12-13.

42 Zaslow, *Northward Expansion*, 80.

43 Ontario Hydro pamphlet, *Hydro in the Northwest* (Toronto: Ontario Hydro, n.d., approximately 1975).

44 "Submission to the Royal Commission on the Northern Environment by Kimberly-Clark of Canada Ltd., Terrace Bay, Ontario" (29 November 1977),

Royal Commission in the Northern Environment (RCNE), Toronto, File 00162, Ex. 133, 1.

45 Department of Indian Affairs Land Registry Office, Reserve General Register.

46 Ibid.

47 Department of Indian Affairs, Ontario Regional Office, Toronto. W. Bethune, Department of Indian Affairs Reserves and Trusts division, to F.W. Beatty, Surveyor General, Division of Surveys, Ontario Dept. of Lands and Forests, 12 August 1959.

48 Department of Indian Affairs Land Registry Office, Reserve General Register.

49 In the early 1930s, gold had been found in the Geraldton area (west of Long Lake) and between 1935 and '55 a mine operated at Theresa, just south of Ginoogaming. With the 1980s' rise in gold prices, areas surrounding the reserve were taken up under exploration licences by Geraldton Longlac Gold Inc., by the Discovery West Corporation, and by Mid-North Engineering Services; D.U. Kresz and B. Zayachivsky, *Precambrian Geology: Northern Long Lake Area* (Toronto: Ministry of Northern Development and Mines, OGS Report 273, 1991), 4.

50 Lake survey summary kindly supplied by the MNR's Geraldton office.

51 Hall, "Treaties, Trains, and Troubled National Dreams," 293.

52 In July 1999 this was pointed out to me even by young men, not the "social element" most likely to be particularly cautious about such matters.

53 Berkes, "Intrinsic Difficulty," 207-208.

54 At around that time, in respect to complaints first lodged in 1953, such protective work was finally being done at neighbouring Long Lake no. 58. Ontario Hydro paid $19,000 in compensation for erosion damage plus $4,245 to cover associated costs (Department of Indian Affairs Land Registry Office, Reserve General Register).

55 Ontario Hydro Archives, Toronto, G.A. Gorman to M.H. Pryce, Ontario Hydro memo of 29 September 1977.

56 Ontario Hydro Archives, Toronto, L.V. Doran, Operating Superintendent, Ontario Hydro Northwest Region (Thunder Bay), to Chief Victor Chapais, 10 September 1981.

57 Long Lake no. 77, Band Administration files. Band council resolutions of 21 July 1983 and 10 February 1986.

58 Long Lake no. 77, Band Administration files. Gestalt Orthophoto Services, "Project Report" dated 11 February 1987.

59 Long Lake no. 77, Band Administration files. Letter from Christine Cram, Director, Specific Claims East/Central, Department of Indian Affairs, to Chief Gabriel Echum, Ginoogaming First Nation, 12 August 1994.

60 Ernest J. Weinrib, "The Fiduciary Obligation," *University of Toronto Law Journal* 25, no. 1 (1975): 7.

61 Huntley Schaller, *Loss of Use Considerations in Determining Compensation for Specific Claims* (Ottawa: Indian and Northern Affairs Canada, Research and Analysis Directorate, 1992), 5.

62 James B. Waldram, *Cumberland House and the E.B. Campbell Dam: An Economic Impact Study* (Thunder Bay: Lakehead University, Centre for Northern Studies Research Report no. 24, 1991), 3.

63 Chief Andrew Rickard, "Submission to the Royal Commission on the Northern Environment by Grand Council Treaty 9" (1 February 1978), Royal Commission on the Northern Environment (RCNE), File 00341, Ex. 297, 14.

64 Missabay quoted by Scott, "The Last of the Indian Treaties," 578; also Government of Canada, *The James Bay Treaty*, 5.

65 J. Dickson (with Beetz, Chouinard, and Lamer concurring) as quoted by Kulchyski, *Unjust Relations*, 159.

66 Kulchyski, *Unjust Relations*, 212, 187.

67 Easterbrook and Aitken, *Canadian Economic History*, 553-54.

68 Other projects involving northern Ontario include the Decker (Great Lakes-Pacific Waterways) Diversion Scheme, the Central North American (Great Bear Lake-US Southwest) Water Plan, and the 1984 T.W. Kierans (Harricanaw-Nipissing) GRAND Canal Scheme; see Richard C. Bocking, "Canadian Waster: A Commodity for Export?" in *Canadian Aquatic Resources*, ed. Healey and Wallace.

69 Ginoogaming First Nation, *Community Information Book, 1998*, 7.

70 Ibid., 9.

CHAPTER 11

1 The "Aboriginal Peoples of Canada" are defined as "the Indian, Inuit and Métis peoples of Canada" by section 35(2) of the Constitution Act, 1982, being Schedule B to the Canada Act 1982, (U.K.) 1982, c.11. The Métis people originated from unions between Indian women and European fur traders, and so their status in Canadian law and their Aboriginal rights probably have to be assessed differently from the status and rights of the Indians and Inuit whose presence in Canada predated the arrival of Europeans: see *R. v. Van der Peet*, [1996] 2 S.C.R. 507, per Lamer C.J. at 558 (para. 67); compare L'Heureux-Dubé J. at 598 (para. 169). Accordingly, the discussion of Aboriginal title in this chapter may not be directly applicable to the Métis. On Métis hunting rights, see *R. v. Powley*, [2001] 2 C.N.L.R. 291 (Ont. C.A.). For acknowledgement of Aboriginal land rights, see, for example, the Royal Proclamation of 1763, reproduced in R.S.C. 1985, App. II, No. 1.

2 *St. Catherine's Milling and Lumber Co. v. The Queen* (1888), 14 App. Cas. 46 (P.C.), at 54.

3 Ibid., at 55, 59; *Roberts v. Canada*, [1989] 1 S.C.R. 322, at 340; *Chippewas of Sarnia Band v. Canada* (1999), 40 R.P.R. (3d) 49, at para. 377, 419, affirmed [2001] 1 C.N.L.R. 56 (Ont. C.A.).

4 *Guerin v. The Queen*, [1984] 2 S.C.R. 335, per Dickson J. at 382.

5 [1997] 3 S.C.R. 1010.

6 At trial the claims were to ownership and jurisdiction, but by the time the case reached the Supreme Court they had been modified to Aboriginal title and self-government.

7 For commentary on the issue of use of oral histories as evidence, see Lori Ann Roness and Kent McNeil, "Legalizing Oral History: Proving Aboriginal Claims in Canadian Courts," *Journal of the West* 39, no. 3 (2000): 66; John Borrows, "Listening for a Change: The Courts and Oral Tradition," *Osgoode Hall Law Journal* no. 39 (2001): 1.

8 This is due to section 91(24) of the Constitution Act, 1867, 30 and 31 Vict. (U.K.), c.3, which gives the parliament of Canada exclusive jurisdiction over "Indians, and Lands reserved for the Indians."

9 For discussion, see Kent McNeil, *Defining Aboriginal Title in the 90s: Has the Supreme Court Finally Got It Right?* (Toronto: Robarts Centre for Canadian Studies, York University, 1998); Kent McNeil, *Emerging Justice? Essays on Indigenous Rights in Canada and Australia* (Saskatoon: University of Saskatchewan Native Law Centre, 2001), 71-81,102-60, 249-80; Kerry Wilkins, "Of Provinces and Section 35 Rights," *Dalhousie Law Journal* 22 (1999): 165.

10 At the end of his judgment, Lamer C.J. expressed the hope that Aboriginal land claims, including the claims of the Gitksan and Wet'suwet'en, could be settled by negotiation: *Delgamuukw v. British Columbia*, [1997] 3 S.C.R. 1010, at 1123-24 (para. 186). To date, no new trial has taken place, and negotiations have bogged down due to fundamental differences between the parties.

11 In a couple of recent decisions, the British Columbia Court of Appeal has acknowledged this problem and forced the province to consult with the Aboriginal people concerned in situations like this. See *Taku River Tlingit First Nation v. British Columbia (Project Assessment Director)*, [2002] 2 C.N.L.R. 312; *Haida Nation v. British Columbia, (Minister of Forests)*, [2002] 2 C.N.L.R. 212.

12 Chief Justice Lamer delivered the main judgment, for himself, and Justices Cory and Major. Justice La Forest, L'Heureux-Dubé J. concurring, delivered a separate judgment that differed from Lamer's in some respects. Justice McLachlin concurred with Lamer, but said she was "also in substantial agreement with the comments of Justice La Forest": *Delgamuukw v. British Columbia*, [1997] 3 S.C.R. 1010, at 1135 (para. 209).

13 Ibid., at 1080 (para. 111). Lamer accordingly held that the test the Supreme Court had laid down for identification and definition of other Aboriginal rights in *R. v. Van der Peet*, [1996] 2 S.C.R. 507, was inapplicable to Aboriginal title. (That test requires proof that an activity was integral to the distinctive culture of the Aboriginal society in question at the time of contact with Europeans.)

14 *Delgamuukw v. British Columbia*, [1997] 3 S.C.R. 1010, per Lamer C.J. at 1083 (para. 117), 1086-87 (para. 122).

15 Ibid., at 1088, heading above para. 125 (italics and capitalization removed).

16 Ibid., at 1089 (para. 128).

17 Ibid., per Lamer C.J. at 1111-12 (para. 166) (emphasis in original).

18 Ibid., per Lamer C.J. at 1082 (para. 114).

19 Ibid., per Lamer C.J. at 181-83 (para. 113, 115). For discussion of inalienability, see Kent McNeil, "Self-Government and the Inalienability of Aboriginal Title," *McGill Law Journal* 47 (2002): 473.

20 *Delgamuukw v. British Columbia*, [1997] 3 S.C.R. 1010, per Lamer C.J. at 1091-93 (para. 133-37).

21 The decision not to constitutionalize other property rights was consciously made in 1982, after debate on the issue. See Alexander Alvaro, "Why Property Rights Were Excluded from the Canadian Charter of Rights and Freedoms," *Canadian Journal of Political Science* 24, no. 2 (1991): 309.

22 [1990] 1 S.C.R. 1075; [1996] 2 S.C.R. 723. Briefly, the *Sparrow* test requires the Crown to prove a valid legislative objective for the infringing measure that is substantial and compelling, and to show that the Crown's fiduciary obligations to the Aboriginal people in question have been respected. For critical commentary, see Kent McNeil, "Envisaging Constitutional Space for Aboriginal Governments," *Queen's Law Journal* 19 (1993): 95; Kent McNeil, "How Can Infringements of the Constitutional Rights of Aboriginal Peoples Be Justified?" *Constitutional Forum* 8, no. 2 (1997): 33. See also the works cited in note 9.

23 *Delgamuukw v. British Columbia*, [1997] 3 S.C.R. 1010, per Lamer C.J. at 1101 (para. 149), quoting from Brian Slattery, "Understanding Aboriginal Rights," *Canadian Bar Review* 66 (1987): 727 at 758.

24 *Delgamuukw v. British Columbia*, [1997] 3 S.C.R. 1010, at 1100 (para. 148), 1105 (para. 157).

25 Ibid., per Lamer C.J. at 1104-06 (para. 155-58).

26 Ibid., at 1098 (para. 145).

27 Moreover, he did not address the issue of whether the date for proof of Aboriginal title in the parts of Canada originally colonized by France is the assertion of French or British sovereignty. For further discussion, see Kent McNeil, "Aboriginal Rights in Canada: From Title to Land to Territorial Sovereignty," *Tulsa Journal of Comparative and International Law* 5 (1998): 253 at 274-76.

28 *Delgamuukw v. British Columbia*, [1997] 3 S.C.R. 1010, at 1098 (para. 145).

29 For critical commentary, see John Borrows, "Frozen Rights in Canada: Constitutional Interpretation and the Trickster," *American Indian Law Review* 22
(1997): 37; Russel Lawrence Barsh and James Youngblood Henderson, "The
Supreme Court's *Van der Peet* Trilogy: Naive Imperialism and Ropes of
Sand," *McGill Law Journal* 42 (1997): 993.

30 *Delgamuukw v. British Columbia*, [1997] 3 S.C.R. 1010, at 1098 (para. 145). This,
in fact, is doubtful: see Kent McNeil, "Sovereignty and the Aboriginal
Nations of Rupert's Land," *Manitoba History* no. 37 (Spring/Summer 1999):
2; Kent McNeil, "Sovereignty on the Northern Plains: Indian, European,
American and Canadian Claims," *Journal of the West* 39, no. 3 (2000): 10.

31 *Delgamuukw v. British Columbia*, [1997] 3 S.C.R. 1010, at 1103 (para. 153).

32 Ibid. The quoted words are actually from the decision of the High Court of
Australia in *Mabo v. Queensland [No. 2]* (1992), 175 C.L.R 1, from which they
were adopted by Lamer (somewhat inappropriately, in my opinion, since
the context for their use in *Mabo* had not been *proof* of Aboriginal title, but
loss of that title through loss of connection with the land).

33 *Delgamuukw v. British Columbia*, [1997] 3 S.C.R. 1010, at 1103 (para. 154).

34 Ibid., at 1097 (para. 143-44).

35 For detailed discussion, see Kent McNeil, *Common Law Aboriginal Title*
(Oxford: Clarendon Press, 1989), 6-78.

36 Another way of stating this is that, in the absence of contrary evidence, possession in fact entails possession in law. The former is a factual matter
involving physical occupation and control, whereas possession in law is
possession that is recognized as such by the law. See Frederick Pollock and
Robert Samuel Wright, *An Essay on Possession in the Common Law* (Oxford:
Clarendon Press, 1888), 16-20.

37 See *Whale v. Hitchcock* (1876), 34 L.T. 136 (Div. C.A.); *Emmerson v. Maddison*,
[1906] A.C. 569 (P.C.), at 575; *Allen v. Roughley* (1955), 94 C.L.R. 98 (Aust.
H.C.), at 136-41.

38 This rule has been part of the common law since at least the thirteenth century. See Samuel E. Thorne, ed. and trans., *Bracton on the Laws and Customs
of England* (Cambridge: Belknap Press of Harvard University Press, 1968-
77), 3: 134 ("everyone who is in possession, though he has no right, has a
greater right [than] one who is out of possession and has no right"). See
also Edward Coke, *The First Part of the Institutes of the Laws of England; or a
Commentary upon Littleton*, 19th ed., ed. Charles Butler (London: J. and W.T.
Clarke et al., 1832), 239n. 1; William Blackstone, *Commentaries on the Laws of
England*, 16th ed. (London: T. Cadell and J. Butterworth and Son, 1825), 2:
196, 3: 177, 180; Pollock and Wright, *An Essay on Possession in the Common
Law* (Oxford: Clarendon Press, 1888), 22-25, 91-100; John M. Lightwood, *A
Treatise on Possession of Land* (London: Stevens and Sons, 1894), 125, 146-47,

294-95; Robert Megarry and H.W.R. Wade, *The Law of Real Property*, 5th ed. (London: Stevens and Sons, 1984), 102-109, 1158-59; E.H. Burn, *Cheshire and Burn's Modern Law of Real Property*, 15th ed. (London: Butterworths, 1994), 25-29. For discussion and further references, see McNeil, *Common Law Aboriginal Title* (Oxford: Clarendon Press, 1989), 42-43, 46-49, 56-58.

39 See *Goodtitle d. Parker v. Baldwin* (1809), 11 East 488 (K.B.), at 495; *Asher v. Whitlock* (1865), L.R. 1 Q.B. 1; *Danford v. McAnulty* (1883), 8 App. Cas. 456 (H.L.), at 460-61, 462, 464-65; *Perry v. Clissold*, [1907] A.C. 73 (P.C.), at 79-80; *City of Vancouver v. Vancouver Lumber Company*, [1911] A.C. 711 (P.C.), at 720; *McAllister v. Defoe* (1915), 8 O.W.N. 175 (Ont. K.B.), affirmed (1915), 8 O.W.N. 405 (Ont. C.A.); *Swaile v. Zurdayk*, [1924] 2 W.W.R. 555 (Sask. C.A.); *Pinder Lumber and Milling Co. v. Munroe*, [1928] S.C.R. 177.

40 See *Perry v. Clissold*, [1907] A.C. 73 (P.C.); *Nireaha Tamaki v. Baker*, [1901] A.C. 561 (P.C.); *Wallis v. Solicitor-General for New Zealand*, [1903] A.C. 173 (P.C.). In *Bristow v. Cormican*, [1878], 3 App. Cas. 641 (H.L.), grantees of the Crown who were not in actual possession failed in an action of trespass because they did not prove that the Crown had title to the land at the time their grant had been issued.

41 See Kent McNeil, "The Onus of Proof of Aboriginal Title," *Osgoode Hall Law Journal* 37 (1999): 775. The principle that title is presumed from possession was applied by Justice Hall (dissenting on other grounds) in *Calder v. Attorney-General of British Columbia*, [1973] S.C.R. 313, at 368, 375, in the context of a claim to Aboriginal title by the Nishga (now spelled Nisga'a) Nation in British Columbia. While the Nishgas' claim was dismissed because they had failed to get permission from the provincial Crown before suing it, six judges acknowledged the existence of their Aboriginal title at common law (Hall J. with Justices Laskin and Spence concurring, thought it still existed, whereas Judson J. , Justices Martland and Ritchie concurring, thought it had been legislatively extinguished prior to British Columbia joining Confederation in 1871).

42 The presumption would be of Aboriginal title, rather than some common law interest, because the occupation I am envisaging would be by the Aboriginal people *as a community*, and so would support their *sui generis* communal title.

43 See *Attorney-General v. Brown* (1847), 1 Legge 312 (N.S.W.S.C.); *The Queen v. Symonds* (1847) [1840-1932] N.Z.P.C.C. 387 (N.Z.S.C.), per Chapman J. at 388-90, Martin C.J. at 393; *Falkland Islands Company v. The Queen* (1863) 2 Moo. P.C. (N.S.) 266, at 272; *Mabo v. Queensland [No. 2]* (1992), 175 C.L.R 1 (H.C. Aust.), per Brennan J. at 53, Deane and Gaudron JJ. at 88, Toohey J. at 180-82, 211-12. For discussion, see McNeil, *Common Law Aboriginal Title*, (Oxford: Clarendon Press, 1989), 134-36.

44 *Delgamuukw v. British Columbia*, [1997] 3 S.C.R. 1010, at 1101 (para. 149); see also 1082 (para. 114).

45 See *Catteris v. Cowper* (1812), 4 Taunt. 547 (C.P.); *Doe d. Osborne v. M'Dougall* (1848), 6 U.C.Q.B. 135; *Lessee of Smith v. McKenzie* (1854), 2 N.S.R. (James) 228 (N.S.S.C.); *Doe d. Eaton v. Thomson* (1860), 9 N.B.R. (4 Allen) 461 (N.B.S.C.); *Wogama Pty. v. Harris* (1968), 89 W.N.N.S.W. (Pt. 2) 62 (N.S.W.C.A.), esp. 64. For discussion, see McNeil, *Common Law Aboriginal Title* (Oxford: Clarendon Press, 1989), 39-63, esp. 42-43. Where there are two or more presumptive titles arising from two or more possessions, in the absence of other evidence the earliest possession will prevail; see *Doe d. Harding v. Cooke* (1831), 7 Bing. 346, esp. per Park J.; *Freeman v. Allen* (1866) 6 N.S.R. 293 (C.A.); *Whale v. Hitchcock,* [1876], 34 L.T. 136 (Div. C.A.), at 137; *Donnelly v. Ames* (1896), 27 O.R. 271 (Q.B.); *Poulin v. Eberle* (1911), 20 O.W.R. 301 (Div. Ct.).

46 While this might be done in the context of an action for declaration of Aboriginal title, it might be more effective for the Aboriginal people in question to simply bring an action to recover possession, as that would not prejudice third party rights (arising, for example, from overlapping Aboriginal title claims): see McNeil, "The Onus of Proof of Aboriginal Title," *Osgoode Hall Law Journal* 37 (1999): 44.

47 It is well established that the onus of proving that Aboriginal rights (which include Aboriginal title: see *R. v. Adams*, [1996] 3 S.C.R. 101) have been extinguished is on the party so alleging, and that the legislative intention to extinguish must be clear and plain. See *R. v. Sparrow*, [1990] 1 S.C.R. 1075, at 1098-99; *R. v. Badger*, [1996] 1 S.C.R. 771, per Cory J. at 794 (para. 41); *Delgamuukw v. British Columbia*, [1997] 3 S.C.R. 1010, per Lamer C.J. at 1120 (para. 180). Similar principles would seem to apply to an allegation that Aboriginal title has been surrendered by treaty, given that treaties have to be interpreted in a generous and liberal fashion in favour of the Aboriginal parties. See *Nowegijick v. The Queen*, [1983] 1 S.C.R. 29, at 36; *Simon v. The Queen*, [1985] 2 S.C.R. 387, at 402; *R. v. Sioui*, [1990] 1 S.C.R. 1025, at 1035-36; *Mitchell v. Peguis Indian Band*, [1990] 2 S.C.R. 85, per La Forest J. at 142-43, Dickson C.J. at 98-100; *R. v. Badger*, [1996] 1 S.C.R. 771, per Cory J. at 794 (para. 41); *R. v. Marshall*, [1999] 4 C.N.L.R 161 (S.C.C.), per Binnie J. at 172-73 (para. 11-14); *R. v. Sundown*, [1999] 1 S.C.R. 393, at 406-407 (para. 24).

48 See *St. Catherine's Milling and Lumber Co. v. The Queen* (1888), 14 App. Cas. 46 (P.C.), at 55, 59; *Delgamuukw v. British Columbia*, [1997] 3 S.C.R. 1010, per Lamer C.J. at 1098 (para. 145).

49 For detailed discussion in the context of Native title in Australia, see Kent McNeil, "Racial Discrimination and Unilateral Extinguishment of Native Title," *Australian Indigenous Law Reporter* 1 (1996): 181; Kent McNeil, "Extinguishment of Native Title: The High Court and American Law," *Australian Indigenous Law Reporter* 2 (1997): 365. Compare *Chippewas of Sarnia Band v. Canada*, [2001] 1 C.N.L.R. 56 (Ont. C.A.). This case is critiqued in Kent

McNeil, "Extinguishment of Aboriginal Title in Canada: Treaties, Legislation, and Judicial Discretion," *Ottawa Law Review* 33 (2001-2002): 301.

50 The inherent limit is discussed earlier. Common law restrictions might arise
    from the law of nuisance and riparian rights of other landholders. Statu-
    tory restrictions, such as environmental laws, would apply only if constitu-
    tionally *intra vires* and justifiable (to the extent that they infringed
    Aboriginal rights) under the *Sparrow* test.

51 Whether they would be able to recover possession depends on complex
    legal issues, including the applicability of statutes of limitation. See *Chippe-
    was of Sarnia Band v. Canada*, [2001] 1 C.N.L.R. 56 (Ont. C.A.), and McNeil,
    "Extinguishment of Aboriginal Title in Canada: Treaties, Legislation, and
    Judicial Discretion," *Ottawa Law Review* 30 (2001-2002): 301.

52 It should be noted that, under old law that may or may not still be valid,
    the dignity of the Crown prevented it from acquiring possession, whether
    rightfully or wrongfully, by physically occupying land. Unless possession
    was cast upon it by law, for the Crown to have possession it generally had
    to have a title that was of record, i.e., a title recorded as a memorial of a
    court or legislative body. This rule complemented the provision in c.29 of
    Magna Carta, 17 John (as re-enacted by 9 Hen. III), that the Crown cannot
    disseise (i.e. dispossess) freeholders (this is now subject to statutes of limita-
    tion). It protected landholders against arbitrary exercise of power by a sov-
    ereign that enjoyed immunity in its own courts prior to the enactment of
    modern Crown liability statutes. See McNeil, *Common Law Aboriginal Title*
    (Oxford: Clarendon Press, 1989) 93-95.

53 For example, see *Wuta-Ofei v. Danquah*, [1961] 3 All E.R. 596 (P.C.), where the
    plaintiff succeeded in an action of trespass by proving occupation, mainly
    by marking boundaries and protesting the defendant's intrusion on the
    land, even though the West African Court of Appeal had dismissed her
    additional claim for a declaration of title (this aspect of the Court of
    Appeal's decision was not appealed to the Privy Council). It is also clear
    from the case law that even wrongful occupation will prevail in an action of
    trespass against a defendant who cannot prove a right to enter or do the
    acts of trespass. See *Graham v. Peat* (1801), 1 East 244 (K.B.); *Catteris v. Cowper*
    (1812), 4 Taunt. 547 (C.P.); *Asher v. Whitlock* (1865), L.R. 1 Q.B. 1; *Glenwood
    Lumber v. Phillips*, [1904] A.C. 405 (P.C.); *Swaile v. Zurdayk*, [1924] 2 W.W.R.
    555 (Sask. C.A.); *Pinder Lumber and Milling Co. v. Munroe*, [1928] S.C.R. 177;
    Nicholls v. Ely Beet Sugar Factory, [1931] 2 Ch. 84.

54 If they can prove occupation *at the time* the Crown asserted sovereignty, of
    course they will be able to prove Aboriginal title in accordance with the *Del-
    gamuukw* test without relying on the presumptions.

55 Letter dated 28 March 1949, reproduced in Frank Waters, *Book of the Hopi*
    (New York: Ballantine Books, 1963), 393-95.

CHAPTER 12

1 Northern populism has its own legitimate grievances against southern domination and exploitation, its own concerns about stable community life and
   sustainable resource use, and its own democratic claims against outside
   Ministry of Natural Resources (MNR) control over public resources. But in
   Temagami it acted for some time, primarily to revive the resource industry
   status quo ante bellum, unmaking in the process TAA self-government proposals and fighting environmentalism as exclusionary and both elite and south-
   ern-derived. (Thomas Dunk, "Talking about Trees: Environment and Society
   in Forest Workers' Culture," *Canadian Review of Sociology* 31, no. 1 [1994]: 14-
   34. See also Roger Fiset et al., *Temagami Workshop*, ed. Barrie Solandt Maxwell
   [Toronto: Canadian Environmental Law Association, and Ryerson Polytechnical Institute, 1992]; Roger Fryer, "Some Comments on Temagami Issues,"
   in *Temagami: A Debate on Wilderness*, ed. Matt Bray and Ashley Thomson
   [Toronto: Dundurn, 1990], 61-64; Judith Skidmore, "Canadian Values and
   Priorities: A Multiple Use Perspective," in *Temagami: A Debate on Wilderness*,
   ed. Bray and Thomson, 65-68.)

2 Much has been written about Temagami country and N'Daki Menan, so
   much so that they are probably the dominant manner in which outsiders
   have come to know about Temagami. But the "Temiskaming area" also
   deserves attention. The Temagami area not only incorporates the nearby
   Tri-Towns and beyond them the Clay Belt, but centres on these and other
   "mini-metropoles" rather than on Lake Temagami. In land-use politics, this
   space, and the forces generating it, came to serve a vision bent primarily on
   reviving the area's resource economy. Increasingly, this vision laid the
   blame for thirty years of resource decline on Aboriginal and environmental
   politics, and less on the general transformation of the work processes in the
   resource industries themselves (Douglas Baldwin, "Imitation vs. Innovation: Cobalt as an Urban Frontier Town," *Laurentian University Review* 11,
   no. 2 [February 1979]: 23-42; Bruce W. Hodgins, "Contexts of the Temagami
   Predicament," in *Temagami: A Debate on Wilderness*, ed. Bray and Thomson,
   123-39, especially 135.)

3 See for example Robert J. Burrows, *The Strategy of Non-violent Defense*
   (Albany: State University of New York Press, 1996); and B.H. Liddell Hart,
   Strategy: The Indirect Approach (London: Faber and Faber, 1967), 18.

4 M.K. Gandhi, *Non-violent Resistance*, ed. Bharatan Kumarappa (New York:
   Schocken, 1951), 132-35.

5 Burrows, *Strategy*, 36-41.

6 Richard Gregg, *The Power of Nonviolence* (New York: Schocken, 1966).

7 Gandhi, *Non-violent*, 57. If armed forces recognized that their own morale
   would be damaged from a violent confrontation with non-violent activists,

they would not be surprised, and could avoid such situations. At the same
time, this approach to non-violent action succeeds only if its practitioners
either demoralize their enemy willingly, or fail to recognize that this is
indeed why they are effective. Non-violent resistance may require putting
such ideas out of one's head: that is, love of enemy may constitute a kind of
necessary "Sorelian" myth, in Gramsci's sense of a necessary fiction that
sustains a movement through a deep crisis. Gandhi's writing on *satyagraha*,
for instance, repeatedly stresses the importance of not embarrassing enemies or treating them with hostility. The enemy's only defeat is their conversion, without even moral coercion.

8 Site of more recent clashes between Toronto Police and the Ontario Coalition Against Poverty.

9 In fact, Hart argues, this link between surprise and identifying an opponent's weakness in space is not absolute. For example, an opponent's weak-
est point in space may be obvious, and yet its use as a focal point of attack
could be unsurprising (and so less effective) to everyone.

10 Liddell Hart, foreword to Sun Tzu, *The Art of War*, trans. Samuel B. Griffith
(Oxford: Oxford University Press, 1963), v.

11 Griffin in Sun Tzu, *Art of War*, 42.

12 Sheldon Wolin, "The Economy of Violence," in *The Prince* by Machiavelli,
ed. Robert M. Adams (New York: W.W. Norton, 1977), 185-94.

13 Sun Tzu, *Art of War*, 88 (my emphasis).

14 Bruce W. Hodgins, *Wanapitei on Temagami: A Story of Adventures* (Peterborough: Wanapitei, 1996), 110-11.

15 Sun Tzu, *Art of War*, 124, 130.

16 See, for example, William Cronin, *Changes in the Land: Indians, Colonists, and
the Ecology of New England* (New York: Hill and Wang, 1983); David Harvey,
"The Nature of Environment" in *Socialist Register: Real Problems, False Solutions*, ed. Ralph Miliband and Leo Panitch (London: Merlin Press, 1993), 48-
57; and James O'Connor, "The Second Contradiction of Capitalism," in *The
Greening of Marxism*, ed. Ted Benton (New York: Guilford, 1996).

17 Fernand Braudel, *On History* (Chicago: University of Chicago Press, 1980);
M. Davis, *Ecology of Fear* (New York: Henry Holt, 1998).

18 For eample, Mary Laronde, "Co-management of Lands and Resources in
N'Daki Menan," in *Rebirth: Political, Economic, and Social Development in First
Nations*, ed. Anne-Marie Mawhiney (Toronto: Dundurn, 1990), 96.

19 Antonio Gramsci, *Selections from the Prison Notebooks*, trans. Quintin Hoare,
Geoffrey Nowell Smith (New York: International, 1971), 175-85.

20 Gordon Baskerville and A.J. Kayll, *An Audit of Management of the Crown
Forests of Ontario* (Toronto: Ontario Ministry of Natural Resources, 1986).

21 Donald Mackay, *Heritage Lost: The Crisis in Canada's Forests* (Toronto:
Macmillan, 1985), 28-57.

22 David Harvey, *Justice, Nature and the Geography of Difference* (Oxford: Blackwell, 1996), 19-45.

23 See Russell S. Uhler, *Canada-United States Trade in Forest Products* (Vancouver: UBC Press, 1991).

24 M. Storper and R. Walker, *The Capitalist Imperative: Territory, Technology, and Industrial Growth* (Oxford: Basil Blackwell, 1989).

25 Bruce W. Hodgins and Jamie Benidickson, *The Temagami Experience: Recreation, Resources, and Aboriginal Rights in the Northern Ontario Wilderness* (Toronto: University of Toronto Press, 1989), 249-66.

26 See K.J. Rea, *The Prosperous Years: The Economic History of Ontario, 1939-1975* (Toronto: University of Toronto Press, 1985) and R.M. Campbell, *Grand Illusions* (Peterborough: Broadview Press, 1991).

27 The spatial practices of the Lake Temagami Plan also had deeper roots: the zoning technique and the creation of rights delimited and enforced by centrally surveyed boundaries were all intensified northwards during the postwar. But their roots had spread first from Europe to the farming landscapes of nineteenth-century southern Ontario. These spatial patterns differed, both before and after the war, from spatial practices of northern mining and logging communities, as well as from the deepest spatial traditions of the Anishnabai. In turn, both of these spatial practices differed from one another, and from the spatial practices of northern resource communities during periods of explosive resource booms.

28 See, for example, Ian Steedman, "Trade Interest versus Class Interest," *Economica Politica* 3, no. 2 (August 1986): 187-206.

29 Gilles Deleuze and Felix Guattari, *Anti-Oedipus: Capitalism and Schizophrenia*, trans. Robert Hurley et al. (Minneapolis: University of Minnesota Press, 1983); *A Thousand Plateaus: Capitalism and Schizophrenia*, trans. Brian Massumi (Minneapols: University of Minnesota Press, 1987). See also Brian Massumi, translator's foreword, *A Thousand Plateaus*, and Christopher Miller, "The Postidentitarian Predicament in the Footnotes of *A Thousand Plateaus*," *Diacritics* 23, no. 3 (Fall 1993): 6-35.

30 See also Bob Jessop, *State Theory: Putting the Capitalist State in Its Place* (University Park: Pennsylvania State University Press, 1990).

31 Deleuze and Guattari, *A Thousand Plateaus*, 385 and 508-509.

32 Recall here the earlier mention of Canada as the "peaceable kingdom."

33 Deleuze and Guattari, *A Thousand Plateaus*, 432-36.

34 See Miller, "Postidentitarian."

35 Deleuze and Guattari, *A Thousand Plateaus*, 404-15.

36 Pierre Clastres, *Society against the State*, trans. Robert Hurley and Abe Stein (New York: Zone, 1987) and Deleuze and Guattari, *A Thousand Plateaus*, 440, 509.

37 Clastres, *Society*, 189-218; Deleuze and Guattari, *A Thousand Plateaus*, 440.

38 R.W. Dunning, *Social and Economic Change among Northern Ojibwa* (Toronto: University of Toronto Press, 1959), 174-98; Hodgins and Benidickson, *The Temagami*, 13; Edward S. Rogers, "Leadership among the Indians of Eastern Subarctic Canada," in *Persectives on the North American Indians*, ed. Mark Nagler (Toronto: McClelland and Stewart, 1972), 57-71; Rupert Ross, *Dancing with a Ghost* (Markham: Octopus, 1992); and Frank Speck, "The Family Hunting Band as the Basis of Algonkian Social Organization (1915)," in *Cultural Ecology*, ed. Bruce Cox (Toronto: McClelland and Stewart, 1973), 62-67.

39 Deleuze and Guattari, *A Thousand Plateaus*, 410.

40 Diana Gordon, "Prehistoric Occupations at Lake Temagami," in *Temagami: A Debate on Wilderness*, ed. Bray and Thomson, 157.

41 Basil Johnston, *The Manitous: The Spiritual World of the Ojibway* (New York: Harper Collins, 1995), 178-237; J.A. Kleinfelder and A. Yesno, *The People North of 50: In Quest of Understanding* (paper produced for the Royal Commission on the Northern Environment, 1984); and Ross, *Dancing with a Ghost*.

42 Denis McLean Watson. "Frontier Movement and Economic Development in Northeastern Ontario, 1850-1914" (master's thesis, UBC, 1971).

43 James Lawson, "Nastawgan or Not? First Nations Land Management in Temagami and Alginquin Park," in *Sustainability—The Challenge: People, Power, and the Environment*, ed. L. Anders Sandberg and Sverker Sörlin (Montreal: Black Rose, 1998); see also Jonathan Murdoch and Terry Marsden, "The Spatialization of Politics: Local and National Actor-Spaces in Environmental Conflict," *Transactions of the Institute of British Geographers* no. 20 (1995): 368-80.

44 B. Bucknall, *"An Overview of the Legislation"* (paper presented for "Registration Revisited," a continuing legal education conference, Toronto, 1987).

45 Brian Back, *The Keewaydin Way* (Temagami: Keewaydin Camp, 1983); and Hodgins, *Wanapitei*.

46 Terry Fiset, Bruce W. Hodgins, et al., *Temagami Workshop* (Toronto: Canadian Environmental Law Association and Ryerson Polytechnic Institute, 1992); Bruce W. Hodgins, Shawn Heard, and John S. Milloy, eds., *Co-Existence? Studies in Ontario-First Nations Relations* (Peterborough: Trent University, Frost Centre, 1992).

47 Enzo di Matteo, "Nations Divided by Logging," NOW 19-25 September 1996, 22; and Thomas Walkom, "Temagami Battle Is about Who Uses Bush Best," *Toronto Star*, 26 October 1989.

48 "Temagami Land Battle Climaxing, Natives Say," *Toronto Star*, 23 March 1993: A1O; "Native Leader Wants Temagami Deal Salvaged," *Globe and Mail*, 16 November 1993: A3; "Natives Reject Deal Again," *Globe and Mail*, 3 March 1994; Jamie Benidickson, "Temagami Old Growth: Pine, Politics and Public

Policy," *Environments* 23, no. 2 (1996): 41-50; and ONAS.

49 Becker and Hassan-Gordon, "Interview"; David Brazeau, "Native Families Fight to Reclaim Land," *Sudbury Star*, 2 February 1993; Darcy Henton, "49 Arrested as Temagami Road Blocked," *Toronto Star*, 13 November 1989: A10; Katt, Massabi, and Friday, "Temagami Natives."

50 Fiset et al., *Temagami Workshop*; Hodgins, *Wanapitei*.

51 For example, Paul Leach, qtd. in Karen Unland, "Temagami Remains a Tinderbox," *Globe and Mail*, 2 September 1996, A6.

52 "Northwatch Structure Paper" (photocopy, 12 August 1995).

53 Benidickson, "Temagami Old Growth"; Patrick Matakala, "Decision-Making and Conflict Resolution in Co-management: Two Cases from Temagami, Northeastern Ontario" (Ph.D. diss., UBC, 1955).

54 Ron Arnold, "Loggerheads over Land Use," *Logging and Sawmilling Journal* (April 1988); Bruce Clark, "Bruce Clark Archives—Letter to Verna Friday" <http://kafka.uvic.ca/~vipirg/SISIS/Clark/vernal.html> 11 December 1995; Ma-Kominising Anishnabaeg; Mark S. Winfield and Greg Jenish, "Ontario's Environment and the 'Common Sense Revolution,'" *Studies in Political Economy* 57 (Autumn 1998): 129-47.

55 Michael M'Gonigle and Ben Parfitt, *Forestopia: A Practical Guide to the New Forest Economy* (Madeira Park: Harbour, 1994).

CHAPTER 13

1 Gerald Woods, "The Quality of Mercy: The Reform Tradition in Canadian Federal Corrections" (manuscript), c.1992.

2 In J.T.L. James, *A Living Tradition: Penitentiary Chaplaincy* (Ottawa: Ministry of Supply and Service, 1990), 171.

3 Interview with "Swiss," Warkworth Institution, May 1999.

4 Art Solomon, *Eating Bitterness: A Vision Beyond the Prison Walls* (Toronto: NC Press, 1994), 84.

5 Interview with "Little Joe," Warkworth Institution, May 1999.

6 Solomon, *Eating Bitterness*, 84.

7 Ibid.

8 Peggy Shaughnessy, journal entry, December 1998.

9 Peter Matthiessen, *In the Spirit of Crazy Horse* (New York: Viking, 1983), 521.

10 Quoted in James Waldram, *The Way of the Pipe: Aboriginal Spirituality and Symbolic Healing in Canadian Prisons* (Peterborough: Broadview Press, 1997), 13.

11 Joseph Couture, *Aboriginal Behavioural Trauma: Towards a Taxonomy* (Saskatoon: Corrections Canada, 1994).

12 Interview with "Slaco," Warkworth Institution, June, 1997.

13 Michel Foucault, *Discipline and Punish: The Birth of the Prison* (New York: Vintage, 1977), 188-89.

14 Foucault, *Discipline*, 19.

15 Solomon, *Eating Bitterness*, 84.

CHAPTER 14

1 For the significance of food in relationship to ceremony, see Basil Johnston, *Ojibway Heritage* (Toronto: McClelland and Stewart, 1998), 34-38, 42. For the significance of the use of licorice among the Ojibway, see the chapter "Licorice and Metaphysics" in Louise Erdrich, *The Blue Jay's Dance: A Birth Year* (New York: Harper Collins, 1995), 22-23.

2 Conversation with Louise Erdrich in her bookstore, Birchbark Books, Minneapolis, 10 April 2002.

3 *The New Shorter Oxford English Dictionary on Historical Principles*, ed. Lesley Brown (Oxford: Clarendon Press, 1993), vol. 2: 3685 .

4 See, for example David T. McNab, "'Time is a Fish.' The Spirit of Nanapush and the Power of Transformation in the Stories of Louise Erdrich," *(Ad)dressing Our Words: Aboriginal Perspectives on Aboriginal Literature*, ed. Armand Garnet Ruffo (Penticton: Theytus Press, 2001), 181-204.

5 A.S. Byatt, *On Histories and Stories, Selected Essays* (London: Chatto and Windus, 2000), 4.

6 See, for example, the writings of Catherine Parr Traill. Her work reveals the pragmatic approach of a European woman in adapting to a new way of life and making use of native plants for food and medicine. The subject of food was a dominant theme in her writings. The writings of Louise Erdrich reveal how an Aboriginal woman uses food as a source of resistance in her writings.

7 Johnston, *Ojibway Heritage*, 34.

8 Maria Tippett, *Emily Carr: A Biography* (Markham: Penguin, 1982).

9 Maria Tippett, *Becoming Myself: A Memoir* (Toronto: Stoddart, 1996), 1.

10 Ibid., 200.

11 Stephanie Kirkwood Walker, *This Woman in Particular: Contexts for the Biographical Image of Emily Carr* (Waterloo: Wilfrid Laurier University Press, 1996), 131.

12 Alberto Manguel, *Reading Pictures: A History of Love and Hate* (Toronto: Alfred A. Knopf, 2000), 6.

13 Jonathan Bordo, Peter Kulchyski, John Milloy, and John Wadland, eds. "Introduction," *Journal of Canadian Studies* 33, no. 2 (1998): 4.

14 Simon Schama, *Landscape and Memory* (Toronto: Vintage, 1996), 574.

15 Ibid.

16 Natalie Zemon Davis gives the perspectives of women through a biographical approach of European women in North and South America, specifically Marie de l'Incarnation in the colony of New France and Maria Sibylla

Merian in the Dutch colony of Surinam. Davis shows that these women had a different approach to the new world based on their gender. Natalie Zemon Davis, *Women on the Margins: Three Seventeenth-Century Lives* (Cambridge: Harvard University Press, 1995).

17 Schama, *Landscape*, 75.

18 Robert Pogue Harrison, *Forests: The Shadow of Civilization* (Chicago: University of Chicago Press, 1972), 164.

19 Cited in Gordon Craig, *The Germans* (New York: Meridian, 1991), 191.

20 Ibid.

21 Ibid.

22 Ibid., 193.

23 Harrison, *Forests*, 173-74.

24 See, for example, John M. MacKenzie, *The Empire of Nature: Hunting, Conservation and British Imperialism* (Manchester: Manchester University Press, 1988), 7-24.

25 Harrison, *Forests*, 70.

26 Ibid., 173-75.

27 Ibid., 180.

28 Schama, *Landscape*, 578.

29 On the family's clans, see Heid Ellen Erdrich, *Fishing for Myth, Poems by Heid E. Erdrich* (Minneapolis: New Rivers Press, 1997). The Chippewa are identified by anthropologists as part of the Algonquian speakers, also known in Canada as Ojibwa (variously spelled, Ojibway). Among themselves, they are known as Anishinabe people of the Anishinabek Nation. They have resided in birch bark country in the Great Lakes, and connecting waterways, on both sides of the international boundary between Canada and the United States since time immemorial. Their neighbours, the Cree, are also Algonquian speakers, who continue to reside north and northwest of the Anishinabe people in present-day Quebec, Ontario, and the prairie provinces of Canada as well as the northwestern States of the USA, especially the Dakotas and Montana. See also Erdrich, *The Blue Jay's Dance*, 98-99.

30 David T. McNab, "'Gathering Gum from the Silver Pine': A Cree Woman's Dream and the Battle of Belly River Crossing, (1869-1870)," *Saskatchewan History* 52, no. 2 (2000): 15-27.

31 Louise Erdrich, *The Birchbark House* (New York: Hyperion Books for Children, 1999), 189-92.

32 Colin G. Calloway, *New Worlds for All Indian, Europeans, and the Remaking of Early America* (Baltimore: Johns Hopkins Press, 1997), 155.

33 Ibid.

34 Franz Kafka, *Erzählungen* (Stuttgart: Reclam, 1995), 43. The story is in the section entitled "Betrachtungen," observations, and is entitled, "Wunsch, Indianer zu werden," the wish to become an Indian. The translation is mine.

35 Calloway, *New Worlds*, 155.

36 Erdrich, *The Blue Jay's Dance*, 88.

37 Louise Erdrich, *The Antelope Wife* (New York: Harper Perennial, 1998), 1.

38 Ibid., 240.

39 Calloway, *New Worlds*, 155.

40 Robert F. Gish, "Life into Death, Death into Life: Hunting as Metaphor and Motive in *Love Medicine*," in *The Chippewa Landscape of Louise Erdrich*, ed. Allan Chavkin (Tuscaloosa: University of Alabama Press, 1999), 67-83.

41 Interview, *Newsweek*, 23 March 1998, 69.

42 Mickey Pearlman and Katherine Usher Henderson, eds., *Inter/View: Talks with America's Writing Women* (Lexington: University Press of Kentucky, 1989), 151-52.

43 Calloway, *New Worlds*, 152-57.

44 Erdrich, *The Antelope Wife*, 132-33.

45 Ibid., 138-39.

46 Ibid., 110.

47 Ibid., 114-17.

48 Ibd., 120-21.

49 Ibid.

50 Erdrich, Louise, *The Last Report on the Miracles at Little No Horse* (New York: Harper Collins, 2001).

CHAPTER 15

1 Most of the material on the Wenjack issue at Trent University comes from the Trent University papers, in the Trent archives. In very muted form, some of the information is also in A.O.C. Cole, *Trent: The Making of a University: 1957-1987* (Peterborough: Trent, 1992), especially 85-93; also 122-25.

2 The *Maclean's* article is reprinted in Carl Mollins, ed., *Maclean's Canada's Century: An Illustrated History of the People and Events that Shaped Our History* (Toronto: Key Porter, 1999), 235-36.

3 John S. Milloy, *"A National Crime": The Canadian Government and the Residential School System, 1879 to 1986* (Winnipeg: University of Manitoba Press, 1999), 118 and 285-89, documentation 375-76.

4 Ian Adams, *The Poverty Wall* (Toronto: McClelland and Stewart, 1971).

EPILOGUE

1 Bruce W. Hodgins, "Background to the Current State of Negotiations on the Native Land Settlement," *Temagami Times*, November 2001; "Fact Sheet" (ONAS, TFN, and TAA), 15-16 August 2001, plus the newsletter *The Temagami Land Claims Report* nos. 1-5 (2000-2003); and Bruce W. Hodgins, personal participation.

2 Bruce W. Hodgins and Kerry Cannon, *On the Land: Aboriginal Self-Determination in Northern Quebec and Labrador* (Toronto: Betelgeuse, 1995) and Bruce W. Hodgins, "The Northern Boundary of Quebec: The James Bay Cree as Self-Governing Canadians," in *English Canada Speaks Out*, ed. J.L. Granatstein and Kenneth McNaught (Toronto: Doubleday, 1991).

3 Ken Coates, *The Marshall Decision and Native Rights* (Montreal and Kingston: McGill-Queen's University Press, 2000).

4 "Nunavut: An Inuit Homeland: Resource Guide" (Durham, NC, Canadian Studies Program, Duke University, 16-17 April 1999), and Jens Dahl, Jack Hicks, and Peter Jull, *Inuit Region's Control of Their Lands and Their Lives* (Copenhagen: IWGIA, 2000).

5 Paul Havemann, ed., *Indigenous Peoples' Rights in Australia, Canada and New Zealand* (Auckland: Oxford University Press, 1999); Noel Loos, *Edward Koiki Mabo: His Life and Struggle for Land Rights* (St. Lucia: University of Queensland Press, 1996).

6 Alan Ward, *An Unsettled History: Treaty Claims in New Zealand Today* (Wellington: Bridgett, 1999); see also Havemann, *Indigenous Peoples*.

7 Curtis Cook and Juon D. Lindau, eds., *Aboriginal Rights and Self-Government: The Canadian and Mexican Experience in North American Perspective* (Montreal and Kingston: McGill-Queen's University Press, 2000).

8 "Teme-Augama Anishnabai: Last-Ditch Defence of a Priceless Homeland," in *Drumbeat: Anger and Renewal in Indian Country*, ed. Boyce Richardson (Toronto: Assembly of First Nations and Summerhill Press, 1989), 227-28.